Growth Centers in the American Urban System

Volume I

Community Development and Regional Growth in the Sixties and Seventies

"This volume is part of a two-volume set. Volume I is the basic research report. Volume II contains the detailed research results, organized to facilitate further investigations and planning uses.

Final Report of a Research Program into Regional Development Processes and Policies, under Contract OER-019-G-71-12 between the Economic Development Administration, U.S. Department of Commerce and The Center for Urban Studies, University of Chicago.

Research Assistants: *Quentin Gillard*
Donald Jones
Richard Lamb
John Pershing

Growth Centers in the American Urban System

Volume I

Community Development and Regional Growth in the Sixties and Seventies

Brian J. L. Berry

Irving B. Harris Professor of Urban Geography
The University of Chicago

Ballinger Publishing Company • Cambridge, Mass.
A Subsidiary of J.B. Lippincott Company

Library of Congress Catalog Card Number 73-10362

International Standard Book Number 0-88410-400-1

Printed in the United States of America

Library of Congress Cataloging in Publication Data

Berry, Brian Joe Lobley, 1934-

Growth centers in the American urban systems, 1960-1970.

Vol. 2 has also special title: Working materials on the U.S. urban hierarchy and on growth center characteristics, organized by economic region.

Bibliography: p.

1. Economic zoning–United States. 2. Cities and towns–United States. 3. Regional planning–United States. I. Title.

HC110.Z6B47 301.36'1'0973 73-10362

ISBN 0-88410-400-1 (v. I)

0-88410-401-x (v. II)

Contents

List of Figures vii

List of Tables xi

Preface xiii

Chapter One
Urban and Regional Growth: The Classical Theory and Some Contradictory Empirical Evidence

Traditional Regional Growth Concepts 6
The Changing Nature of Regional Growth: The United States in the 1960s 9
A Unit for Analysis: The Daily Urban System 10
Growth Characteristics of the DUSs, 1960–1970 17
Patterns of Intraregional Growth and Expansion 21

Chapter Two
Development of a Research Strategy 41

An Urban-Rural Growth Strategy for Appalachia 42
Strategic Development Principles 43
Programs to Change Accessibility 45
Service Delivery Systems 48
Growth Centers, Development Districts, and a Concentrated Investment Policy 48
Some Early Results of the Concentrated Investment Program 53
Growth Centers for the Upper Great Lakes Region 55
Initial UGLRC Attempts to Define Growth Areas 56
Bases of the Hierarchical Definitions 59
The Urban Hierarchy of the Upper Great Lakes Region 60
Labor Markets, Spread Effects, and Gradients of Urban Influence 63
Patterns of Change 91
Synthesis: Growth Regions and the Lagging Periphery 104
The Proposed Growth and Service Centers 108

Chapter Three
The Nation's Growth Centers in the 1960s 117

The U.S. Urban Hierarchy 117
Gradients of Urban Influence and Change 122
Growth Centers, Both Continuing and Emergent 136
The National Patterns 140

Chapter Four
The Patterns Analyzed 149

The Upper Midwest Case 149
Urban-Related Growth 149
Special Investment Areas 150
High Amenity Areas 150
Metropolitan Decentralization, Megalopolitan Evolution and High-Amenity Growth: Leading Elements in the Nationwide Pattern 150
Filtering of Manufacturing Industries 151
Synthesis: The Regional Geography of Growth 155

Chapter Five
Review and an Agenda 157

Appendix:
Growth Center Schemes Evaluated 165

The USDA Proposals 165
EDA's Designated Growth Centers 173
Appalachia's Concentrated Investment Centers 185

References 189

Index 193

About the Author 197

List of Figures

1-1 National Market Access in 1960 2
1-2 Manufacturing Areas in 1962 3
1-3 The National Pattern of Urban Commuting Fields in 1960 12
1-4 Commuting Areas Classified by the Size of their Central Cities 13
1-5 Regionalization of the United States According to Nature of Economic Centers 14
1-6 The OBE Economic Areas 16
1-7 Growth Rate of the DUSs 1960-1970 Related to Their Population in 1960 22
1-8 Growth Rate Related to Agricultural Earnings 29
1-9 Growth Rate Related to Manufacturing Earnings 29
1-10 Growth Rate Related to Residentiary Earnings 30
1-11 Growth Rate Related to Federal Earnings 30
1-12 Population Growth Rate Related to Per Capita Incomes 32
1-13 Population Growth Rate Related to Growth Rate of Per Capita Incomes 32
1-14 Population Growth Rate Related to Growth Rate of Earnings from Wholesale and Retail Trade 33
1-15 Population Growth Rate Related to Growth Rate of Earnings from Services 33
1-16 Population Growth Rate Related to Growth Rate of Federal Civilian Earnings 34
1-17 Population Growth Rate Related to Growth Rate of Manufacturing Earnings 34
1-18 Zones of Above-National Population Growth 1960-1970 35
1-19 Zones of Net Immigration, 1960-1970 37
1-20 Zones of Net Emigration, 1960-1970 38
2-1 Metropolitan Areas with Commuting Fields Extending into Appalachia 46
2-2 Zones of Appalachia Lying Outside Metropolitan Commuting Fields 47
2-3 The Appalachian Development Highways 49
2-4 Service Delivery System Model 50
2-5 Initial UGLRC Proposals for Growth Areas 57
2-6 The Urban Hierarchy of the Upper Great Lakes Region 64
2-7 Rand McNally City Ratings and Economic Classification 65
2-8 Metropolitan Trade and Service Areas (after Borchert) 66
2-9 Wholesale-Retail Trade and Service Areas (after Borchert) 67
2-10 Rand McNally Major Trade Areas 68
2-11 Rand McNally Basic Trade Areas 69
2-12 Hierarchy of Market Areas of Centers Occupying the Three Top Levels of the Urban System 70

2-13 Three-digit Zip-Code Areas and Sectional Center Cities 71
2-14 Metropolitan Labor Markets 72
2-15 Labor Markets of Non-Metropolitan Centers 73
2-16 Hierarchical Diffusion of TV Stations 75
2-17 Nielsen Television Market Areas 76
2-18 TV Market Penetration in 1953 77
2-19 TV Market Penetration in 1956 78
2-20 TV Market Penetration in 1959 79
2-21 TV Market Penetration in 1962 80
2-22 TV Market Penetration in 1965 81
2-23 Detroit-Alpena Gradients 82
2-24 Detroit-Sault Ste. Marie Gradients 83
2-25 Detroit-Traverse City Gradients 84
2-26 Chicago-Marquette Gradients 85
2-27 Chicago-Ironwood Gradients 86
2-28 Chicago-Eau Claire Gradients 87
2-29 Minneapolis-Duluth Gradients 88
2-30 Fargo-Duluth Gradients 89
2-31 Duluth-Sault Ste. Marie Gradients 90
2-32 Rate of Population Change of Smaller Urban Centers Related to Distance from Duluth 92
2-33 Population Change and Migration Rates Compared 93
2-34 Counties with Lagging Population and Labor Force 94
2-35 Counties with Growing Disadvantaged Population 95
2-36 Counties with an Aging Population 96
2-37 Counties with Above-Average Income Growth 97
2-38 Counties with Positive Agricultural Change 98
2-39 Counties with Expanding Service and Transport Functions, and Related Residential Growth 99
2-40 Counties with Greatest Manufacturing Employment Growth 100
2-41 Counties with Growing Manufacturing Payrolls and Value Added 101
2-42 Counties with Greatest Changes in Manufacturing Establishments 102
2-43 Counties with Greatest Changes in Wholesale Employment 103
2-44 Spatial Variations of Wage Rates in Wisconsin 105
2-45 Ratio of Income of Farm Residents from Non-Agricultural Sources to Farm Products Sold 106
2-46 Synthesis of Regional Growth Characteristics 107
2-47 Economic Status of the Rural Population in 1960 111
2-48 The Proposed Growth Centers and their Areas of Influence 112
3-1 Centers of Metropolitan Status in the U.S. Urban Hierarchy 118
3-2 The Metropolitan-Status Daily Urban Systems of the U.S. in 1960, as indexed by the Commuting Fields of Central Cities in that Year 119
3-3 A Distinction is Made Within Each OBE Area Between Counties Lying *Within* and Counties Lying *Beyond* the Commuting Area of the Central City 120
3-4 The Urban Hierarchy in the Memphis Region. The Highways that are noted are used as Traverses for Plotting Socio-Economic Gradients 121
3-5 Classification of Counties on a Scale of Urbanization and Population Densities in 1960 123

3-6 Variation of Per Capita Incomes along the Scale of Urban Orientation in 1960 124
3-7 Percentage of Families with Incomes Less Than $3,000 in 1960 Related to Urban Orientations 124
3-8 Concentration of the Elderly in Areas with Differing Urban Orientations in 1960 124
3-9 Variations in Newspaper Market Penetration and Daily Commuting Along the Traverse Between Jackson and Paducah 125
3-10 Population Change and Migration, 1960-1970, Along the Same Traverse as in Figure 3-9 126
3-11 Spatial Interdependencies Along a Traverse Between Little Rock and Nashville 127
3-12 Gradients of Change Along the Little Rock-Nashville Traverse 128
3-13 Spatial Interdependencies, Jonesboro to Tupelo 129
3-14 Changes in the 1960s, Jonesboro to Tupelo 130
3-15 Newspaper Market Penetration by the Nation's Metropolitan-Level Centers 131
3-16 Newspaper Market Penetration by Centers Occupying the Top Two Levels of the Urban Hierarchy 132
3-17 Socioeconomic Transect Network 135
3-18 A Sample of the Set of Gradients Presented in Volume II 137
3-19 Changes in Median Family Income, 1960-1970 138
3-20 Changes in the Percentage of Families Beneath the Poverty Line, 1960-1970 139
3-21 Continuing Foci for Regional Growth 144
3-22 Population Growth Points 146
3-23 Income/Welfare Growth Points 147
3-24 Non-Metropolitan Growth Patterns in the 1960's 148
4-1 Changing Income Gradients as the Metropolitan Order is Replaced by that of the Megalopolis 152
4-2 Filtering of Manufacturing Employment into the Inter-Metropolitan Periphery: (a) Employment Expansion in More Urbanized Counties 153
4-3 Filtering of Manufacturing Employment into the Inter-Metropolitan Periphery: (b) Employment Expansion in More Rural Counties 154
4-4 Synthesis of Growth Patterns in the 1960's 156
5-1 Market Penetration by Television in 1953 159
5-2 Market Penetration by Television in 1956 160
5-3 Market Penetration by Television in 1959 161
5-4 Market Penetration by Television in 1962 162
5-5 Market Penetration by Television in 1965 163

List of Tables

1-1 Population of Daily Urban Systems, 1960 and 1970, with Percentage Rate of Change, 1960 to 1970 18
1-2 Basic and Residentiary Earnings of the Daily Urban Systems in 1967, Expressed as a Percentage of Total Earnings 23
1-3 Median Growth Rates of Various Types of Economic Areas, 1960–1970 31
2-1 Growth Characteristics of Places in the Borchert-Adams Hierarchy 60
2-2 Hierarchical Position of Urban Centers in the Upper Great Lakes Region 61
2-3 Labor Market Populations, 1960 74
2-4 Incomes of Standard Metropolitan Statistical Areas, 1929–1966 109
2-5 Source, Type, and Growth Rate of Standard Metropolitan Statistical Area Incomes, 1959–1966 110
2-6 Proposed Growth and Service Centers 113
3-1 Urban Hierarchy of the Memphis, Tenn. (Miss.-Ark.) Economic Area (OBE 046) 133
3-2 Urban Hierarchy of Salina, Kans., Economic Area (OBE 109) 141
3-3 Growth Centers in the Salina, Kans., Economic Area (OBE 109) 142
A-1 Population Growth in 1960 Census Area, Discounting Effects of Annexation (Number of Towns) 166
A-2 Population Growth in 1960 Census Area, Discounting Effects of Annexation (Number of Towns) 167
A-3 Change in Number of Manufacturing Employees, Counties, 1963–1967 167
A-4 Change in Industrial Composition, Counties, 1950–1960 169
A-5 Number of Towns Located on the Interstate Highway System 170
A-6 Reasons for Vitality or Apparent Vitality 171
A-7 Reasons for Vitality or Apparent Vitality (Percentage of Towns) 172
A-8 Growth Categories of Designated EDA Growth Center in Each OBE Area 174
A-9 District Centers in Appalachia 185

Preface

The development of firmly-based positions on national growth policy and community development will be a matter of increasing urgency during the decade of the 1970s. Increasing effort will have to be devoted in both the public and private arenas to clarification of exactly what is meant by a national growth policy, the governmental role in such a policy, the efficacy and impact of present federal programs, and the range of programs likely to be productive of alternative futures. It is hoped that this study will be a contribution to this effort.

Among the questions that will have to be resolved are whether there can be any consensus about what a national growth policy means that transcends the competitive interest-group nature of American politics, and what the content of "balanced and orderly growth" (the definition stressed by Congress) is or should be. Still to be worked out is the relationship of a national growth policy to other national policies, such as economic stability at full employment, environmental protection and resource conservation, and, in particular, community development.

The idea of a growth policy carries with it the corollary idea of a policy that seeks to combat decline. Likewise, congressional interest in balanced and orderly growth carries with it the desire to combat "unbalanced" and "disorderly" growth. Both corollaries involve the regional distribution and spatial pattern of development. Several issues are intertwined, for example whether or not processes of transportation improvement and land development can be changed to accommodate higher standards, and whether or not locationally-specific policies can contribute to the elimination of regional inequities.

One such locationally-specific policy is the growth center strategy, now being applied or currently proposed for application by the Economic Development Administration, the Appalachian Regional Commission, the Department of Transportation and the U.S. Department of Agriculture. There is little consistency to these efforts. Indeed, in the past, growth center strategies have been predicated on one or more of the following hypotheses, each of which assumes that growth centers provide the opportunity for achieving "concentrated deconcentration" of population and economic activity into presumably lagging regions:

1. Planned development of public infrastructure investment at optimal sites will avoid the undesirable externalities associated with "excessively large" and congested cities, as well

as the high marginal costs of providing public infrastructure to support private growth in minor centers of activity.
2. Growth center policy provides possible population redistribution from major cities which avoids major service dislocation.
3. Public investment in spatially concentrated infrastructure is likely to maximize the inflow of exogenous capital into lagging regions.
4. In the long run, the "spread effects" of a growth center policy are likely to be substantial as the growth areas become regional centers of innovation and technical efficiency, and growth impulses diffuse from them into surrounding areas.
5. A commitment to provide specific amounts and types of public investment in selected sites will facilitate the formulation of regional economic goals and thereby the establishment of priorities for public investment in quantitative and spatial terms.

Underlying each of these hypotheses is the notion that spatially selective public investments are required in preselected growth centers to bring growth into areas which have lagged in their economic performance. Such selectivity involves official encouragement of spatially unbalanced growth within a region in the short run by concentrating it in centers thought to display the desired prospective vitality, in the attempt to simulate the growth characteristics of prosperous centers in fast-growing regions. The overall objectives are those of attracting exogenous capital, of encouraging local product and production innovation, and ultimately of spreading economic improvements into the non-growth center parts of the region. This combination of major public investment, it is claimed, should result in an alleviation of regional balance-of-payments disequilibrium and should also help in substituting intraregional for interregional movements of capital and labor that threaten to denude the lagging region of critical resources.

In short, then, several arguments which a priori have seeming validity, are advanced in favor of growth center strategies:

1. Such a policy contributes in the long run to more rapid concentration of a lagging region's population into a few large urban areas, with the result of creating the conditions for servicing net and replacement demand for social/economic overhead capital at low cost.
2. For a given subsidy cost, spatially concentrated investment is likely to maximize the flow of income to regional earners in the short run; to attract a maximum flow of exogenous enterprise and capital; and to generate a highly productive environment in which an expanded export base can reduce the regional balance-of-payments deficit and provide sufficient job opportunities to restrain the emigration out of the region of the economically active population.
3. The quality of short-term regional planning may be improved if the mix and scheduling of public investment over time is given a rigorous spatial dimension.

The issues that arise are whether these arguments are valid in fact, and if so, whether consistent objectives for a growth center policy can be developed. Of particular interest is whether nationwide criteria can be developed for selection of growth centers, or whether the federal government must leave the definitions to the several states, as was done in the creation of the Appalachian growth center strategy.

It has been the underlying premise of this study that nationwide criteria do exist for growth center identification, and that these criteria can be derived by first defining the regional urban hierarchies that exist in the United States, classifying every urban center in the United States according to its hierarchical status, and analyzing the growth patterns of centers at each echelon of the hierarchy; second, by identifying the areas of influence of the centers of spatial organization that occupy the upper echelons of this hierarchy, and by showing the effects on regional growth and welfare of the influences that spread from these centers within their areas of influence; and third, by isolating and codifying all those cases of accelerated growth that occurred throughout the nation in the 1960s either as a consequence of the diffusion of metropolitan influences outward into the interurban peripheries, or in nonmetropolitan growth centers.

Thus, in this study, materials are provided not only on the nature and growth of the continuing foci of the nation's economic life, but also on the loci of new growth impulses and directions, and trends in urban-regional development. The organization of the volume reflects the ingredients. Chapter 1 reviews the theory of urban-regional growth, and looks in particular at the theoretical basis of growth center strategies: hierarchical diffusion and spread effects within urban systems. Evidence is offered that the classical economic theory is wanting in the United States today, and that new concepts of metropolitan growth and the nature of filtering and spread are required to comprehend the changing nature of regional development.

In Chapter 2, it is asked whether the new forces of metropolitan growth can be harnessed to channel development into those peripheral areas that are lagging behind the nation in incomes, employment opportunities, and the maintenance of a satisfactory way of life. The chapter concerns itself with the way in which a research strategy subsequently applied on a nationwide basis was worked out in two cases, the urban-rural growth strategy for Appalachia and a set of growth center recommendations for the Upper Great Lakes Region.

The nationwide application is outlined in Chapter 3, and the full results are presented in Volume II, the companion publication. First, the U.S. urban hierarchy is described and mapped. Second, gradients of urban influence and change are outlined. Third, continuing centers of spatial organization and the new growth centers of the 1960s are identified and discussed.

In Chapter 4, the results are analyzed. In the Appendix to the volume these results are used to assess a variety of programmatic proposals for growth center strategies made to the Congress by the U.S. Department of Agriculture together with the program evaluation by the Economic Development Administration of its own growth center policies.

Volume I concludes with a brief description of an agenda for future research and policy development. As noted above, the detailed results of the analysis are tabulated in Volume II, the companion volume.

Growth Centers in the American Urban System

Volume I

Community Development and Regional Growth in the Sixties and Seventies

Chapter One

Urban and Regional Growth: The Classical Theory and Some Contradictory Empirical Evidence

The reason why growth center strategies have been proposed as solutions to regional pockets of poverty ultimately is to be found in the highly-structured character of the nation's economic space. The central driving force has long been

> . . . a great heartland nucleation of industry and the national market, the focus of large-scale national-serving industry, the seedbed of new industry responding to the dynamic structure of national final demand, and the center of high levels of per capita income . . .

Standing in a dependent relationship to the heartland,

> . . . radiating out across the national landscape are . . . resource-dominant regional hinterlands specializing in the production of resource and intermediate outputs for which the heartland reaches out to satisfy the input requirements of its great manufacturing plants. Here in the hinterlands, resource-endowment is a critical determinant of the particular cumulative advantage of the region and hence its growth potential. (Perloff and Wingo, 1963).

Figure 1–1 portrays the geographic configuration of national market access in the United States in 1960, and figure 1–2, the related spatial pattern of industrial concentrations. The geography of this relationship—the juxtaposition that constitutes the nation's heartland—was explored at length almost two decades ago by Harris (1954). Subsequent workers have demonstrated the theoretical significance of general access within the country, thus cementing our understanding of industrial location processes (Tidemann, 1968).

To appreciate why the nation's hinterlands developed their dependent relationship to this industrial heartland, one must understand the sequence of stages through which the national economy has evolved:

> . . . throughout the evolution . . . two factors, great migrations and major changes in technology, have particularly influenced the location of relative growth and decline. Both factors have repeatedly been given specific geographical expression through their relationship to resource patterns. Major changes in technology have resulted in critically important changes in the evaluation or definition of particular resources on which the growth of certain urban regions had previously been based. Great migrations have sought to exploit resources—ranging from

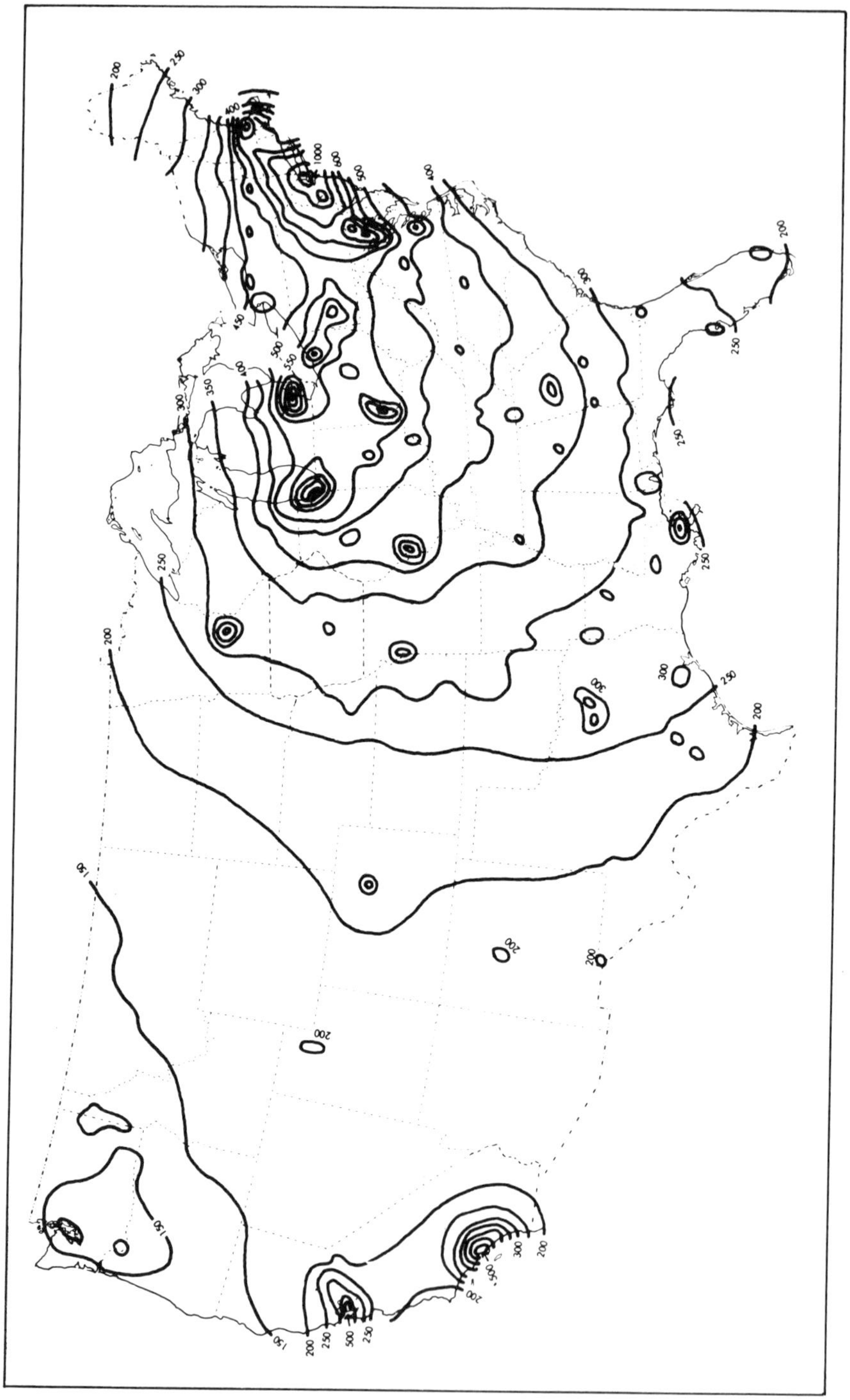

Figure 1-1. National Market Access in 1960. The map contours population potentials.

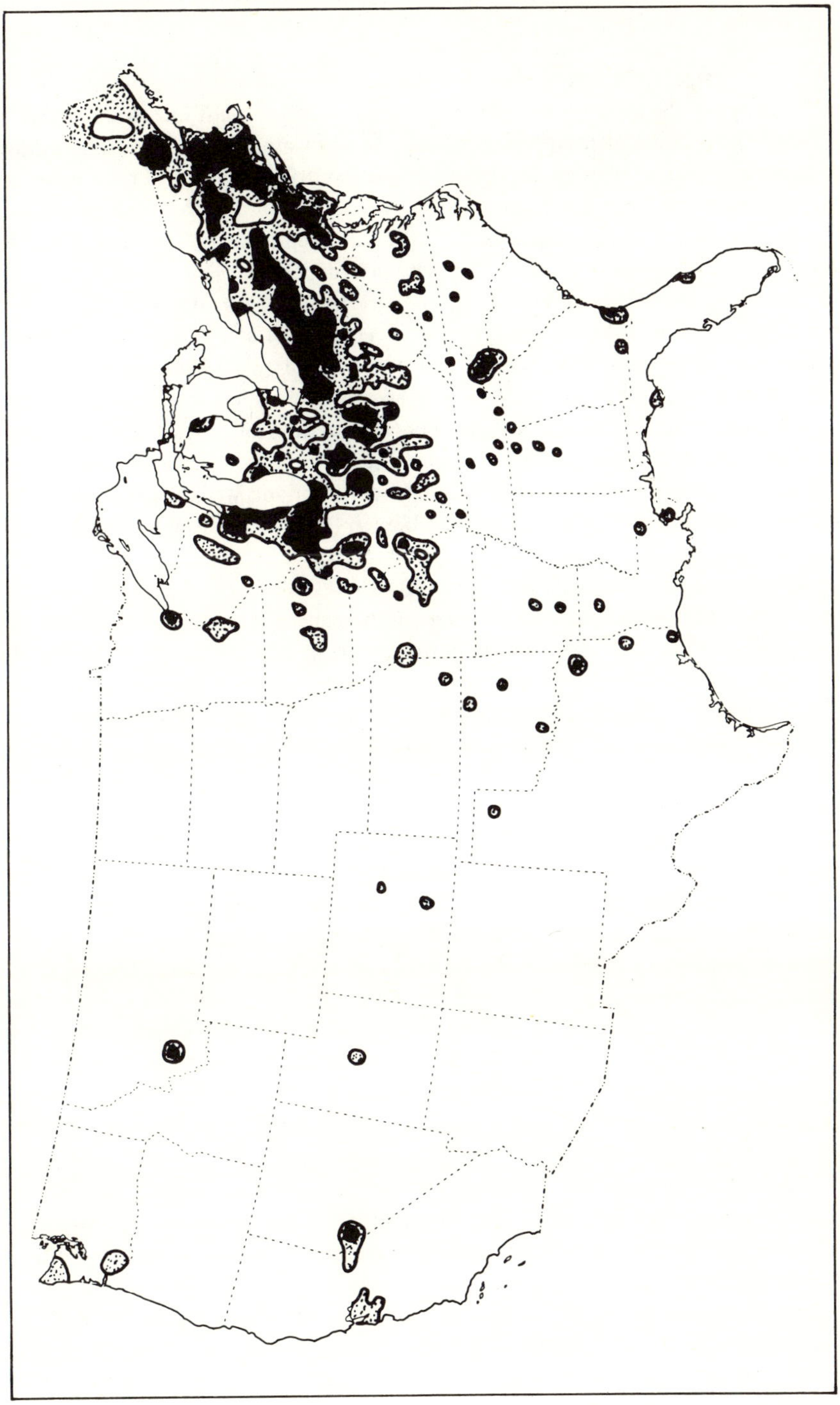

Figure 1–2. Manufacturing Areas in 1962. Shades indicate intensity of manufacturing concentrations.

> climate or coal to water to zinc—that were newly appreciated or newly accessible within the national market. Usually . . . the new appreciation or accessibility has come about, in turn, through some major technological innovation. (Borchert, 1967).

Several stages of "natural resources that count" can be cited in the history of the American economy. In the agricultural period, the natural endowment most valued was arable land with environmental components of climate and water. During industrialization a new set of mineral resources became important. In the twentieth century, service activities and amenity resources have exerted an increasingly strong pull on industry and on people, along with regional differences in governmental expenditures. In each of these stages, urban growth and regional development have been closely interdependent.

America's oldest cities were mercantile outposts of a resource area whose exploitation was organized by the developing metropolitan system of Western Europe. The initial impulses for independent urban growth came at the end of the eighteenth century, when towns were becoming the outlets for capital accumulated in commercial agriculture and the centers of colonial development of the continental interior. Arable land was the resource that counted in regional growth. Regional economies developed a certain archetype: a good deepwater port as the nucleus of an agricultural hinterland well-adapted for the production of a staple commodity in demand on the world market. Growth potentials of regions depended on the extent and richness of the hinterlands accessible to the ports. The prototypic American metropolis thus was a port at a strategic location on long-distance oceanic or riverine trade routes, providing a range of mercantile services, and determining the terms of trade. This agricultural resource-dominated (but city-centered) expansion of the economy set the stage for subsequent developments by establishing a geography of markets, transport routes, and labor forces that conditioned the nature of succeeding growth.

New resources became important from 1840–1850 onwards, and new locational forces came into play. Foremost was a growing demand for iron, and later steel, and along with it rapid elaboration of productive technologies. Juxtaposition of coal, iron ore, and markets afforded the impetus for manufacturing growth in the northeastern United States, localized by both factors in the physical environment (minerals) and environmental components created by prior growth of the urban system (linkages to succeeding stages of production, in turn located closer to markets). The "heartland" of the American manufacturing belt developed westwards from New York in the area bounded by Lake Superior iron ores, the Pennsylvania coalfields, and the capital, entrepreneurial experience, and engineering trades of the north-east, while at the same time New York cemented its dominance by accentuation of its financial, entrepreneurial, and specialized manufacturing roles. This heartland became not only the heavy industrial center of the country, but has remained the center of national demand, determining patterns of market accessibility since (fig. 1–1 and 1–2).

The heartland had initial advantages of both excellent agricultural resources and a key location in the minerals economy. With development, it grew into the urbanized center of the national market. Subsequent metropolitan growth took place in a pattern organized around this national core region until after the Second World War. From 1869 to 1950 there was, for example, a stable pattern of growth in manufacturing employment among the states (Borts, 1967). Continued spread of population and agriculture over the continent pulled processing and servicing activities and new urban growth with them. However, the developmentally-dominant effects still came from growth of the minerals economy until well into the twentieth century, so that a process of "circular and cumulative causation"

(Pred, 1966) strengthened and maintained the relations of the national heartland and hinterlands—of core and periphery—and the new metropolitan centers that did emerge did so in sequence with the overall growth, outward spread, and spatial integration of the economy.

In each case, the basic conditions of regional growth were set by the heartland. It was the lever for successive development of newer peripheral regions by reaching out to them as its input requirements expanded, and it thereby fostered specialization of regional roles in the national economy. The heartland experienced cumulative urban-industrial specialization, while each of the hinterlands found its comparative advantage based on narrow and intensive specialization in a few resource subsectors, only diversifying when the extent of specialization enabled the hinterland region to pass through that threshold scale of market necessary to support profitable local enterprise. Flows of raw materials inward and finished products outward articulated the whole (Ullman, 1957).

Since 1950, growth of the service sector, increase in the number of "footloose" industries (including final processing of consumer goods using manufactured parts, and the aircraft, aerospace, and defense industries), rapid emergence of a "quaternary" sector of the economy (involving, for example, the "research and development" industry), expansion and interregional migration of the non-job-oriented population (for example of retirees to Florida, Arizona, and California), rising governmental expenditures and overall rising real incomes, have all served to produce yet another transformation of the economy and the urban system—and of the traditional export-base concept of hinterland growth. Advantages for economic growth have been found around the "outer rim" of the country, in former hinterland regions (Ullman, 1954), as changing communications technology has reduced the time and costs involved in previous heartland-hinterland relationships. The changes have been cumulative, for regional growth within the context of the national pattern of heartland and hinterland had brought these regions to threshold sizes for internal production of a wide variety of goods and services at the very time that changes in the definition of urban resources made their rapid advance, free of the traditional constraints of heartland-hinterland leverage, possible. Hence the explosive metropolitan growth of the south, southwest, and west, led by the tertiary and quaternary sectors.

The outcome of this latter stage of urban-regional growth is that it is now

> . . . possible to interpret the spatial structure of the United States in ways that will emphasize a pattern consisting of *one*, metropolitan areas and *two*, the inter-metropolitan periphery. Except for thinly populated parts of the American interior, the inter-metropolitan periphery includes all the areas that intervene among metropolitan regions and that are, as it were, the reverse image of the trend towards large scale concentrated settlement that has persisted in this country for over half a century. Like a devil's mirror, much of the periphery has developed a socio-economic profile that perversely reflects the very opposite of metropolitan virility. Economically, the inter-metropolitan periphery includes most of the areas that have been declared eligible for federal area redevelopment assistance . . . They have a disproportionately large share of low-growth and declining industries and a correspondingly antiquated economic structure. Nevertheless, one-fifth of the American people are living in these regions of economic distress.

Friedmann and Miller (1965), the authors of the above quotation, go on to say:

> Demographically, the inter-metropolitan periphery has been subject to a long-term, continuous decline. This trend reflects the movement of people to cities,

> especially to the large metropolitan concentrations. Although the smaller cities on the periphery have to some extent benefitted from migration, their gains have been less, on the average, than for all urban areas. In addition, migration from economically depressed regions has been highly selective, so that the age distribution of the remaining population has become polarized around the very young and the very old . . . Socially, the standard indices of education and health are substantially lower along the periphery than in metropolitan areas. The quality of public services has deteriorated (though their *per capita* cost has increased), the housing stock is older, and the level of educational attainment is significantly below the average for metropolitan America. Rapid and selective outmigration, a declining economic base, the burden of an aging population, and low incomes have rendered many peripheral communities helpless in their desire to adapt to changing circumstances in the outside world. The remaining population is frequently short both on civic leadership and hope. They can neither grasp the scope of events that have overtaken them nor are they capable of responding creatively to the new situations.

It is in the peripheries that growth center strategies are being proposed as instruments for alleviating problems of unemployment and low incomes, while meeting the need for institution building, community organization, and leadership development. Yet the strategies take as their theoretical base the earlier driving mechanism of the heartland-hinterland relationship, failing to include the self-sustaining growth of metropolitan America. It is to this discordance that we should now turn.

TRADITIONAL REGIONAL GROWTH CONCEPTS

The traditional theory of regional growth and classical growth center concepts both stem from the heartland-hinterland dependency relationship. The problem for public policies formulated on the basis of these ideas is, however, that the service-related transformation of the American economic scene in recent decades and the attendant emergence of metropolitan areas and the inter-metropolitan periphery as the basic regional distinction in the nation casts serious doubt on this classical basis of growth center theory. This implies that it is more critical today than ever before that we look in some detail at the nature of growth processes in the American urban system in the 1960s, and on that basis explore alternative theoretical formulations and new approaches to the uses of growth centers as instruments for inducing regional development. It is in the framework of such alternative approaches that our analysis proceeds and policy recommendations are made later in the study.

Following the example of Perloff (1960), Friedmann (1966), and others, the classical theory of regional growth can be set in propositional form, as follows:

1. A regional economy is an interdependent part of a national economy. That differential regional economic growth has been until recently an expression of an open, highly dynamic economy, made up of an industrial heartland and resource-dominant hinterlands is unquestionable. As long as demand and supply conditions change and regions have differing advantages for production, differences in regional growth must be seen as part of the total economic system, just as are economic specialization and the division of labor. All the elements essential to national economic growth therefore are also essential to the economic growth of regions. Chief among these elements are development of natural resources, development of manpower skills, aggressive entrepreneurship, an elaborate infrastructure, and associated external economies. In such circumstances, the degree to which *local* decisions can shape the future of a regional economy depends upon the degree of self-sustaining local autonomy ("closure") of that economy. Greater closure implies greater autonomy of choice; greater openness implies greater dependency upon changes and choices in other regions and the nation. Clearly, the degree of closure is small in resource-oriented hinterland regions, and this in turn implies that sensitivity to external change centered in the national heartland remains substantial in such cases. The significant change noted later in this chapter is that all of the nation's major urban regions achieved substantial closure in the short run during the 1960s, with the result that their growth rates converged on the national growth rate, whatever their economic specializaton.

2. Regional growth is externally induced. Basic to the growth of regions, according to the classical theory, is their capacity for attracting industries that produce goods for export to other regions of the country. Growth impulses in regional economies, come from outside, according to this view, in the form of demands for regional specialities. The nature of these specialities, alternative sources of them, and changes in the structue of demand therefore determine in large measure the nature and extent of regional growth. Expanding national demands spark heartland growth, which in turn directs differential hinterland growth through growing demands for hinterland specialities. What more recent evidence suggests, however, is that the growth of major metropolitan regions is based upon the exercise of innovative leadership as new specialities are invented, producing rapid growth based upon a favorable mix of new industries. Further, there is accumulating evidence that the heartland-hinterland "lever" no longer works by means of heartland demands for regional resource-related specialities, traditionally defined, but is rapidly being replaced by the filtering of older slower-growth industries from the metropolitan regions into the hinterlands as the principal source of hinterland growth.

For this reason, not all of the regions of a country can expect their economic activities and populations to increase at the same rate of speed. Yet, every region *can* hope to enjoy a high and rising per capita income if the nation's output and productivity continue to increase, and as long as filtering works smoothly, and as long as its people are willing to face up to the need for a degree of outmigration when the overall situation calls for it. In most such instances, significantly higher income levels within a lagging hinterland region can be achieved only combining effective economic development with substantial outmigration.

3. Export sector growth translates into residentiary sector growth. Export industries need secondary support in the form of housing, public facilities, retail establishments, service facilities, and many other elements of local infrastructure. In the classical theory, export income supports these local facilities in a basic-nonbasic relationship that involves a simple multiplier linkage between export-industry fortunes and total regional growth.

The essence of the postwar transformation of regional economic relationships is, however, the changing role of the service industries in the traditional tertiary and modern quarternary sectors. Whereas the export-base formulation relegates these industries to a "nonbasic" role, with the magnitude of their growth determined strictly by the multiplier relationship to the export base, more recent evidence conclusively demonstrates that the tertiary and quaternary sectors have become the new propulsive sources of internally-generated growth, as we shall see later.

4. Economic growth takes place in a matrix of urban regions through which the space-economy is organized. The crux of the link between regional growth and modern growth center concepts is that it is cities within the urban system, linked by filtering mechanisms, not the heartland-hinterland lever in the regional system linked by export-base multipliers, that today organize the economy spatially. They are centers of activity and of innovation, focal points of the transport and communications networks, locations of superior accessibility at which firms can most easily reap scale economies and at which industrial complexes can obtain the economies of localization and urbanization. They encourage labor specialization, areal specialization in productive activities, and efficiency in the provision of services. Agricultural enterprise is more efficient in the vicinity of cities. The more prosperous commercialized agricultures encircle the major cities, whereas the peripheries of the great urban regions are characterized by backward lower-income economic systems.

There are two major elements in this city-centered organization of economic activities in space (Berry, 1967b):

a. *A system of cities*, arranged in a *hierarchy* according to the functions performed by each.
b. Corresponding *areas of urban influence* or *urban fields* surrounding each of the cities in the system.

Impulses of economic change have been shown to be transmitted in such a system simultaneously along three planes:

a. Outward from heartland metropoli to those of the regional hinterlands.
b. From centers of higher to centers of lower level in the hierarchy, in a pattern of "hierarchical diffusion."
c. Outward from urban centers into their surrounding urban fields, in radiating "spread effects."

Part of the diffusion mechanism has been shown to reside in the operation of urban labor markets. When growth is sustained over long periods, regional income inequality should be reduced because any general expansion in a high-income area will result in some industries being priced out of the high-income labor market. There will be a shift of that industry to lower income regions, especially to smaller urban centers in more peripheral areas. The significance of this "filtering" or "trickle down" process lies not only in its direct but also in its indirect effects. If the boom originates in the high-income region, as is very likely, the multiplier effects will be larger in the initiating region, although the relative rise in income may be greater in the underdeveloped region. But the induced effects on real income and employment may be considerably greater in the low-income region if prices there are likely to rise less and/or if the increase in output per worker is greater. Both are likely, because of decreasing cost due to external economies stemming from urbanization of the labor force. If the boom can be maintained, industries of higher labor productivity will shift units into lower-income areas, and the low-wage industries will be forced to move into even smaller towns and more isolated areas.

The net result is that the following properties should characterize such urban-regional hierarchical systems:

a. The size and functions of a central city, the size of its urban field, and the spatial extent of developmental "spread effects" radiating outwards from it are proportional.
b. Since impulses of economic change are transmitted in order from higher to lower centers in the urban hierarchy, continued innovation in large cities remains critical for extension of growth over the complete economic system.

c. The resulting spatial incidence of economic growth will be a function of distance from the central city. Troughs of economic backwardness will lie in the most inaccessible areas along the peripheries between the least accessible lower-level centers in the hierarchy.
d. Further, the growth potential of an area situated along an axis between two cities is a function of the intensity of interaction between them, which is in turn a function of their relative location and the quality of transportation arteries connecting them.

It is easy to see how a logical progression of urban growth flows from such conclusions, leading to the following conclusion:

5. When economic growth is sustained over long periods, it results in progressive integration of the space economy. If metropolitan development is sustained at high levels, rural-urban differences will be eliminated and the space-economy should be integrated by outward flows of growth impulses through the urban hierarchy, and inward migration of labor to cities in a reverse stepwise or ratchet fashion. Troughs of economic backwardness at the intermetropolitan periphery are thereby eroded, and each area should then find itself within the spheres of influence of a variety of urban centers of a variety of sizes. Concentric bands of agricultural organization and efficiency around metropolitan centers should be eliminated or reduced in importance, and agricultures also introduce new specialities, taking full advantage of differences in local resource endowments.

It is this full integration of the national space-economy that constitutes the objective of regional development strategy. Essentially, what modern growth theory suggests is that continued urban-industrial expansion in major metropolitan regions should lead to catalytic impacts on surrounding areas. Growth impulses and economic advancement should filter and spread to smaller places and ultimately infuse dynamism into even the most tradition-bound peripheries. Growth center concepts enter the scene if filtering mechanisms are perceived not to be operating quickly enough, if "cumulative causation" leads to growing regional differentials rather than their reduction (see below), or if institutional or historical barriers block diffusion processes. The purpose of spatially-selective public investments in growth centers, it is held, is to hasten the focused extension of growth to lower echelons of the hierarchy in outlying regions, and to link the growth centers more closely into the national system via higher-echelon centers in the urban hierarchy.

THE CHANGING NATURE OF REGIONAL GROWTH: THE UNITED STATES IN THE 1960s

There is an increasing realization that significant changes have occurred in the nature of regional development processes in the United States. These changes indicate the pressing need for new and imaginative approaches to regional policy. We have already noted the rapid rise of the service and quaternary sectors of the economy and the increasing significance of both governmental expenditures and amenity resources in the new growth nexus. Under these conditions, it is now clear that large urban regions (whether possessing heartland or hinterland locations) can free themselves of narrow export dependency, traditionally defined.

The long-run viability of any large metropolitan area, in these new conditions, resides ultimately on its capacity to invent and innovate, i.e., to create new rapid-growth, high-wage activities. What are such activities? Wilbur Thompson (1968) argues as follows:

> the economic base of the larger metropolis is . . . the creativity of its universities and research parks, the sophistication of its engineering firms and financial institutions, the persuasiveness of its public relations and advertising agencies, the flexibility of its transportation networks and utility systems, and all the dimensions of "infrastructure" that facilitate the quick and orderly transfer from old dying bases to new growing ones.

The link between self-sustaining innovation in metropolitan regions and growth in regions not able to attain the threshold conditions for self-sustaining growth is, in such circumstances, clear:

> Larger urban regions combine a favorable industry mix for growth with a steadily declining share of the various growth industries . . . High wage rates of the innovating area, quite consonant with the high skills needed at the beginning of the learning process, become excessive when skill requirements decline, and the industry (or parts of it) "filters down" to the smaller, less industrially sophisticated regions where the cheaper labor can meet the declining skill demands of the filtering industry, thus creating the phenomenon of small towns with low-wage, slow-growth filtered-down industry [at the time when the metropolis has moved on to new bases]. (Thompson, 1968)

The heartland-hinterland lever for growth is thus replaced by the mechanisms of filtering on a regional scale. This possibly can produce convergence and integration of the space-economy; however, far more likely is a circular and cumulative process that leads to the innovating area spiraling away in terms of aggregate growth and incomes, leaving a continuing lag in the peripheral region that only new growth centers can begin to bridge.

At sufficient scale, local markets, infrastructure, and residentiary development thus make the large metropolitan region self-generative of growth. When threshold conditions are reached, however, the metropolis grows at about the rate of the nation. This threshold was argued by Thompson to be a metropolitan area (SMSA) of at least 250,000 population, although we shall show later that a regional population of at least 1,000,000 is probably more accurate. Beneath this scale, growth in the peripheries is related to capturing a share of downward-filtering industry, slow in growth, and yielding lower returns. The basic regional distinction is therefore that between self-generative metropolitan America, and the hand-me-down inter-metropolitan periphery, condemned to progress characterized at best by lagged emulation and second-hand growth.

A Unit for Analysis: The Daily Urban System

The validity of this alternative view of regional growth processes is to be seen quite clearly in the evidence of the 1960s.

At the outset, it is necessary to have a precise functional definition of the nature of the "urban regions" themselves, however, so that there is clarity in the discussion relative to the units of analysis about which generalizations are being made. Only then will we be able to focus clearly on the problems of inducing growth in those areas not participating fully in the strengths and benefits of a dynamic market economy.

Let us pose the definitional problem in the following way. Suppose we had information available about the likely growth of economic activity in certain urban centers during the 1970s. How might we go about forecasting the growth in population that would result? Or suppose we have earnings figures for workers at their place of employment, and want to study expenditure patterns at their places of residence. How might we go about linking earnings and expenditures in a consistent accounting framework?

The problem that arises is the same in both cases. People no longer live next to their workplace; indeed, the separation of residence and work continues to increase year by year as both residential neighborhoods and new industrial estates decentralize further afield from historic concentrations in the central cities. Maps showing the commuting "fields" of the nation's major central cities in 1960 (Berry, 1968) reveal the extensive areas of the country in daily commuting contact with legally-defined central cities of various size categories in that year (fig. 1-3, 1-4 and 1-5).

The commuting fields have surely become more extensive during the 1960–1970 decade. For population projections, this means that the residential areas (housing markets) related to particular employment clusters (job markets) cover zones extending far beyond both legal city limits and the boundaries of, for example, the Bureau of Census's "Standard Metropolitan Statistical Areas," which are explicitly constructed to *exclude* all counties for which the percentage of resident workers commuting to work in the central city drops beneath 15 percent. Population projections based upon assumptions about economic activity thus need a different unit of accounting if changes in employment are to be related properly to changes in the population supported by the jobs. Such an accounting unit is the *Daily Urban System* (DUS).

The term Daily Urban System was coined by C. A. Doxiadis in 1967 when he suggested the delimitation of functional boundaries for the nation's emerging urban areas through use of daily commuting fields. He argued that sixty DUSs were now forming in the United States, each with an average radius of ninety miles "within which people will move the way they now move within well-organized metropolitan areas."

The DUSs used in this study differ from those proposed by Doxiadis in that they are based upon the *actual* 1960 evidence about commuting patterns around existing economic centers.

The delineation procedure was as follows, as developed by the Office of Business Economics, U.S. Department of Commerce (now the Bureau of Economic Analysis, Economic and Social Statistics Administration), on the basis of our earlier studies of commuting (Berry, 1968). First, economic centers were identified. Standard Metropolitan Statistical Areas were chosen where possible. Each SMSA has a large city at its center which serves both as a wholesale and retail trade center and as a labor market center. However, not all SMSAs were made centers of economic areas because some are integral parts of larger metropolitan complexes and evidence a high degree of cross-commuting with other metropoli. The New York City area, for instance, encompasses not only the New York City SMSA, but also Jersey City, Newark, Patterson-Clifton-Passaic, Stanford, Norwalk, and Bridgeport SMSAs. The Seattle economic area includes Seattle-Everett and the Tacoma SMSAs. In rural parts of the country, where there were no SMSAs, cities of from 25,000 to 50,000 population were utilized as economic centers provided that two other criteria were met. These other criteria were: (1) that the city form a wholesale trade center for the area, and (2) that the area as a whole have a population minimum of about 200,000 people. After identifying economic centers, intervening counties were allocated to the centers. This assignment was made primarily on the basis of the journey to work pattern around the economic centers. Comparative time and distance of travel to the economic centers, the interconnection between outlying counties because of the journey to work pattern, the road network, and the linkages of counties by such other economic ties as telephone traffic, bank deposits, television viewing, newspaper circulation, and topography were also used to determine placement of peripheral counties into the appropriate economic area. In places where the commuting pattern of adjacent economic sectors overlapped, counties were included in the economic area containing the center with which there was the greatest commuting connection. In the

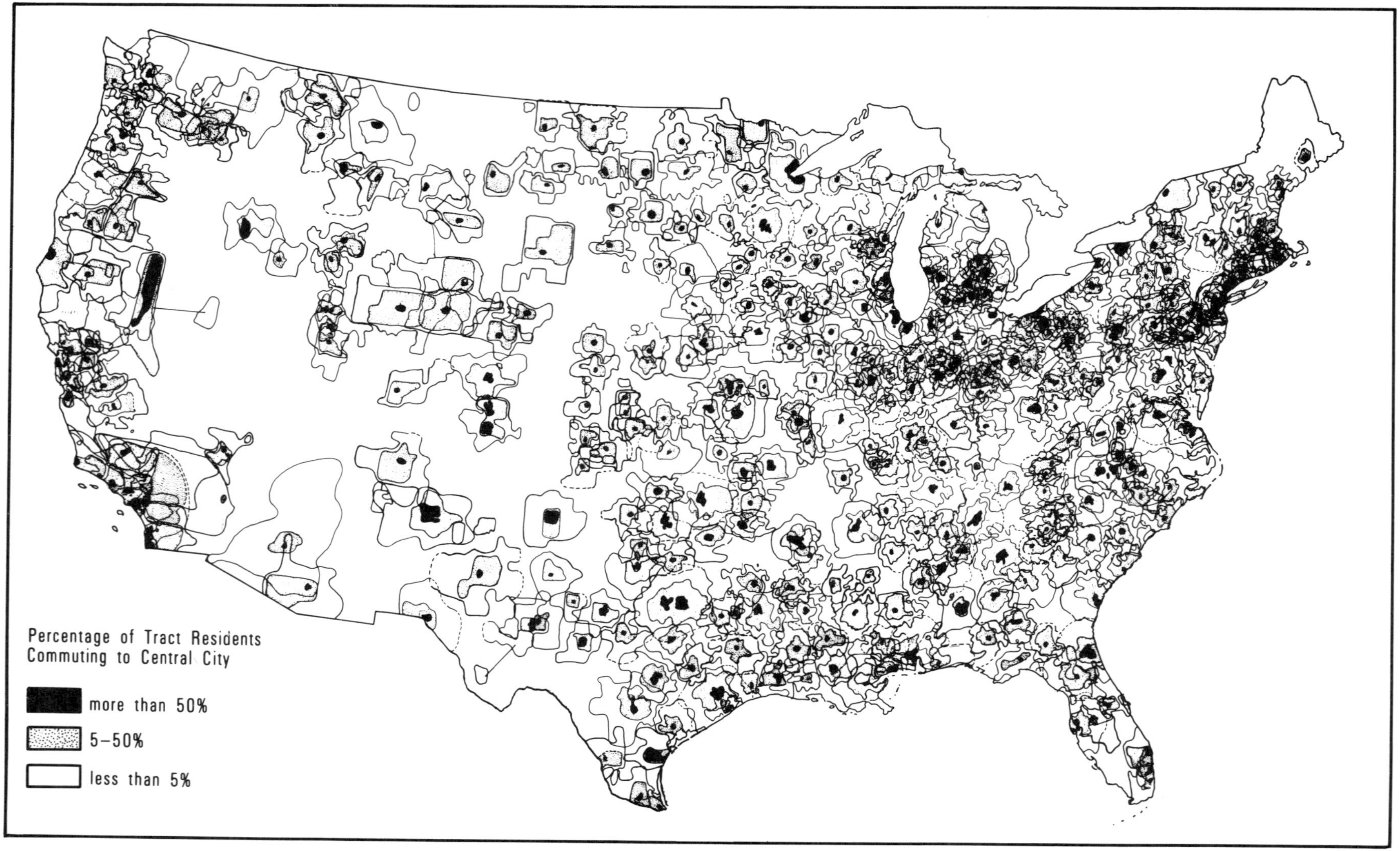

Figure 1–3. The National Pattern of Urban Commuting Fields in 1960.

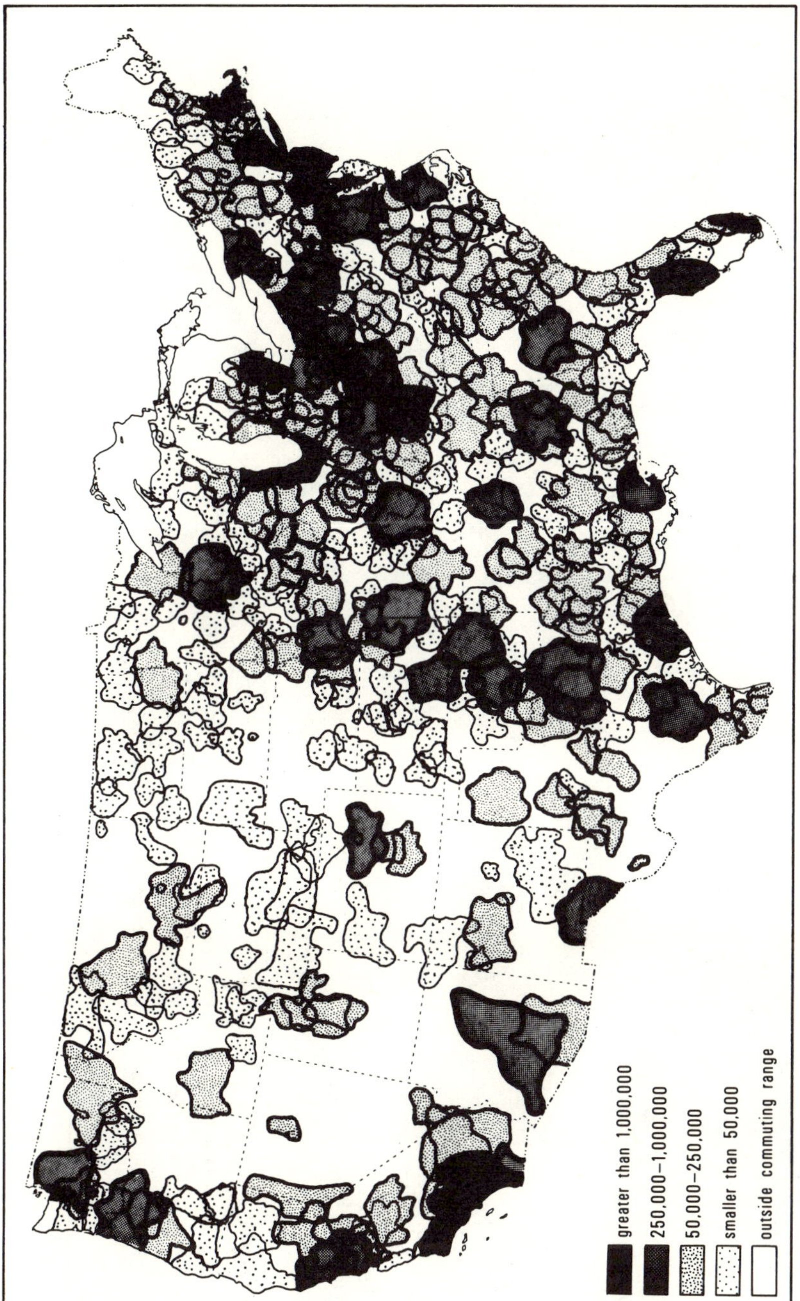

Figure 1–4. Commuting Areas Classified by the Size of their Central Cities.

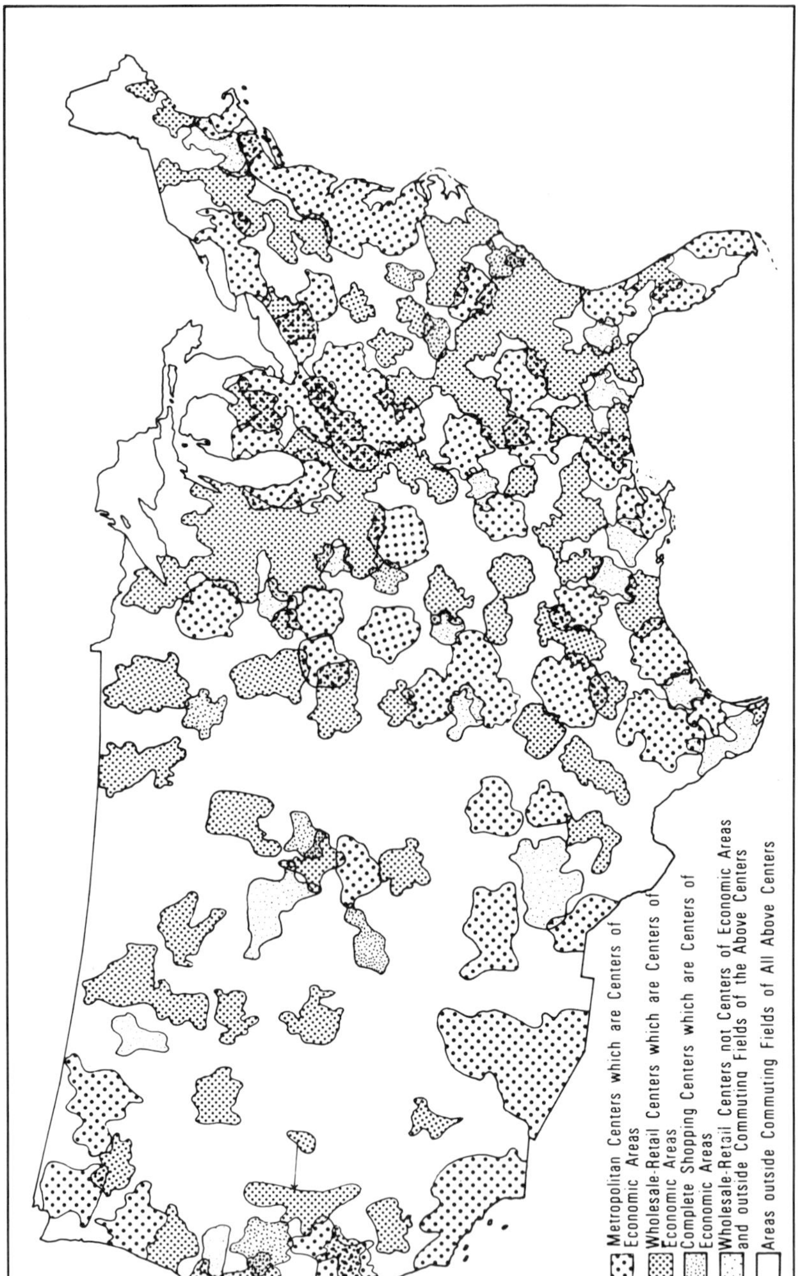

Figure 1–5. Regionalization of the United States According to Nature of Economic Centers.

case of cities where the commuting pattern overlapped to a great degree, no attempt was made to separate the two cities; instead, both were included in the same economic area.

A map of this preliminary division of the United States into OBE Economic Areas was distributed in September 1967 to members of state bureaus of business research, state planning agencies, and to field representatives of federal agencies involved in water resources planning. At the same time, OBE made a series of population forecasts using the preliminary economic area definitions. Reviewing the maps, with reference to the criteria used, several suggestions for revision were made by the states and by federal agencies based on additional data, and the areas were revised accordingly. The revised set of 173 OBE Economic Areas is shown in figure 1-6, dated January 1969.

It is this revised set of OBE areas that are called "Daily Urban Systems" in this study. These areas are used to organize the hierarchy and regional growth data in later chapters and in Volume II. The areas have the following statistical and conceptual advantages for urban and regional analysis:

1. They completely disaggregate the United States into subregions, using county units as convenient building blocks.
2. They have a high degree of "closure" with respect to the job and housing markets, and in the tertiary sector of their economies. This means
   a. that forecasts based on assumptions about the economic base (job market) can be translated into population forecasts (commuting area = housing market);
   b. income earned within each area can be equated with income spent, plus saving;
   c. a tertiary or "residentiary" economic sector can be identified whose growth, according to traditional economic theory, ought to be related to total sales made within the areas, in contrast to the primary and secondary sectors whose growth is in part related to sales made outside the economic area in larger markets, if traditional theory holds.
3. Because they extend beyond the existing commuting areas in many parts of the country, including counties whose orientation is defined by other forms of communication and marketing, the DUSs have the advantage of including the most likely prospective commuting areas within their limits, enabling the definition to remain stable over the time-period of the population projections. The exceptions are to be found in those places where increasing cross-commuting violates the "closure" conditions of section 2 above and suggests that, in the future, adjacent DUSs should be merged as their job and housing markets coalesce.

Each DUS specializes, of course, in the production of certain goods and services in order to take advantage of lower costs of production resulting from the availability of natural resources and from benefits to be derived from location and from internal and external economies. Each also approaches self-sufficiency in its residentiary industries; that is, most of the services and some of the goods required by the household sector and by local business as intermediate products are produced within the area. Thus the DUSs correspond to the closed trade areas of central place theory in which the number and type of establishments and their size and trade areas are bounded by the relative transportation costs from hinterland to competing centers. In other words, the closure with respect to residentiary industries includes general and convenience retail and wholesale trade activities and those other services which are difficult or impossible to transport and are most efficiently consumed in the vicinity of their production. On the other hand, the economic areas are open

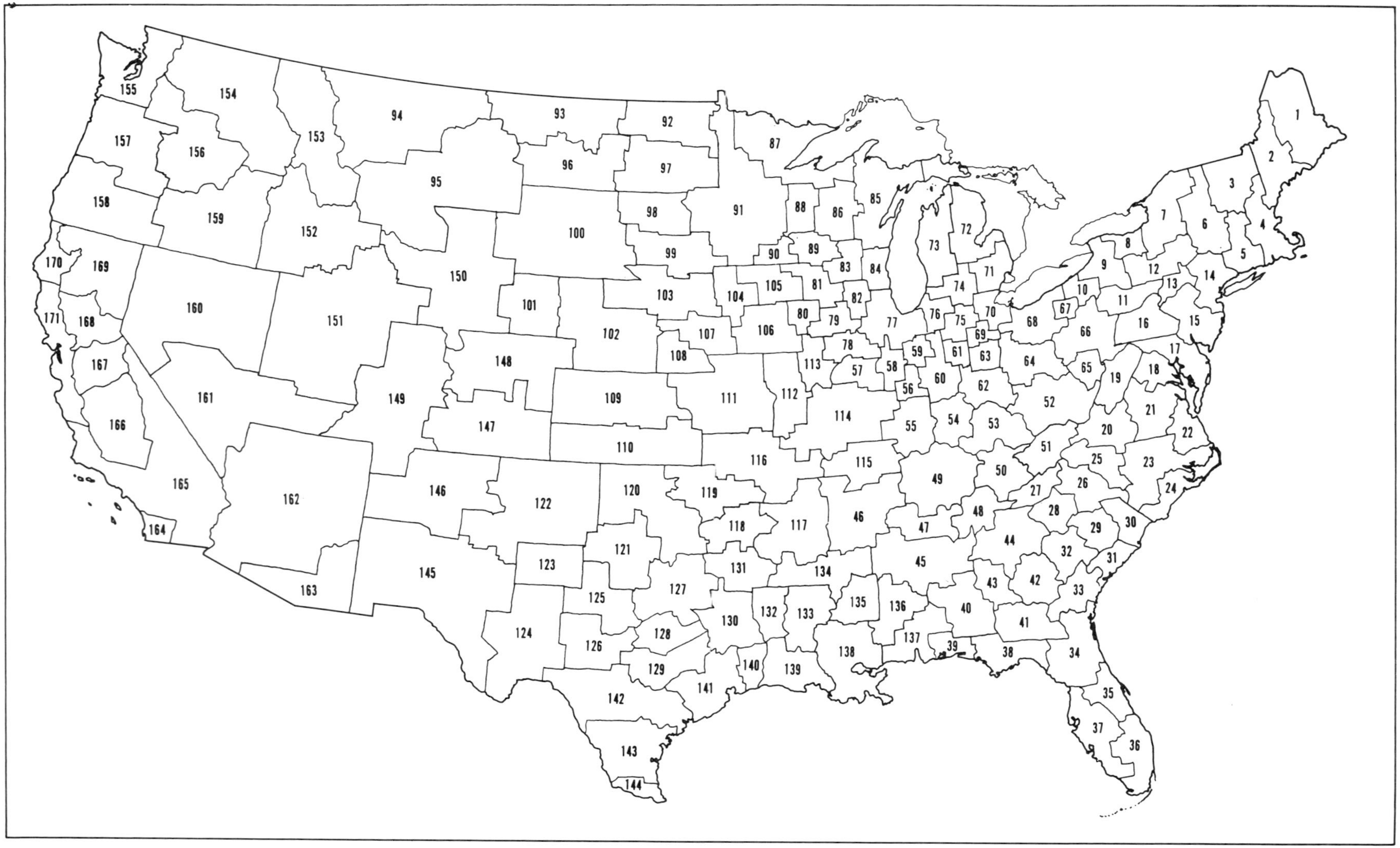

Figure 1–6. The OBE Economic Areas. Names corresponding to the numbers on the map will be found in Table 1–1.

for the most part to the movement of transportable commodities and nontransportable special services such as education at Cambridge and recreation at Miami, as well as to the effects of federal investment. Hence, if tertiary or quaternary activity is, as we have argued, becoming a source of new growth, the regional definition in no way inhibits recognition of this fact.

Growth Characteristics of the DUSs, 1960-1970

Table 1-1 presents the population of each DUS in 1960 and 1970, and shows the decadal percentage changes 1960-1970. There are wide variations in the growth rates. Why is this so?

First, there are clear relationships between growth and size. Figure 1-7 presents the evidence graphically, plotting the growth rate on the ordinate, and the 1960 population on the abscissa (using a logarithmic scale in the latter case). Each dot represents one of the 173 DUSs. Horizontal lines show the national growth rate 1960-1970, and zero change. The observations have been grouped into roughly equal logarithmic intervals (100,000-225, 000; 225,000-500,000; 500,000-1,000,000, etc.), and for each class the graph also shows the median growth rate for the observations within the class, and the upper and lower quartiles for all except the extreme classes with the fewest observations. Several things are immediately apparent:

1. The median growth rate increases progressively with size of DUS to a population of 1,000,000, and stabilizes thereafter at about the national growth rate. This is consistent with the ideas on self-generative development above a threshold.
2. The inter-quartile range is stable for size classes of less than 1,000,000, and above that point also for the lower quartile. However, the upper quartile is markedly greater than elsewhere in the size class 1,000,000-2,250,000, indicating accelerated growth of many centers in this size range in particular, as they pass over the threshold of self-sustained growth and, thereafter, converge again on the national average rate.
3. The median growth rate is negative in the smallest size class, as is the lower quartile in the size range 225,000-500,000, indicating that declining DUSs are disproportionately the smaller ones.

What accounts for some of these relationships? Do certain economic bases result in more ebullient growth, while others produce decline? Graphical comparisons of data from tables 1-1 and 1-2 provide information on shares of regional income derived from employment in different sectors that produces relevant insights:

1. The greater the dependence of a DUS on earnings derived from primary economic activities such as agriculture, the lower the growth rate. Indeed, when agricultural earnings exceed 25 percent of local earnings, there is a declining population (fig. 1-8).
2. As earnings from secondary sources in the manufacturing industries increase, the population growth rate of the DUS stabilizes around the national average, consistent with Thompson's notion of the urban size-ratchet effect (fig. 1-9).
3. The greater the share of local earnings derived from the tertiary sector, involving residentiary activities, the greater the population growth rate (fig. 1-10). One reason is the interregional migration of the more elderly non-job oriented population, supporting a tertiary sector via transfer payments; another is the differential regional growth of R and D, education, and other "brain power" activities.

Table 1-1. Population of Daily Urban Systems, 1960 and 1970, with Percentage Rate of Change, 1960 to 1970.

Daily Urban System	*Population 1960*	*(in thousands) 1970*	*Percentage Change in Population 1960-1970*
1. Bangor, Maine	337	321	-4.7
2. Portland, Maine	691	740	7.1
3. Burlington, Vt.	449	502	11.8
4. Boston, Mass.	5,668	6,338	11.8
5. Hartford, Conn.	2,542	2,966	16.7
6. Albany-Schenectady-Troy, N.Y.	1,192	1,331	11.7
7. Syracuse, N.Y.	1,342	1,444	7.6
8. Rochester, N.Y.	851	1,016	19.4
9. Buffalo, N.Y.	1,590	1,642	3.2
10. Erie, Pa.	444	459	3.6
11. Williamsport, Pa.	405	419	3.5
12. Binghamton, N.Y. -Pa.	695	765	10.1
13. Wilkes-Barre-Hazelton, Pa.	689	692	0.4
14. New York, N.Y.	16,406	18,228	11.1
15. Philadelphia, Pa.-N.J.	6,418	7,281	13.5
16. Harrisburg, Pa.	1,581	1,723	9.0
17. Baltimore, Md.	2,348	2,670	13.7
18. Washington, D.C.-Md.-Va.	2,273	3,090	35.9
19. Staunton, Va.	361	387	7.1
20. Roanoke, Va.	768	803	4.6
21. Richmond, Va.	898	1,004	11.7
22. Norfolk-Portsmouth, Va.	1,002	1,232	23.0
23. Raleigh, N.C.	1,479	1,621	9.6
24. Wilmington, N.C.	448	482	7.5
25. Greensboro-Winston Salem-High Point, N.C.	1,005	1,142	13.6
26. Charlotte, N.C.	1,285	1,489	15.9
27. Asheville, N.C.	350	391	11.6
28. Greenville, S.C.	741	817	10.3
29. Columbia, S.C.	551	610	10.7
30. Florence, S.C.	406	400	-1.3
31. Charleston, S.C.	368	430	16.9
32. Augusta, Ga.	422	461	9.3
33. Savannah, Ga.	403	417	3.5
34. Jacksonville, Fla.	808	946	7.1
35. Orlando, Fla.	648	941	45.3
36. Miami, Fla.	1,644	2,430	47.9
37. Tampa-St. Petersburg, Fla.	1,299	1,797	38.4
38. Tallahassee, Fla.	310	344	10.9
39. Pensacola, Fla.	313	382	21.9
40. Montgomery, Ala.	669	686	2.6
41. Albany, Ga.	453	460	1.6
42. Macon, Ga.	469	496	5.7
43. Columbia, Ga.-Ala.	462	488	5.6
44. Atlanta, Ga.	1,793	2,296	28.0
45. Birmingham, Ala.	1,680	1,660	-1.2
46. Memphis, Tenn.-Ark.	1,613	1,700	5.4
47. Huntsville, Ala.	552	671	21.4
48. Chattanooga, Tenn.-Ga.	650	718	10.4
49. Nashville, Tenn.	1,280	1,426	11.4
50. Knoxville, Tenn.	876	904	3.3
51. Bristol, Va.-Tenn.	718	698	-2.7
52. Huntington-Ashland, W. Va.-Ky.-Ohio	1,422	1,309	-7.9
53. Lexington, Ky.	708	805	13.8
54. Louisville, Ky.-Ind.	1,070	1,204	12.5
55. Evansville, Ind.	747	771	3.1

(continued)

Table 1-1. (continued)

Daily Urban System	*Population 1960*	*(in thousands) 1970*	*Percentage Change in Population 1960-1970*
56. Terre Haute, Ind.	250	252	0.9
57. Springfield, Ill.	471	490	4.0
58. Champaign-Urbana, Ill.	354	390	10.1
59. Lafayette-West Lafayette, Ind.	227	250	10.1
60. Indianapolis, Ind.	1,384	1,613	16.5
61. Muncie, Ind.	501	551	10.1
62. Cincinnati, Ohio-Ky.-Ind.	1,744	1,889	8.3
63. Dayton, Ohio	1,002	1,159	15.7
64. Columbus, Ohio	1,552	1,763	13.6
65. Clarksburg, W. Va.	333	326	-2.1
66. Pittsburgh, Pa.	3,749	3,716	-0.9
67. Youngstown-Warren, Ohio	749	770	2.8
68. Cleveland, Ohio	3,898	4,255	9.2
69. Lima, Ohio	259	276	6.5
70. Toledo, Ohio	967	1,054	8.9
71. Detroit, Mich.	4,582	5,207	13.7
72. Saginaw, Mich.	691	787	14.0
73. Grand Rapids, Mich.	990	1,166	17.8
74. Lansing, Mich.	889	986	10.9
75. Fort Wayne, Ind.	517	597	15.5
76. South Bend, Ind.	681	747	9.6
77. Chicago, Ill.	7,323	8,193	11.9
78. Peoria, Ill.	572	628	9.8
79. Davenport-Rock Island-Moline, Iowa-Ill.	552	605	9.5
80. Cedar Rapids, Iowa	288	330	14.5
81. Dubuque, Iowa	292	301	3.3
82. Rockford, Ill.	492	560	13.7
83. Madison, Wis.	377	455	20.8
84. Milwaukee, Wis.	1,848	2,066	11.8
85. Green Bay, Wis.	831	926	11.4
86. Wausau, Wis.	322	350	8.7
87. Duluth-Superior, Minn.-Wis.	449	429	-4.6
88. Eau Claire, Wis.	205	219	6.9
89. La Crosse, Wis.	257	269	4.8
90. Rochester, Minn.	230	245	6.1
91. Minneapolis-St. Paul, Minn.	2,528	2,935	16.1
92. Grand Forks, N.D.	223	220	-1.3
93. Minot, N.D.	189	170	-9.8
94. Great Falls, Mont.	226	222	-1.7
95. Billings, Mont.	245	246	0.7
96. Bismark, N.D.	149	144	-3.2
97. Fargo-Moorhead, N.D.-Minn.	342	335	-2.0
98. Aberdeen, S.D.	142	132	-7.0
99. Sioux Falls, S.D.	372	365	-2.0
100. Rapid City, S.D.	237	231	-2.5
101. Scotts Bluff, Nebr.	116	105	-9.1
102. Grand Island, Nebr.	322	309	-4.0
103. Sioux City, Iowa-Nebr.	467	454	-2.8
104. Fort Dodge, Iowa	280	266	-5.3
105. Waterloo, Iowa	427	426	-0.3
106. Des Moines, Iowa	759	741	-2.3
107. Omaha, Nebr.-Iowa	720	794	10.3
108. Lincoln, Nebr.	320	323	1.0
109. Salina, Kans.	379	342	-9.8
110. Witchita, Kans.	731	723	-1.1
111. Kansas City, Mo.-Kans.	1,538	1,674	8.9

(continued)

Table 1-1. (continued)

Daily Urban System	*Population 1960*	*(in thousands) 1970*	*Percentage Change in Population 1960-1970*
112. Columbia, Mo.	367	396	7.9
113. Quincy, Ill.	301	299	-0.7
114. St. Louis, Mo.-Ill.	2,945	3,248	10.3
115. Paducah, Ky.	580	558	3.9
116. Springfield, Mo.	777	816	5.1
117. Little Rock-No. Little Rock, Ark.	771	864	12.0
118. Fort Smith, Ark. -Okla.	252	289	14.4
119. Tulsa, Okla.	891	1,014	13.9
120. Oklahoma City, Okla.	1,040	1,156	11.2
121. Wichita Falls, Tex.	460	455	-1.1
122. Amarillo, Tex.	451	437	-3.0
123. Lubbock, Tex.	326	328	0.6
124. Odessa, Tex.	337	319	-5.4
125. Abilene, Tex.	290	264	-9.0
126. San Angelo, Tex.	126	124	-0.9
127. Dallas, Tex.	2,063	2,736	32.6
128. Waco, Tex.	374	403	7.8
129. Austin, Tex.	452	559	23.7
130. Tyler, Tex.	518	545	5.2
131. Texarkana, Tex.-Ark.	315	329	4.6
132. Shreveport, La.	445	453	1.7
133. Monroe, La.	515	532	3.8
134. Greenville, Miss.	556	506	-8.9
135. Jackson, Miss.	489	510	4.4
136. Meridian, Miss.	402	465	15.8
137. Mobile, Ala.	664	724	8.9
138. New Orleans, La.	1,884	2,148	14.0
139. Lake Charles, La.	655	748	14.1
140. Beaumont-port Arthur-Orange, Tex.	373	394	5.6
141. Houston, Tex.	1,758	2,362	34.4
142. San Antonio, Tex.	1,065	1,229	15.4
143. Corpus Christi, Tex.	465	516	11.0
144. Brownsville-Harlingen-San Benito, Tex.	369	355	-3.8
145. El Paso, Tex.	646	681	5.4
146. Albuquerque, N.M.	500	572	14.4
147. Pueblo, Colo.	424	509	20.1
148. Denver, Colo.	1,169	1,523	30.3
149. Grand Junction, Colo.	239	251	5.1
150. Cheyenne, Wyo.	221	229	3.5
151. Salt Lake City, Utah	898	1,061	18.2
152. Idaho Falls, Idaho	286	300	4.9
153. Butte, Mont.	213	234	10.3
154. Spokane, Wash.	659	687	4.1
155. Seattle-Everett, Wash.	1,879	2,363	25.8
156. Yakima, Wash.	398	406	2.0
157. Portland, Ore.-Wash.	1,348	1,637	21.4
158. Eugene, Ore.	458	541	18.0
159. Boise City, Idaho	241	265	9.8
160. Reno, Nev.	142	191	33.9
161. Las Vegas, Nev.	166	317	91.1
162. Phoenix, Ariz.	945	1,316	39.3
163. Tucson, Ariz.	357	454	27.3
164. San Diego, Calif.	1,033	1,357	31.4
165. Los Angeles-Long Beach, Calif.	8,087	10,436	29.0
166. Fresno, Calif.	916	1,036	13.1

(continued)

Table 1-1. (continued)

Daily Urban System	*Population 1960*	*(in thousands) 1970*	*Percentage Change in Population 1960–1970*
167. Stockton, Calif.	537	643	19.6
168. Sacramento, Calif.	854	1,089	27.6
169. Redding, Calif.	153	176	15.3
170. Eureka, Calif.	132	121	-7.9
171. San Francisco-Oakland, Calif.	4,001	5,090	27.2
172. Anchorage, Alaska	226	300	32.8
173. Honolulu, Hawaii	632	768	21.5

4. The greater the earnings derived from governmental sources, the greater the local growth rate (fig. 1-11).

The growth sectors of the decade were the tertiary (traditionally the nonbasic or secondary sectors), and the governmental. Indeed, no DUS with more than 12.5 percent of its earnings derived from federal sources lost population in the decade, and the greater the federal contribution to local earnings, the greater the decadal growth rate. This finding is of particular importance for it emphasizes that among the unplanned consequences of the concentration of governmental expenditures in particular places are systematic impacts on the growth rates of those places. Thus, when we turn to the issue of inducing growth in lagging areas, we must consider what alternative pattern might have been produced by some other pattern of regional expenditures of the federal dollar.

Putting the data together, we find that the joint relationships between DUS size and economic base are as reported in table 1-3. In general, both increased diversification and increasing size produce greater stabilization of the growth rate at the national average. Small size combined with a regional economy specialized in the primary sectors usually means a declining population. The accelerated growth of the upper-quartile DUSs in the 1,000,000+ size range is associated with massive reliance upon governmental expenditures. And because these expenditures produce higher-than-average incomes, the decade was characterized by (a) a positive association between per capita incomes and population growth rates (fig. 1-12), and (b) a stability relationship between growth rates of income and of population (fig. 1-13). The dynamic in these latter two relationships involves positive relations between population growth and growth rates of earnings in retail trade, service activities, and from federal civilian employment on the one hand (figs. 1-14, 1-15 and 1-16), alongside similar positive relationships with the growth rate of manufacturing earnings on the other hand (fig. 1-17).

Such, then, are the bases of the broad regional differences in population growth rates depicted in figure 1-18. But this map also reveals interesting intraregional growth differences, for example the negative growth rates of the traditional core cities, as well as accelerated new growth directions penetrating the former interurban peripheries, and it is to these differences that we now must turn.

Patterns of Intraregional Growth and Expansion

The facts of equally dramatic change *within* the urban systems became unmistakable in the United States in the 1960s. As the Commission on Population Growth and the

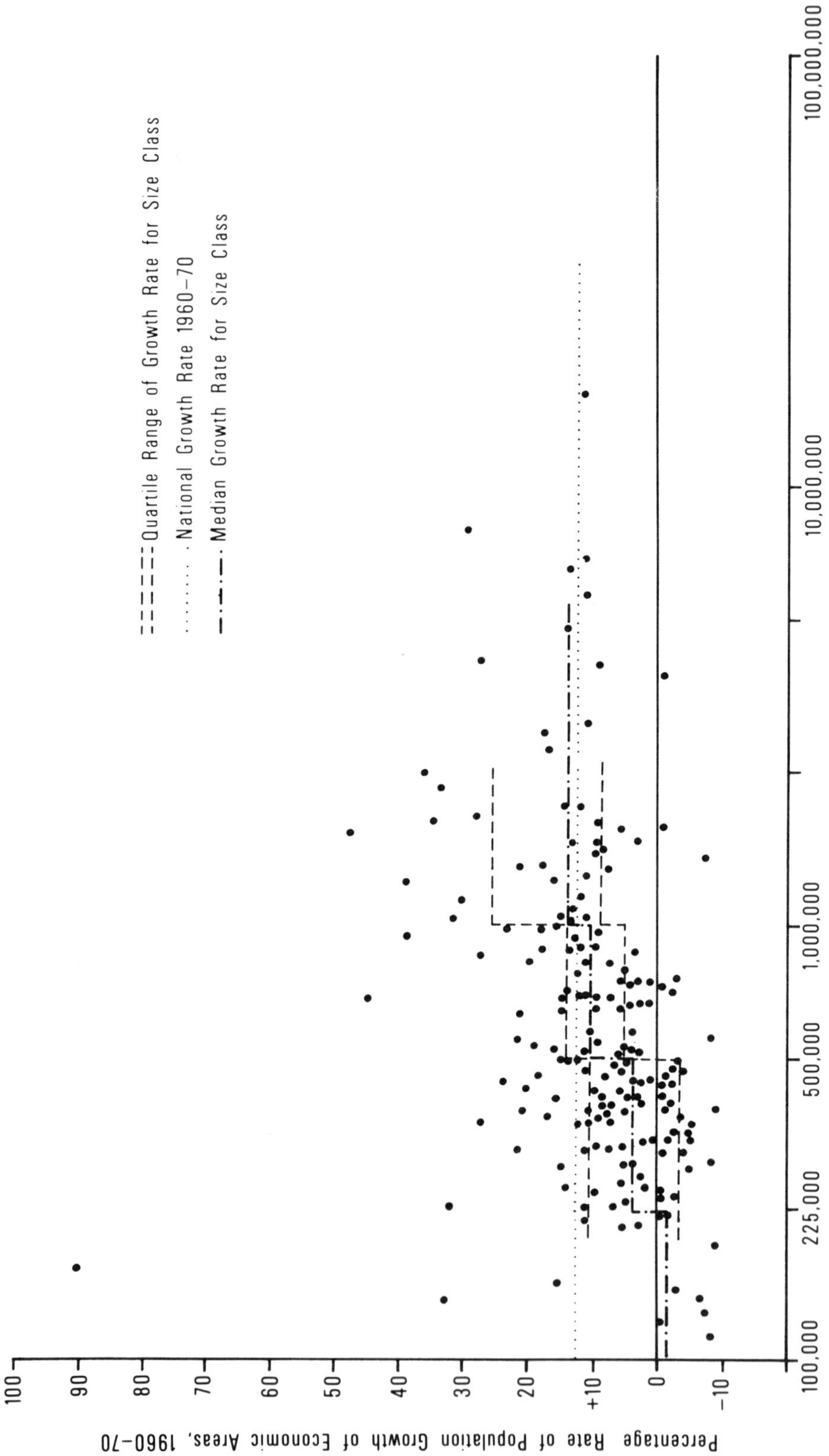

Figure 1–7. Growth Rate of the DUSs 1960–1970 Related to Their Population in 1960.

Table 1-2. Basic and Residentiary Earnings of the Daily Urban Systems in 1967, Expressed as a Percentage of Total Earnings

	Basic						
Economic Area	*Agriculture*	*Mining*	*Manufacturing*	*Federal Govt.*	*Other*	*Total*	*Residentiary*
1. Bangor, Maine	7.49	.09	25.52	10.36	1.26	44.73	55.27
2. Portland, Maine	2.76	.06	33.58	2.32		38.72	61.28
3. Burlington, Vt.	5.09	.69	29.04	.99	3.82	39.64	60.36
4. Boston, Mass.	.72	.06	29.32	2.39	4.34	36.83	63.17
5. Hartford, Conn.	1.20	.10	39.92	1.71	.93	43.86	56.14
6. Albany-Schenectady-Troy, N.Y.	1.96	.45	27.60	8.01	1.85	39.87	60.13
7. Syracuse, N.Y.	3.38	.52	29.47	5.68	1.58	40.63	59.37
8. Rochester, N.Y.	2.88	.23	44.14	.30		47.56	52.44
9. Buffalo, N.Y.	2.10	.35	37.36	1.76	.45	42.02	57.98
10. Erie, Pa.	2.87	.33	45.03	.43	.54	49.21	50.79
11. Williamsport, Pa.	2.16	2.08	38.16	5.03	1.58	49.01	50.99
12. Binghampton, N.Y.-Pa.	4.32	.12	39.77	3.17	.51	47.90	52.10
13. Wilkes-Barre-Hazelton, Pa.	1.60	1.91	33.77	.53	1.44	39.25	60.75
14. New York, N.Y.	.38	.12	24.65	.66	11.38	37.20	62.80
15. Philadelphia, Pa.-N.J.	1.12	.26	32.61	2.20		36.19	63.81
16. Harrisburg, Pa.	3.97	.73	33.81	1.20	1.81	41.52	58.48
17. Baltimore, Md.	2.49	.05	24.04	9.64		36.22	63.78
18. Washington, D.C.-Md.-Va.	.77	.14	2.05	32.08	6.13	41.17	58.83
19. Staunton, Va.	5.74	1.74	30.38	3.20	2.00	43.06	56.94
20. Roanoke, Va.	3.88	.36	37.48	1.03	2.64	45.39	54.61
21. Richmond, Va.	3.33	.20	21.23	7.93	2.94	35.64	64.36
22. Norfolk-Portsmouth, Va.	2.71	.02	12.84	35.72		51.29	48.71
23. Raleigh, N.C.	12.99	.31	18.07	13.72		45.09	54.91
24. Wilmington, N.C.	10.45	.05	13.56	29.44		53.50	46.50
25. Greensboro-Winston Salem-High Point, N.C.	3.49	.17	42.12	.75	1.94	48.47	51.53

(continued)

Table 1-2. (continued)

Economic Area	Basic: Agriculture	Basic: Mining	Basic: Manufacturing	Basic: Federal Govt.	Basic: Other	Basic: Total	Residentiary
26. Charlotte, N.C.	2.06	.17	40.56	.63	1.75	45.17	54.83
27. Asheville, N.C.	4.37	.40	36.85	.81	1.05	43.47	56.53
28. Greenville, S.C.	1.45	.14	46.84	.83		49.26	50.74
29. Columbia, S.C.	5.63	.24	18.36	16.29		40.52	59.48
30. Florence, S.C.	14.63	.22	29.85	3.38	.48	48.57	51.43
31. Charleston, S.C.	3.69	.03	12.98	34.16	.30	51.16	48.84
32. Augusta, Ga.	6.20	.41	26.54	22.77		55.93	44.07
33. Savannah, Ga.	9.99	.06	21.80	6.32	3.39	41.56	58.44
34. Jacksonville, Fla.	3.72	.55	12.49	13.46	6.58	36.80	63.20
35. Orlando, Fla.	5.29	.06	19.03	4.24	8.80	37.42	62.58
36. Miami, Fla.	4.49	.24	10.86	2.43	17.98	36.00	64.00
37. Tampa-St. Petersburg, Fla.	4.69	1.28	13.60	2.38	11.91	33.86	66.14
38. Tallahassee, Fla.	6.17	.11	11.56	27.26		45.11	54.89
39. Pensacola, Fla.	1.52	.15	15.72	33.17		50.55	49.45
40. Montgomery, Ala.	6.96	.19	19.00	16.27	.04	42.47	57.53
41. Albany, Ga.	20.87	.35	17.88	6.57		45.67	54.33
42. Macon, Ga.	11.90	1.98	18.20	16.63		48.71	51.29
43. Columbus, Ga.-Ala.	3.17	.12	22.45	27.20		52.93	47.07
44. Atlanta, Ga.	1.55	.29	24.05	1.89	8.42	36.20	63.80
45. Birmingham, Ala.	4.27	1.51	30.29	3.34	1.12	40.52	59.48
46. Memphis, Tenn.-Ark.	13.86	.20	19.55	2.97	3.04	39.62	60.38
47. Huntsville, Ala.	6.64	.31	25.56	11.40	4.99	48.89	51.11
48. Chattanooga, Tenn.	3.37	.64	41.95	.67		46.62	53.38
49. Nashville, Tenn.	5.88	.38	23.53	6.10		35.90	64.10
50. Knoxville, Tenn.	1.95	2.80	31.04	4.29	.43	40.50	59.50
51. Bristol, Va.-Tenn.	3.00	10.15	28.51	.96	1.75	44.37	55.63
52. Huntington-Ashland, W. Va.-Ky.	1.02	11.77	24.01	3.14	3.61	43.55	56.45
53. Lexington, Ky.	11.84	3.19	18.59	4.37	.48	38.47	61.53
54. Louisville, Ky.-Ind.	3.25	.26	28.44	8.46	1.17	41.58	58.42
55. Evansville, Ind.	8.08	6.24	26.38	.53	.93	42.17	57.83
56. Terre Haute, Ind.	8.75	3.32	19.90	4.31	4.99	41.27	58.73

57. Springfield, Ill.	10.48	.93	19.70	5.46	4.02	40.59	59.41
58. Champaign-Urbana, Ill.	11.25	.40	16.79	16.05	.48	44.96	55.04
59. Lafayette, West Lafayette, Ind.	13.80	.25	26.46	8.65	.94	50.09	49.91
60. Indianapolis, Ind.	3.17	.32	33.02	1.57	1.17	39.26	60.74
61. Muncie, Ind.	3.67	.17	50.71	.35		54.90	45.10
62. Cincinnati, Ohio-Ky.-Ind.	1.83	.16	34.50	.54	.97	38.00	62.00
63. Dayton, Ohio	2.25	.19	40.71	5.94		49.10	50.90
64. Columbus, Ohio	1.69	.80	28.91	3.94	.50	35.84	64.16
65. Clarksburg, W. Va.	1.22	14.30	19.66	4.45	4.91	44.54	55.46
66. Pittsburgh, Pa.	.79	2.87	36.53	.45	2.87	43.50	56.50
67. Youngstown-Warren, Ohio	.96	.42	50.46	.41	.60	52.85	47.15
68. Cleveland, Ohio	1.12	.39	41.70	.37	.67	44.24	55.76
69. Lima, Ohio	8.43	.21	38.69	.36	.50	48.20	51.80
70. Toledo. Ohio	4.22	1.00	36.14	.40	1.04	42.80	57.20
71. Detroit, Mich.	.48	.09	42.94	.39	.17	44.07	55.93
72. Saginaw, Mich.	4.42	1.04	37.66	4.78	.31	48.21	51.79
73. Grand Rapids, Mich.	3.33	.17	38.85	.42	.44	43.21	56.79
74. Lansing, Mich.	2.95	.15	38.15	4.95	.42	46.62	53.38
75. Fort Wayne, Ind.	5.26	.23	40.52	.35	.73	47.08	52.92
76. South Bend, Ind.	3.86	.09	45.11	.36		49.42	50.58
77. Chicago, Ill.	1.09	.27	32.12	.99	4.04	38.52	61.48
78. Peoria, Ill.	9.52	1.22	30.31	.32	.63	42.00	58.00
79. Davenport-Rock Island-Moline, Iowa-Ill.	8.74	.20	34.12	.47		43.52	56.48
80. Cedar Rapids, Iowa	11.70	.43	29.68	.36		42.17	57.83
81. Dubuque, Iowa	22.86	.91	17.75	.50		42.02	57.98
82. Rockford, Ill.	7.06	.24	43.84	.27		51.42	48.58
83. Madison, Wis.	9.05	.26	15.85	12.43	1.70	39.30	60.70
84. Milwaukee, Wis.	2.28	.15	39.58	.47	.23	42.71	57.29
85. Green Bay, Wis.	5.76	2.94	32.04	3.68		44.43	55.57
86. Wausau, Wis.	9.79	.23	28.37	3.25	.37	42.01	57.99
87. Duluth-Superior, Minn.-Wis.	.42	13.28	15.54	6.75	8.31	44.30	55.70

(continued)

Table 1-2. (continued)

Economic Area	Basic						Residentiary
	Agriculture	Mining	Manufacturing	Federal Govt.	Other	Total	
88. Eau Claire, Wis.	10.15	.26	23.66	5.74	2.64	42.46	57.54
89. La Crosse, Wis.	12.69	.60	19.95	5.31	2.72	41.27	58.73
90. Rochester, Minn.	12.64	.26	25.50	.38	7.53	46.31	53.69
91. Minneapolis-St. Paul, Minn.	5.41	.16	23.46	.63	5.42	35.08	64.92
92. Grand Forks, N.D.	30.49	.18	3.56	10.62	1.40	46.26	53.74
93. Minot, N.D.	27.04	2.89	.91	11.25	1.61	43.71	56.29
94. Great Falls, Mont.	21.90	.87	3.11	12.58	2.64	41.09	58.91
95. Billings, Mont.	15.80	3.42	4.77	4.94	6.04	34.97	65.03
96. Bismarck, N.D.	18.62	1.63	1.42	7.24	8.50	37.42	62.58
97. Fargo-Morrhead, N.D.-Minn.	19.12	.16	2.33	5.69	11.71	39.00	61.00
98. Aberdeen, S.D.	33.79	.18	2.96	3.53	2.08	42.54	57.46
99. Sioux Falls, S.D.	26.86	.25	8.21	2.13	2.59	40.03	59.97
100. Rapid City, S.D.	28.41	3.69	2.34	13.13	.39	47.96	52.04
101. Scotts Bluff, Nebr.	30.67	1.88	2.74	2.43	4.75	42.47	57.53
102. Grand Island, Nebr.	31.46	.25	9.61	.54	2.26	44.12	55.88
103. Sioux City, Iowa-Nebr.	26.21	.14	11.52	1.36	1.81	41.03	58.97
104. Fort Dodge, Iowa	34.43	.24	9.14	.41	1.27	45.50	54.50
105. Waterloo, Iowa	17.80	.51	27.35	.60		46.26	53.74
106. Des Moines, Iowa	11.65	.38	16.03	1.66	5.28	35.00	65.00
107. Omaha, Nebr.-Iowa	9.58	.40	14.84	4.64	8.01	37.46	62.54
108. Lincoln, Nebr.	16.57	.10	10.06	5.50	3.28	35.51	64.49
109. Salina, Kans.	26.83	4.05	5.58	3.45	1.96	41.87	58.13
110. Witchita, Kans.	10.23	2.17	25.89	2.56	.86	41.72	58.28
111. Kansas City, Mo.-Kans.	5.90	.21	19.30	3.86	5.83	35.10	64.90
112. Columbia, Mo.	17.68	.42	10.23	11.27	1.67	41.27	58.73
113. Quincy, Ill.	15.41	.37	29.75	.42	.61	46.56	53.44
114. St. Louis, Mo.-Ill.	1.86	1.57	28.86	2.90	1.23	36.41	63.59
115. Paducah, Ky.	20.08	1.08	17.38	3.57	1.21	43.31	56.69

116. Springfield, Mo.	7.02	1.14	21.53	3.87	5.16	38.71	61.29
117. Little Rock-North Little Rock, Ark.	8.53	.88	17.56	3.92	5.35	36.24	63.76
118. Fort Smith, Ark.-Okla.	3.38	1.60	23.57	4.52	.70	33.77	66.23
119. Tulsa, Okla.	2.62	10.42	20.48	.80	2.39	36.72	63.28
120. Oklahoma City, Okla.	7.62	4.89	9.00	12.07	2.01	35.59	64.41
121. Wichita Falls, Tex.	11.11	4.36	5.76	30.52		51.75	48.25
122. Amarillo, Tex.	19.91	5.01	7.84	8.44	2.22	43.42	56.58
123. Lubbock, Tex.	33.91	2.20	3.75	2.57	.23	42.66	57.34
124. Odessa, Tex.	7.74	24.28	5.70	2.94	1.43	42.09	57.91
125. Abilene, Tex.	12.20	6.23	7.04	9.74	4.24	39.45	60.55
126. San Angelo, Tex.	16.21	3.20	4.90	12.24	1.62	38.15	61.85
127. Dallas, Tex.	1.22	1.81	25.35	1.80	7.21	37.40	62.60
128. Waco, Tex.	5.06	.31	10.99	33.96		50.32	49.68
129. Austin, Tex.	5.56	.93	6.88	22.35	.95	36.67	63.33
130. Tyler, Tex.	1.52	5.18	25.39	5.49	1.97	39.55	60.45
131. Texarkana, Tex.-Ark.	3.92	1.28	27.72	8.61	1.27	42.80	57.20
132. Shreveport, La.	3.63	5.52	18.73	6.21	2.98	37.06	62.94
133. Monroe, La.	15.80	1.93	13.61	8.85	1.12	41.32	58.68
134. Greenville, Miss.	24.39	1.79	23.42	.78		50.38	49.62
135. Jackson, Miss.	8.97	1.54	17.14	1.29	4.70	33.64	66.36
136. Meridian, Miss.	6.32	2.31	24.76	5.52	1.32	40.24	59.76
137. Mobile, Ala.	2.34	.22	23.48	14.95	1.13	42.13	57.87
138. New Orleans, La.	2.29	5.72	16.88	.70	9.99	35.58	64.42
139. Lake Charles, La.	8.97	11.13	9.91	12.71	3.57	46.29	53.71
140. Beaumont-Port Arthur-Orange, Tex.	.88	2.58	36.18	.78	8.81	49.23	50.77
141. Houston, Tex.	1.65	5.87	19.66	.70	11.59	39.47	60.53
142. San Antonio, Tex.	3.98	1.47	7.38	24.56	.51	37.90	62.10
143. Corpus Christi, Tex.	8.31	8.32	7.78	13.28	.72	38.41	61.59
144. Brownsville-Harlingen-San Benito, Tex.	21.06	2.09	5.01	7.85	4.17	40.18	59.82
145. El Paso, Tex.	7.68	6.39	7.63	19.97	2.55	44.23	55.77
146. Albuquerque, N.M.	1.56	2.49	5.24	16.92	3.83	30.05	69.95
147. Pueblo, Col.	5.55	.79	10.44	25.65	1.71	44.14	55.86

(continued)

Table 1-2. (continued)

Economic Area	Basic						Residentiary
	Agriculture	*Mining*	*Manufacturing*	*Federal Govt.*	*Other*	*Total*	
148. Denver, Col.	4.00	1.98	13.83	5.80	7.99	33.60	66.40
149. Grand Junction, Col.	7.87	12.21	4.53	6.62	8.09	39.32	60.68
150. Cheyenne, Wyo.	8.10	9.76	5.91	10.82	7.15	41.74	58.26
151. Salt Lake City, Utah	3.74	3.93	12.75	13.74	2.53	36.68	63.32
152. Idaho Falls, Idaho	21.59	.97	9.26	1.11	6.65	39.58	60.42
153. Butte, Mont.	4.49	6.84	17.90	4.73	6.85	40.81	59.19
154. Spokane, Wash.	14.04	1.62	12.60	6.88	1.30	36.43	63.57
155. Seattle-Everett, Wash.	1.25	.15	27.23	6.12	1.37	36.13	63.87
156. Yakima, Wash.	17.57	.14	13.52	4.78	1.15	37.17	62.83
157. Portland, Ore.-Wash.	3.44	.18	22.48	2.44	3.97	32.50	67.50
158. Eugene, Ore.	2.52	.75	31.19	3.80	1.42	39.68	60.32
159. Boise City, Idaho	14.52	.14	11.04	5.34	5.40	36.45	63.55
160. Reno, Nev.	2.89	3.88	2.50	8.94	23.44	41.65	58.35
161. Las Vegas, Nev.	1.32	1.26	3.39	4.74	35.64	46.35	53.65
162. Phoenix, Ariz.	6.77	2.18	17.63	5.99	2.39	34.97	65.03
163. Tucson, Ariz.	1.20	7.61	7.43	18.69	3.30	38.23	61.77
164. San Diego, Calif.	1.56	.12	14.97	26.59	.96	44.21	55.79
165. Los Angeles-Long Beach, Calif.	1.54	.58	27.91	1.99	4.34	36.37	63.63
166. Fresno, Calif.	20.76	3.61	7.29	7.91		39.57	60.43
167. Stockton, Calif.	13.22	.27	14.55	11.01	.68	39.72	60.28
168. Sacramento, Calif.	4.57	.17	8.23	22.36	3.01	38.33	61.67
169. Redding, Calif.	1.38	.37	21.83	14.46	5.54	43.58	56.42
170. Eureka, Calif.	4.43	.19	28.81	9.95	.96	44.34	55.66
171 San Francisco-Oakland, Calif.	1.96	.23	17.19	7.97	5.42	32.77	67.23
172. Anchorage, Alaska	2.47	3.13	3.73	32.44	8.10	49.86	50.14
173. Honolulu, Hawaii	5.12	.01	4.55	22.86	6.09	38.63	61.37

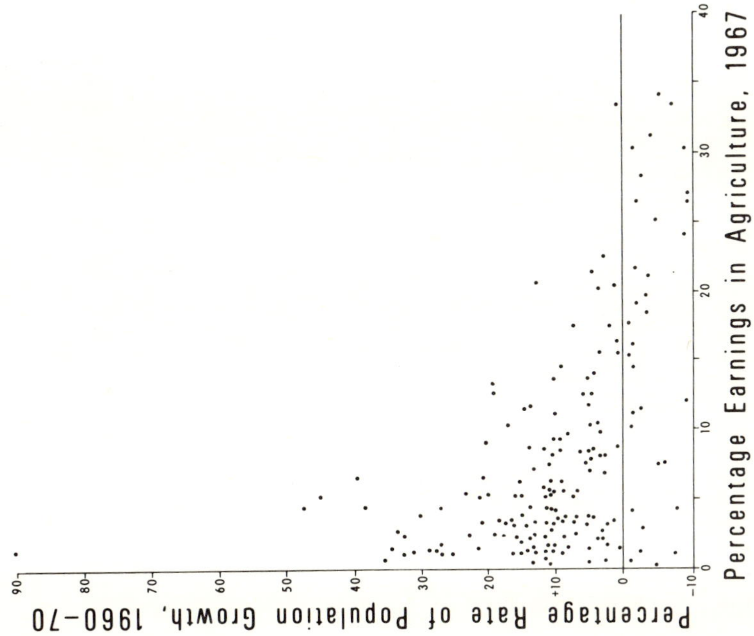

Figure 1–8. Growth Rate Related to Agricultural Earnings.

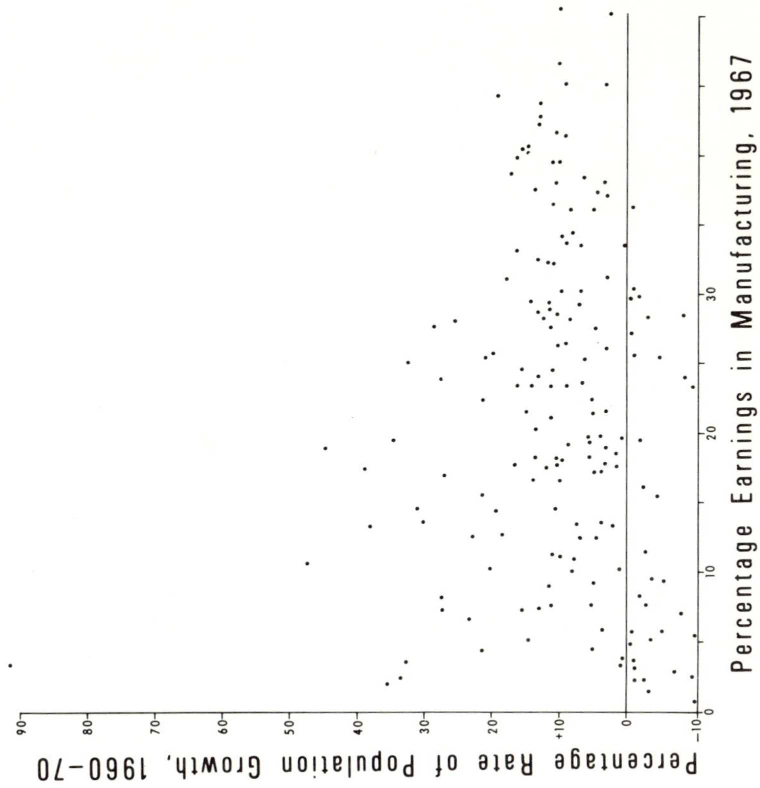

Figure 1–9. Growth Rate Related to Manufacturing Earnings.

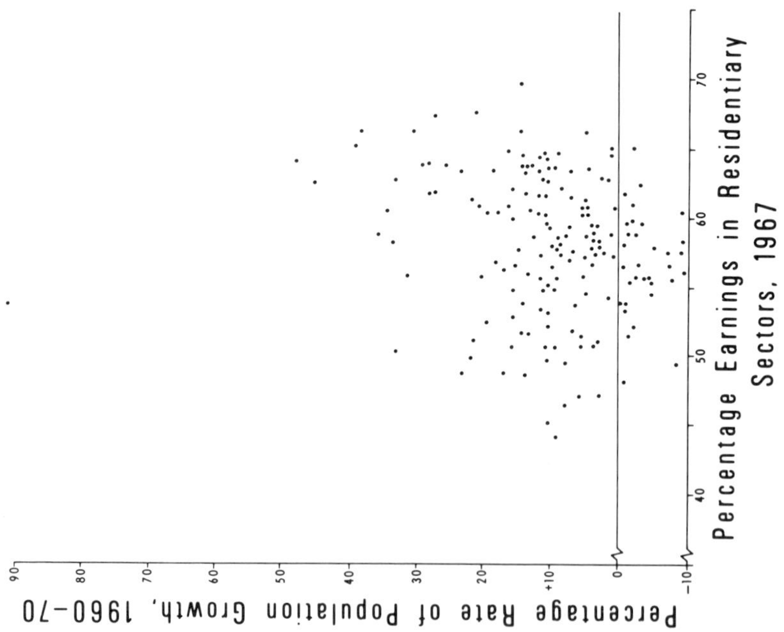

Figure 1–10. Growth Rate Related to Residentiary Earnings.

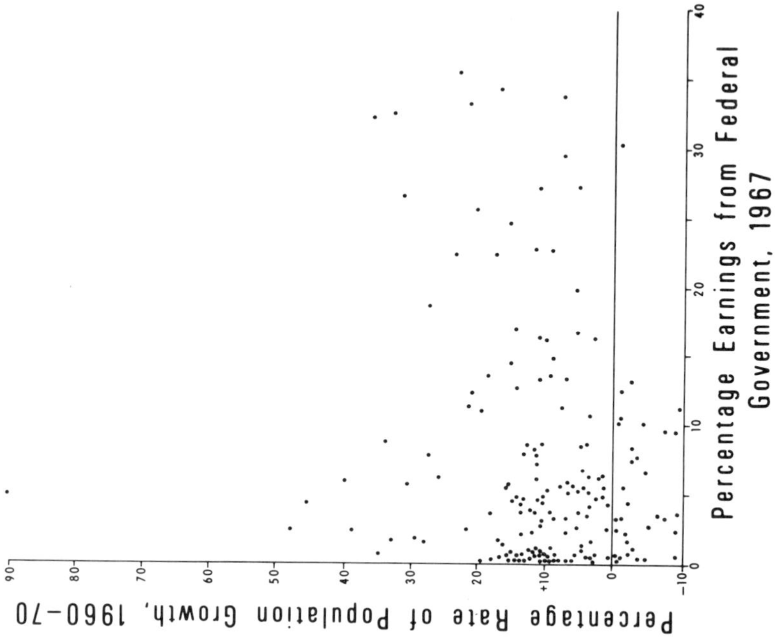

Figure 1–11. Growth Rate Related to Federal Earnings.

Table 1-3. Median Growth Rates of Various Types of Economic Areas, 1960–1970

Population Size-Class of Economic Area in 1970 (in thousands)	Economic Area Focuses Upon:										
	Center of Metropolitan Status				Center of Less Than Metropolitan Status						
	and Source of Earnings of Area was Derived in 1967 From:										
	12.5% Federal Government	60% Residentiary	Federal and Residentiary	Diversified Sources	12.5% Federal Government	60% Residentiary	Federal and Residentiary	Diversified	25% Agriculture	Federal and Agriculture	12.5% Mining
1. 100–225	a	a	a	a	15.3	-2.05	b	8.6	-8.05	b	b
2. 225–500	b	1.7	23.7	-3.0	9.7	4.9	b	4.0	-4.0	-2.5	-4.6
3. 500–1,000	7.2	11.0	18.2	15.5	10.7	12.0	b	9.6	b	b	b
4. 1,000–2,250	27.2	18.9	15.4	11.8	9.6	b	11.7	9.0	b	b	b
5. 2,250–5,000	35.9	14.9	b	11.5	a	a	a	a	a	a	a
6. 5,000–10,000	b	12.7	b	b	a	a	a	a	a	a	a
7. 10,000 and over	b	11.1	b	b	a	a	a	a	a	a	a

[a]No centers of this level.

[b]No centers of this type.

National Growth Rate 1960–1970 was 13.3%.

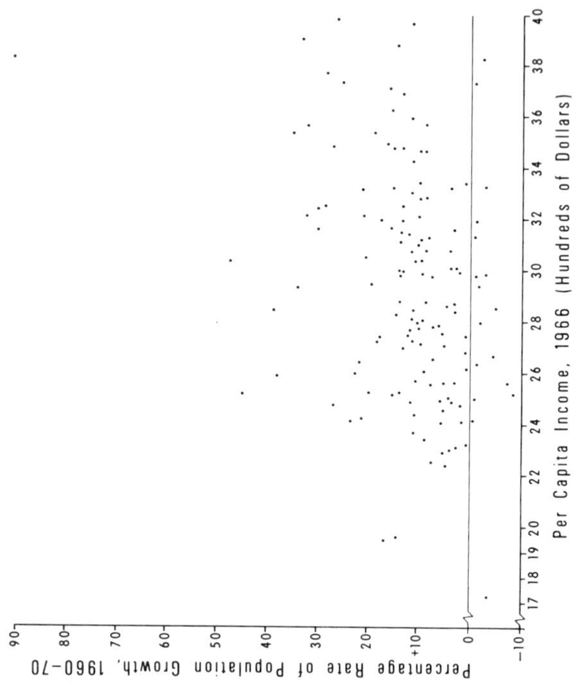

Figure 1–12. Population Growth Rate Related to Per Capita Incomes.

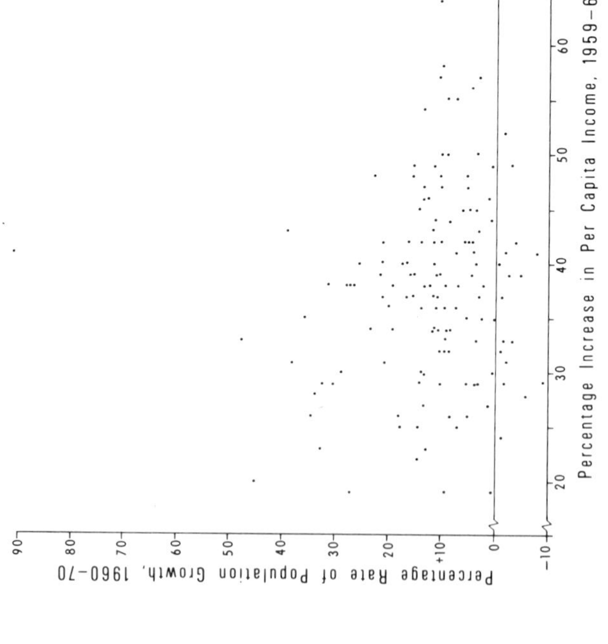

Figure 1–13. Population Growth Rate Related to Growth Rate of Per Capita Incomes.

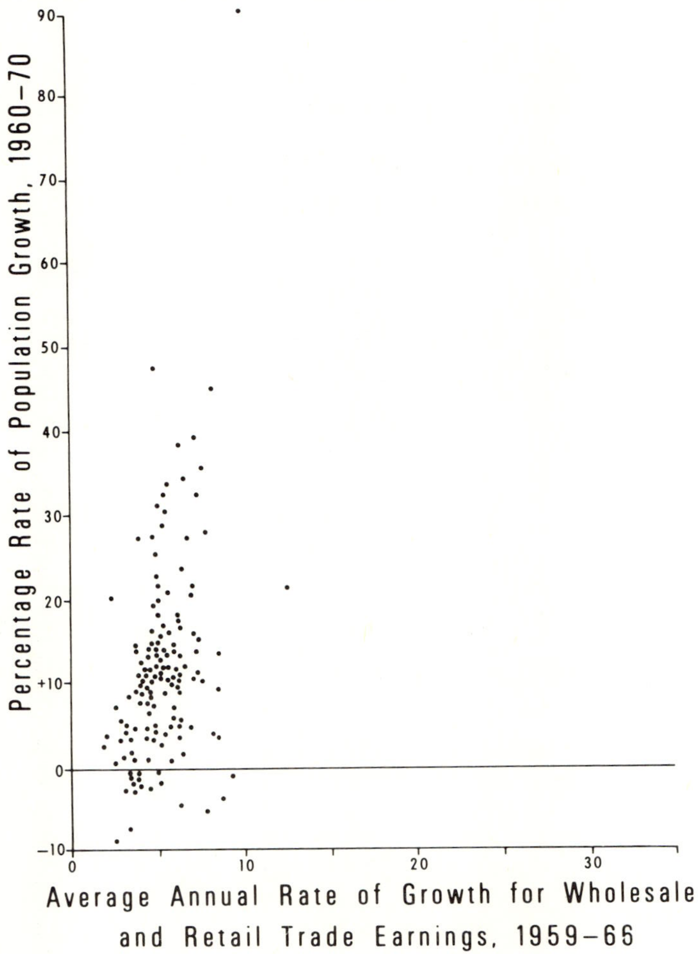

Figure 1-14. Population Growth Rate Related to Growth Rate of Earnings from Wholesale and Retail Trade.

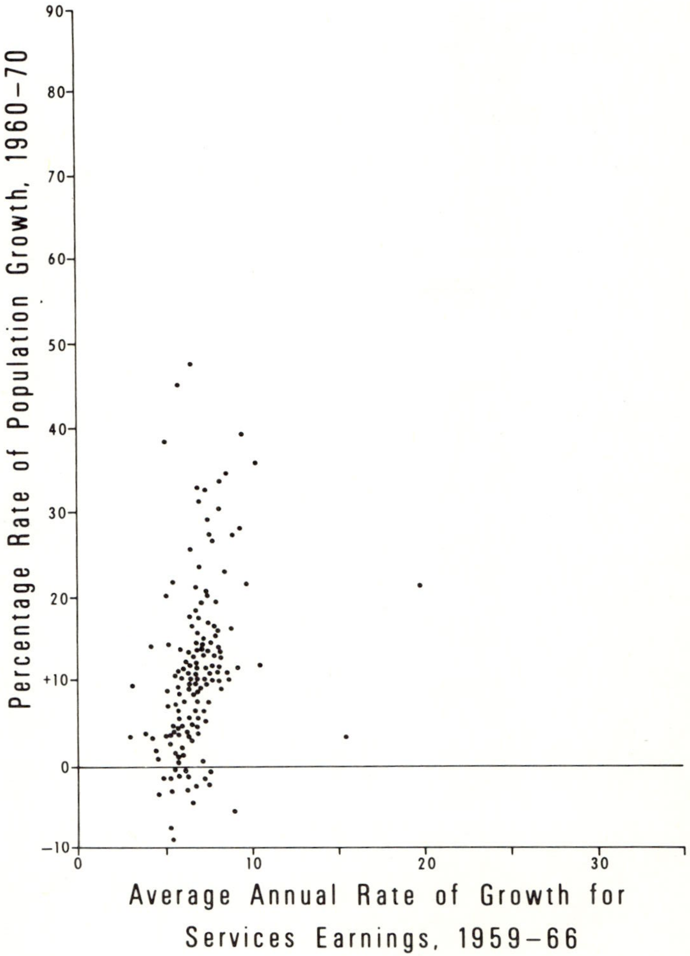

Figure 1-15. Population Growth Rate Related to Growth Rate of Earnings from Services.

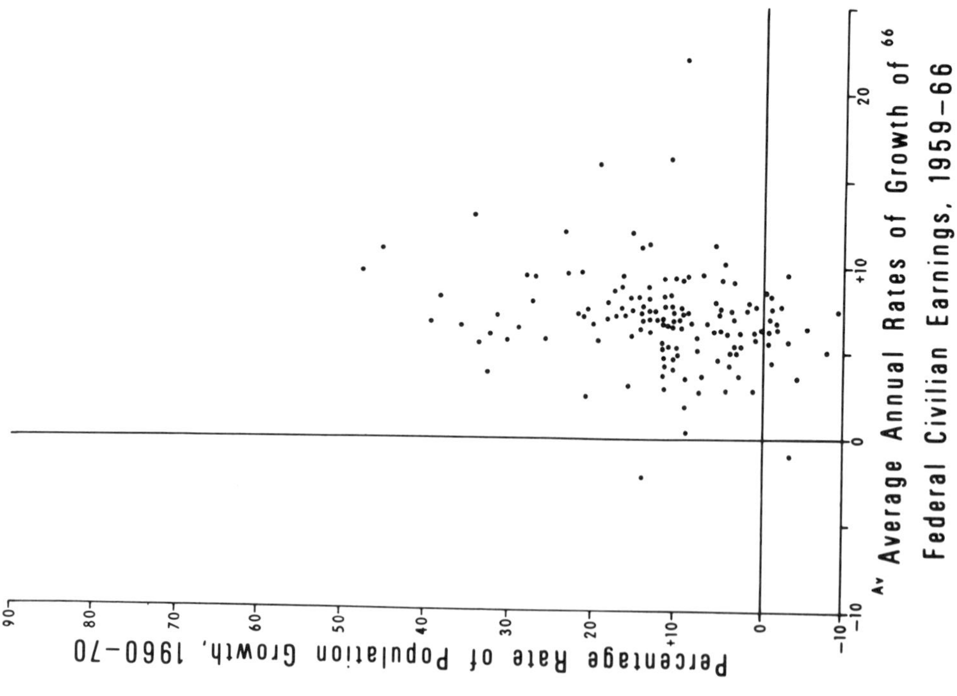

Figure 1–16. Population Growth Rate Related to Growth Rate of Federal Civilian Earnings.

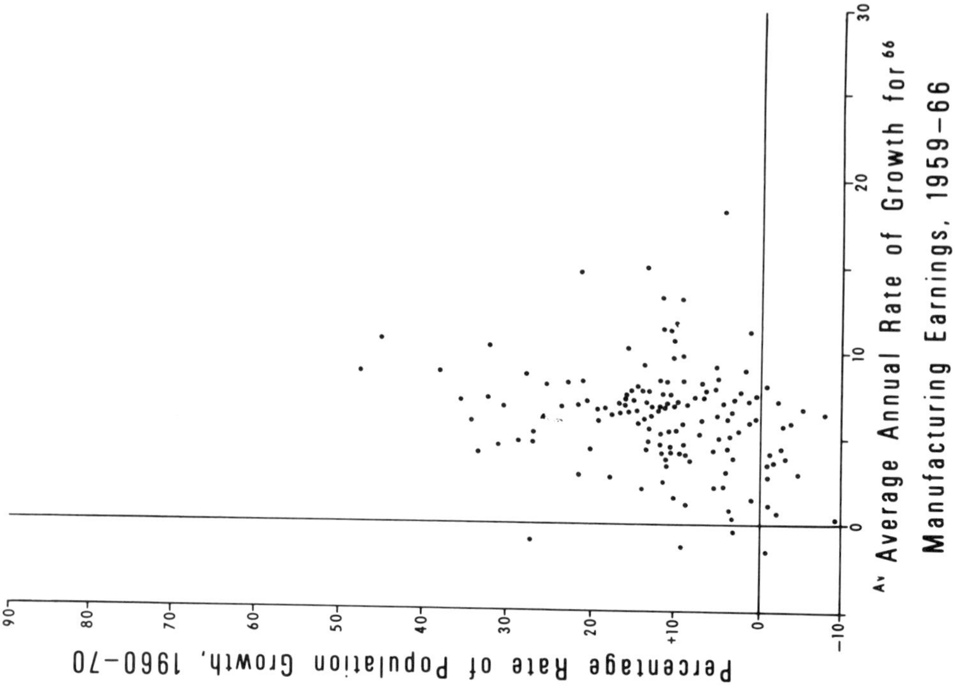

Figure 1–17. Population Growth Rate Related to Growth Rate of Manufacturing Earnings.

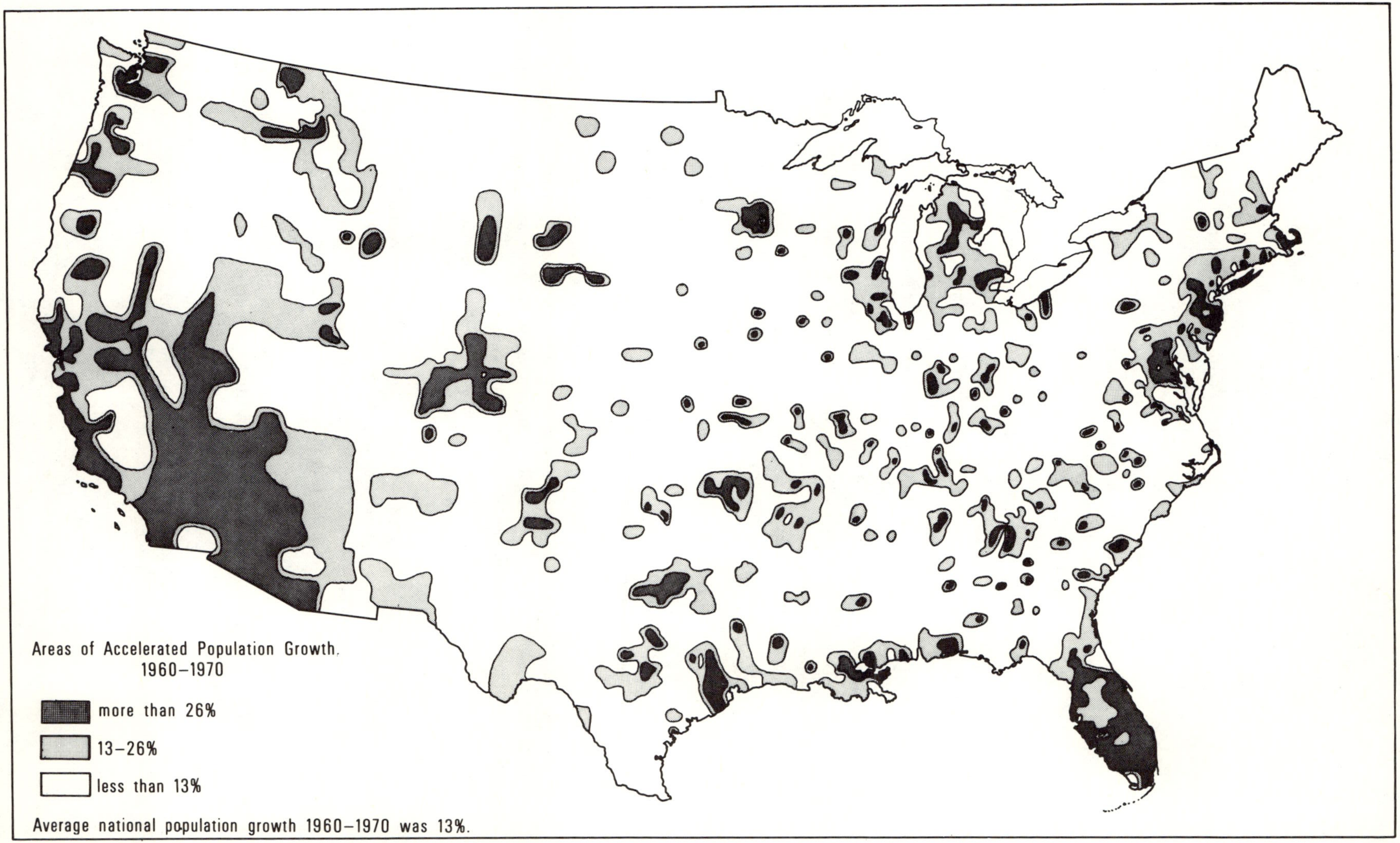

Figure 1–18. Zones of Above-National Population Growth 1960–1970.

American Future pointed out, the population of metropolitan areas grew by 26 millions, two-thirds from growth within constant boundaries, but one-third by annexation of the expanding peripheries into which the population is now dispersing. Of the growth inside 1960 boundaries, three-quarters was due to natural increase, and of the one-quarter due to immigration, more came from overseas than from rural areas. The zones of population growth due to net immigration were the outer suburbs, and the interurban peripheries in major megalopolitan regions (fig. 1–19) whereas net emigration was from the least densely-settled agricultural plains, the Mississippi Delta, Appalachia and the Deep South (fig. 1–20). Only 5 percent of the nation's population—less than 10 million people—was engaged in farming in 1970, and it is expected that perhaps 4 millions of these will contribute to further metropolitan concentration in the next two decades, less than a quarter of a million a year.

Growth in the United States is now largely self-generated metropolitan growth in all the larger urban regions; the concentrative migration process resulting from industrial urbanization has ended. Migration takes place between metropolitan areas on an interregional scale, and intraregionally through an accelerating dispersion of people and jobs outward into the expanding metropolitan periphery. Nearly 40 million Americans change their homes each year. Roughly one in 15 Americans—a total of 13 million people—migrate across a county line. And the outward urge dominates, into zones of superior residential amenity. In the two decades 1950–1970 the average population density of all urbanized areas in the United States dropped from 5,408 persons per square mile to 3,376; for central cities the decline was from 7,786 to 4,463. Many of the central cities that grew in the wave of industrial urbanism are now experiencing declining populations. Declining central cities lost more people in the decade than were lost due to migration by declining rural counties. The list includes Baltimore, Boston, Philadelphia, Pittsburgh, Chicago, Detroit, and St. Louis; fifteen of the twenty-one central cities with a population exceeding one-half million in 1960 lost population in the decade. Almost all metropolitan growth was, as a result, concentrated in the decade in rapidly-dispersing suburban territory.

In short, there has been a shift in the locus of new growth—residential, industrial, commercial—to the expanding suburban and exurban segments of the daily urban systems on an intraregional scale, as well as to the nation's "rimland" on the interregional scale. Many suburban areas now provide all the essential services formerly concentrated in the city core; new outlying locations provide for shopping needs, jobs, entertainment, medical care and the like. And along with suburbanization has come an extensive sorting-out process. Suburban communities are internally homogeneous, while highly differentiated from each other along class, age, and ethnic lines, just as the white suburbs are differentiated in their turn from the central cities in which the nation's blacks and other racial minorities are increasingly concentrated.

The essential driving force resides in *social* rather than economic dynamics. David McClelland (1961) has pointed out that the drive for achievement is a variable of key importance within the "mainstream" American culture—a culture in which status and self respect some from what a person *does*, in the material world, rather than from his ancestry or his holiness.

Social and spatial mobility are one key, built into and interrelated within individuals' nervous systems as a result of the attitudes and pressures of the culture. Children must "get ahead" and "improve themselves" through education. Workers must ascend the job hierarchy. Earnings must be spent on the best possible homes and material possessions in the best possible neighborhoods. Any increase in job or financial status must be matched by a move to a better neighborhood. "Downgrading" of the neighborhood through entry of

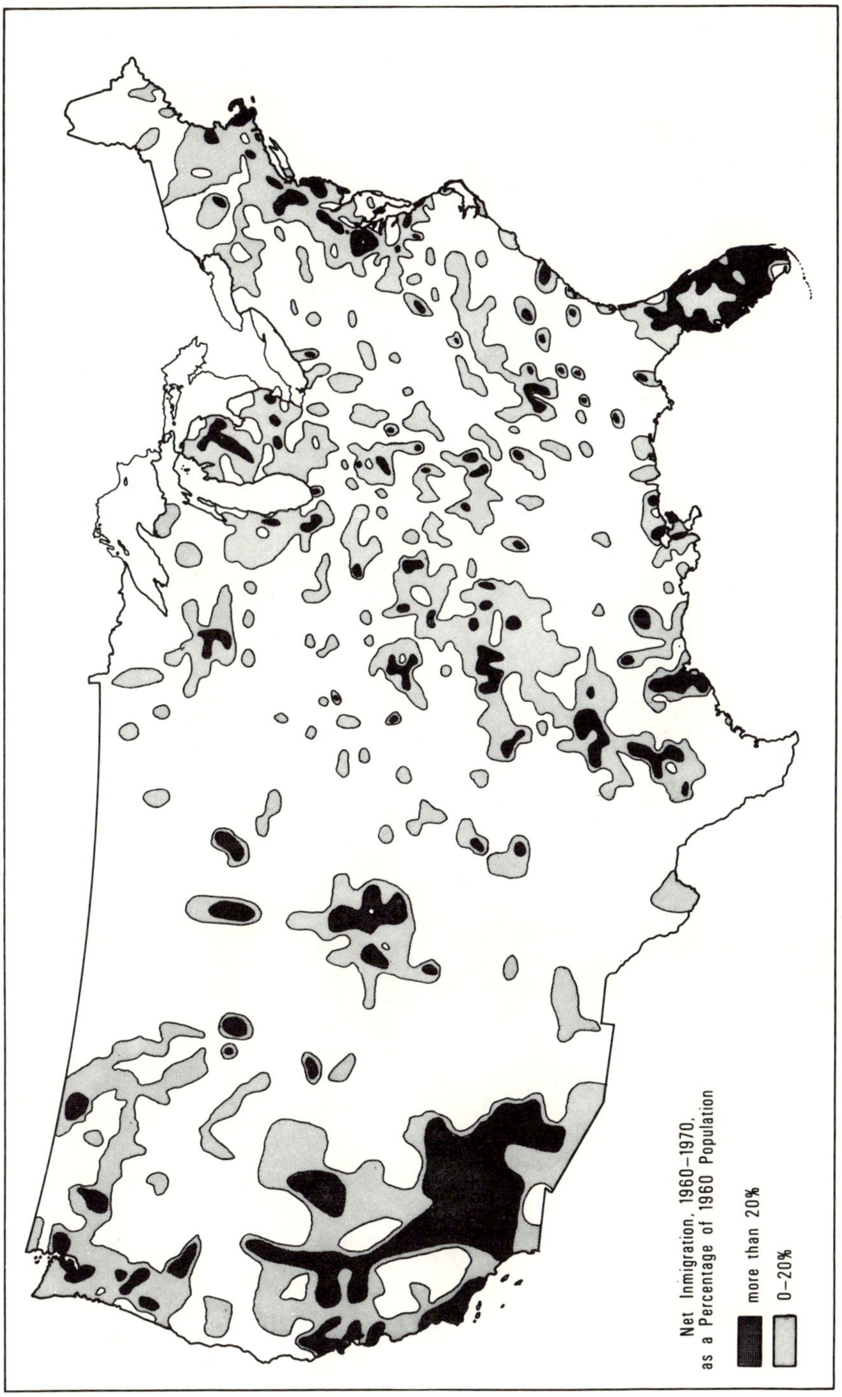

Figure 1–19. Zones of Net Immigration, 1960–1970.

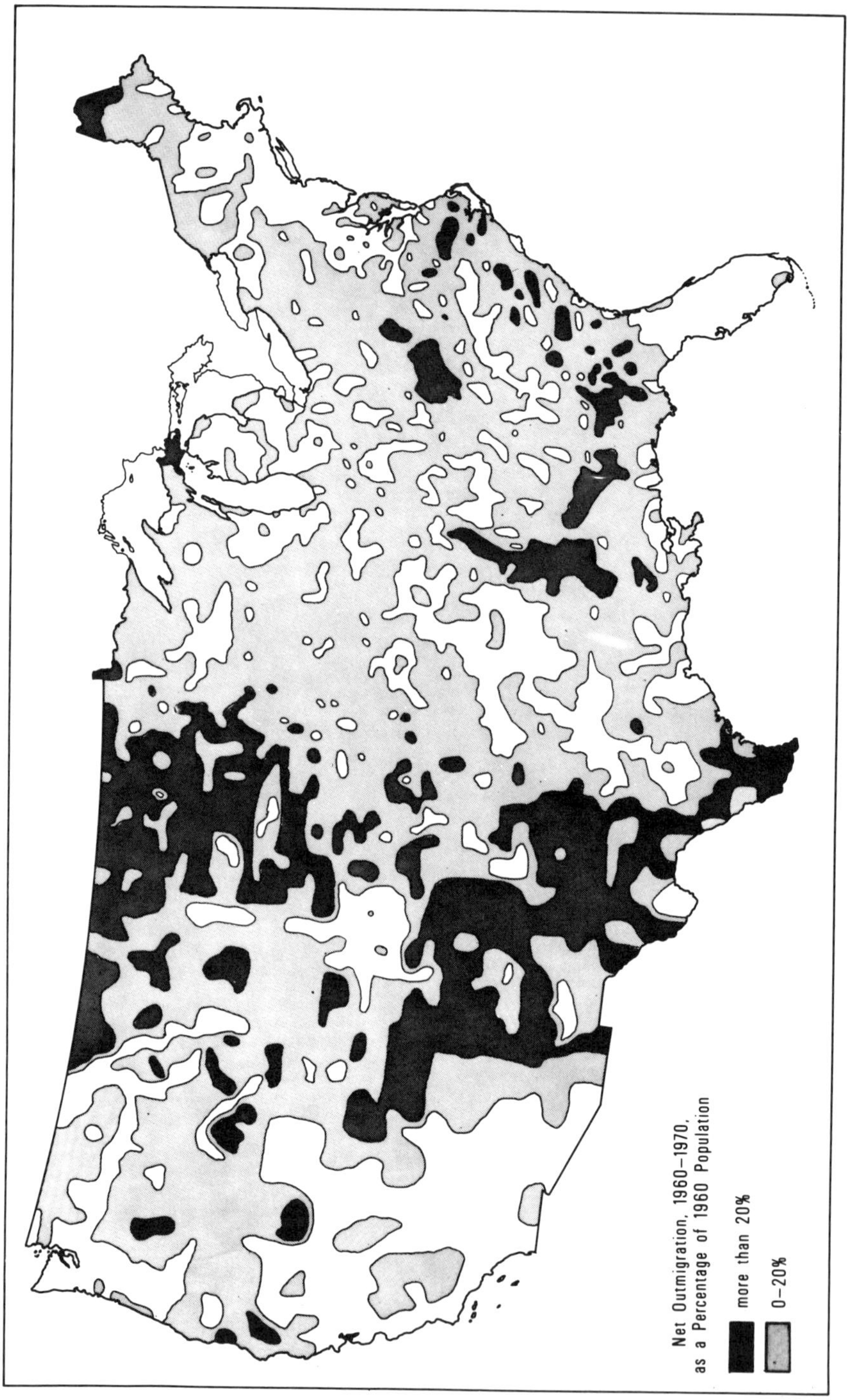

Figure 1–20. Zones of Net Emigration, 1960–1970.

those perceived to be of lower status must be fought, and if it cannot be contained one must flee to avoid the inevitable resulting loss of status. To do otherwise would be to abandon the aggressive pursuit and the outward display of "success;" one must always "fight" to "win."

When a family seeks a home they look for other things too, of course. The prime decision relates to the home–its price and type, determined by achieved status, and by the family's needs at the stage in life cycle that the choice is made. Since a large number of homes qualify within these first bounds for all but the poor, neighborhood considerations then come into play. The scale of urban regions has brought complexity and the rapidity of urban change produces uncertainty and insecurity. The whole is too large for the individual to comprehend. In the search for self-identity in a mass society, he seeks to minimize disorder by living in a neighborhood in which life is comprehensible and social relations predictable. Indeed, he moves out of "his" neighborhood when he can no longer predict the consequences of a particular pattern of behavior. He seeks an enclave of relative homogeneity: a territory free from status competition because his neighbors are at similar stages in the life cycle; a safe area, free from status-challenging ethnic or racial minorities; a haven from complexity, to be protected and safeguarded by whatever means: legal, institutional, and frequently illegal violence, each a symptom of defensive territoriality protecting that which has been achieved.

The resulting homogeneous niches are exquisitely reticulated in geographic space. High-status neighborhoods seek out zones of superior residential amenity near water, trees, and higher ground, free from the risk of floods and away from smoke and factories, and increasingly in the furthest accessible peripheries. Middle-status neighborhoods press as close to the high-status as feasible. To the low-status resident, least able to afford costs of commuting, are relinquished the least desirable areas adjacent to industrial zones radiating from the center of the city along railroads and rivers, the zones of highest pollution and the oldest, most deteriorated homes. In the cores of the ghettos, widespread abandonment of properties marks the extremes of neglect.

The whole is more a Balkanization than a melting pot, and many see deepening schisms resulting. President Johnson's *Commission on Crimes of Violence* reported:

> If present trends are not positively redirected by creative new action, we can expect further social fragmentation of the urban environment, formation of excessively parochial communities, greater segregation of different racial groups and economic classes . . . and polarization of attitudes on a variety of issues. It is logical to expect the establishment of the "defensive city," the modern counterpart of the fortified medieval city, consisting of an economically declining central business district in the inner city protected by people shopping or working in buildings during nighttime hours. Highrise apartment buildings and residential "compounds" will be fortified "cells" for upper-, middle-, and high-income populations living at prime locations in the inner city. Suburban neighborhoods, geographically removed from the central city, will be "safe areas," protected mainly by racial and economic homogeneity and by distance from population groups with the highest propensities to commit crimes. Many parts of central cities will witness frequent and widespread crime, perhaps out of police control.

What all of this means is that the black resident of the metropolis finds himself in a central-city ghetto abandoned both by whites and, increasingly, by employment. The flight of white city-dwellers into the expanding peripheries of metropolitan regions is an accelerating phenomenon as minorities move towards majority status in the city centers, and all evidence points to industry following population into the higher-status suburbs at an accelerating rate. The exurban fringes of many of the nation's urban regions have now pushed one hundred miles and more from the traditional city centers. More important, the core-orientation implied in use of the terms "central city" and "central county" is fast on the wane. Today's daily urban systems appear to be multi-nodal multi-connected social systems in action, in which the traditional centralization of the population into metropolitan areas has been counterbalanced by a reverse thrust of racially-fed decentralization. The situation is very different from the period at the end of the nineteenth century from which we derive the traditional theories of urbanization and economic growth. Decentralization and an outward urge have replaced centralization and core-orientation; differentiation and segregation substitute for the integrative role of the melting pot; social dynamics mould industrial location choices as well as those of residence.

The essence of the daily urban system is therefore its linkages and interactions, as changed by changing modes of communication. Both places of residence and places of work are seen to be responding to social dynamics. At the same time, new communications media, notably television, have contributed to cognitive changes by providing the universal perception of decaying central cities, the new home of the former residents of the now-emptied periphery; the immediate on-the-spot experience of their riots; the careful documentation of their frustrations; and acute awareness of emerging separatist feelings. It is no accident that the suburbanization of white city dwellers has increased, supported by rising real incomes and increased leisure time. Gradients of distance accretion are now beginning to replace those of core-centered distance-decay within the larger megalopolitan complexes as persons of greater wealth and leisure seek homes and work among the more remote environments of hills, water, and forest, while most aspire to such settings as an ideal. In consequence core-dominated concentration is on the wane; the multi-node multi-connection system is the rule. It is the spontaneous creation of new communities in zones of superior residential amenity, the flows that respond to new transportation arteries, the waves emanating from growth centers, the mutually-repulsive interactions of antagonistic social groups, the reverse commuting resulting from increasing segregation along city boundary lines as employment decentralizes, and all the other facets of social dynamics that today combine to constitute today's urban systems in America.

It is these dynamics that produced significantly different patterns of regional growth in the 1960s, and call for a different theory of regional development than has traditionally been used.

Chapter Two

Development of a Research Strategy

How might an orderly basis for the development of growth center strategies be provided under the changed set of regional growth processes that characterized the nation during the 1960s? The problem is, of course, that of the new distinction between self-sustaining growth of major metropolitan regions and the second-hand development of lesser regions on the one hand, and the multi-nodal multi-connected decentralization dynamics of the major daily urban systems pushing outwards into former peripheral regions on the other. The question is whether this new set of forces can be used as a basis for channelling growth into those peripheral areas that are lagging behind the nation in incomes, employment opportunities, and development necessary to maintain a satisfactory way of life. Can a spatial policy extend the unfolding spatial process, hastening existing trends, and reshaping or redirecting them where appropriate?

The research strategy we have developed and which is applied to the United States as a whole in Chapter 3 was worked out in two cases. The first was that of the development of an urban-rural growth strategy for Appalachia, to which I contributed, but which was largely the work of Ralph Widner. The second involved my developing a set of growth center recommendations for the Upper Great Lakes Region. Each of these cases will be reviewed in some detail before we turn to the nationwide materials.

The Appalachian case is of interest because it showed the necessity of distinguishing between growth strategies for outlying areas *within* metropolitan labor markets and growth strategies for the inter-urban peripheries, while linking them together via the Appalachian Development Highways. Furthermore, it pointed out how essential it was to have a sound understanding of the dynamics of spatial growth, and a firm base of understanding of the role of the urban hierarchy in the spatial organization of social and economic life in Appalachia.

In Appalachia, however, the definition of the urban hierarchy was left to the individual states. While this was understandable in terms of the Appalachian Regional Commission, it meant that there was no guarantee of consistency in the definitional process. Such a consistent basis for definition was worked out and applied to the Upper Great Lakes Region, and it led to a distinction being drawn between *primary growth centers*, existing centers of spatial organization and sources of continuing self-sustaining growth, *secondary growth centers*, those places with growth prospects, and *service centers*, those places strategically placed to maintain adequate levels of services for the population remaining in peripheral areas, but lacking in real growth prospects. It was the definitional procedure developed in the Upper Great Lakes case that provided the basis for the procedures applied nationwide in the present study.

AN URBAN-RURAL GROWTH STRATEGY FOR APPALACHIA

In the Appalachian Regional Development Act of 1965, Congress recognized the Appalachian Region as an area which, although rich in natural resources and economic potential, had seriously lagged behind the rest of the nation in its economic development and improvements in its average standard of living. The Act further stated that the region, historically dependent on a few basic industries and a marginal agricultural sector, did not have the economic base required for a strong self-sustaining pattern of growth. Therefore, Congress created the Appalachian Regional Commission as a federal-state partnership for the purpose of inducing orderly, accelerated economic development in the region.

At the time of the commission's organization, the problems of the region were stated as follows:

1. *Low Income*. One Appalachian family in three had an annual income of less than $3,000 compared to a national figure of one family in five. Less than 9 percent of Appalachia's families had an income of more than $10,000 per year compared to nearly 16 percent in the rest of the nation. Appalachian per capita income was $1,450 while the nation's per capita income was $1,850.

2. *High Unemployment.* While unemployment in the U.S. measured 5.5 percent, over 8.7 percent of the Appalachian labor force was unemployed in 1960. Estimates indicate that in some portions of West Virginia, unemployment may have been as high as 30-40 percent.

3. *Lack of Urbanization*. While 70 percent of the nation's population was located in urban areas, only 47 percent of Appalachia's population was urbanized. Appalachia has one of the highest concentrations of rural nonfarm population in the United States, reflecting the dispersed settlement patterns accompanying a resource-dependent economy. It is more difficult and more costly to provide dispersed populations with adequate public services.

4. *Deficiencies in Education*. In 1960, 41 out of 100 people in the United States over age 25 had completed high school. In Appalachia, the figure was only 33 out of 100. Similar patterns are exhibited for dropout rates, number of college graduates, and literacy levels. The Appalachian high school graduate generally finds himself less employable than the graduate from non-Appalachian areas.

5. *Deficits in Standards of Living.* The 1960 census indicated that the average Appalachian bought fewer services, fewer automobiles, and fewer retail goods than was true for the rest of the nation. His housing was of significantly lower quality and value than the national average.

6. *Changing Population.* The 1960 census showed that the region had experienced considerable outmigration, losing 12.7 percent of its total population between 1950 and 1960. Those most able to leave the region in search of new economic opportunity were the young, working-age adults having the most education. Not only did this represent a drain on the region's manpower resources, but the resulting population was heavily distributed toward the very old with obsolete skills and the very young who were still in school. This type of population requires a higher level of public services and is less able to provide the taxes to support them than is the case with a more normally distributed population.

Appalachia's problems in the early sixties were the result of a blend of forces. The national economy was sluggish and demand in general was insufficient to stimulate vigorous economic growth. The impact of this generally sluggish economy was much harsher in Appalachia than in the nation as a whole. This was the result of structural problems in the Appalachian economy which combined with a lack of adequate public services and associated social problems to make the region unable to compete economically with other areas of the nation.

Historically, there have been four main sectors of the Appalachian economy—agriculture, the railroads, mining, and primary manufacturing. Thus, Appalachia's economic base was heavily concentrated in the very sectors of economic activity which for several decades have experienced declining employment due to technological changes or shifting markets. A second, related problem is the lack of diversity in Appalachia's economic base. Many areas ranging from small towns to metropolitan complexes rely on one or two predominant industries for their economic livelihood. This makes the area highly sensitive to technological change, shifts in markets or changes in the national business cycle.

For example, thirty five years ago 10 percent of Appalachia's labor force (approximately 476,895 men) worked in the mines. New technologies have greatly increased labor productivity in the mines and have also allowed other power sources to capture many of the markets once served by coal. As a result, by 1960 the mines only accounted for 3.5 percent of Appalachian employment of 198,488 jobs.

Technological change and market shifts are not peculiar to Appalachia but are occurring all over the United States, although the degree of their occurrence is perhaps greater in Appalachia. However, other parts of the nation have shown themselves to be capable of responding to these changes. They have reached a stage in their development which enables them to attract and develop new types of economic activity to replace the old. But regions such as Appalachia did not develop the social and economic infrastructure necessary for this kind of flexibility.

Strategic Development Principles

Four basic assumptions were accepted as underlying the strategic principles for development that were fashioned by the Appalachian Regional Commission (ARC, 1970):

1. Substantial investment in human capital is required not only because the principal concern is the people of the region rather than geography, but because without investments in the health and skills of the people, resources would remain inert and capital would never appear.
2. The location of the region between the major metropolitan regions of the East made it possible to integrate much of the Appalachian economy with the national mainstream by strengthening transportation linkages with major nearby centers.
3. Development of a well-articulated economy, particularly with respect to local-serving services, required a growth strategy which recognized the relationship between urbanization and the potential for growth in a local area.
4. Public services and facilities provide the necessary supporting infrastructure for most private investments in manufacturing plants and services. A proper investment strategy would be attuned to that relationship and place highest priority upon those public investments in each area most likely to push the area economy over the threshold of growth.

These assumptions were synthesized in two general goals:

1. *Social Goal*–To provide the people of Appalachia with the health and skills they require to compete for opportunity wherever they choose to live.
2. *Economic Goal*–To develop in Appalachia a self-sustaining economy capable of supporting the people with rising incomes, improving standards of living, and increasing employment opportunities.

To achieve these goals, the commission decided that it was necessary to understand the patterns of economic development in the United States and, to the best of its ability, to work *with* these trends instead of against them so that ultimately the region could develop the capacity to contribute its fair share to national economic growth by offering competitive services and locations for new enterprise.

It was recognized that a selective strategy would have to be pursued that was most likely, given the limited resources available, to develop a self-sustaining economy in Appalachia. The commission defined a self-sustaining economy as one "capable of fostering its own growth through continuing development of its own resources, market advantages, and internal economic structure." It went on to assert that "a self-sustaining economy also means one that does not require massive infusions of welfare and other transfer payments from the rest of the country to sustain its population at acceptable standards of living with rising incomes."

Obviously, to undertake such a strategy, it was necessary to understand clearly the pattern of economic growth that was occurring nationally and to help induce similar patterns in the region. After careful deliberation, the commission concluded:

1. That major employment growth in Appalachia, as in the nation, will be in the service sector of the economy, though this employment will rest on manufacturing and extractive activities which export to the rest of the nation and world markets.
2. That this future employment growth, by definition, will be closely related to urbanization, though the form and character of that urbanization may differ in the future from what we know today.
3. That the region is substantially underurbanized compared to the rest of the country and that it, therefore, lacks both the service base and the concentrations of population required to support modern economic development.
4. That modern transportation and technology has substantially changed the economic geography of the United States (and thus of Appalachia) enlarging effective markets, service areas, and commuting sheds.

A principal component of the Appalachian strategy therefore became to strengthen selectively those ubran centers, either existing or to be created, which on the basis of performance, location and potential were the most likely ones to grow in service employment. The necessity of selectivity was emphasized by the House Committee on Public Works in its elaboration on the directive in the Appalachian Regional Development Act of 1965 to "concentrate its investments in areas with a significant potential for future growth where the return on public dollars invested will be the greatest:"

> This language is intended to direct the Appalachian Commission and those agencies charged with the implementation of the Appalachian program to allocate funds to locations which show promise for future economic growth. It would be obviously impossible to ask this Congress to appropriate the funds necessary to bring every single location in Appalachia up to acceptable economic standards.

While such an objective would be a worthy one, Federal dollar resources are obviously insufficient to accomplish such a task.

The Senate report further elaborated by pointing out the need to take a regional approach within each commuting area so that rural jurisdictions could pool their resources in building quality schools and hospitals and in providing access for their citizens to nearby jobs.

In directing the Appalachian Regional Commission to take such an approach to regional development, the Congress made a dramatic break with past approaches to rural development. It recognized that the automobile and modern technology had drastically changed the conditions under which rural people live in the United States, i.e., that fewer people will be employed in agriculture and mining and that more will be employed in manufacturing and services. In addition, thanks to the automobile, they can reach jobs and services each day many miles away.

The commission decided that two aspects of urban development were of significance in constructing the new strategy. First, it was recognized that a certain degree of agglomeration or aggregation of activity must occur in a given area if self-sustaining growth is to be achieved. This is to say that some minimum level of urbanization must take place if economic growth is to be supported. In Appalachia, there are many cases where this "critical mass" does not exist in any real sense, despite the existence of a large and dense rural nonfarm population. In such areas urbanization, perhaps of unique character, must be induced. The large populations of such areas in Appalachia may make such an approach feasible where, under other conditions, such a "new towns" strategy would prove unworkable. Continued de-population in these areas, voluntary or involuntary, is the inevitable alternative if some such approach is not adopted.

The other characteristic of urban development which was taken into account is the tendency of urban centers, once they reach a certain size, to disperse into surrounding rural hinterlands. These forces create revenue problems for the centers and frequently impose higher costs for services on the metropolitan areas as a whole, but they spell certain advantages for Appalachia where these forces are pressing into the region from the outside.

After careful consideration, the commission therefore concluded that its major emphasis should not be on large metropolitan areas, since it was going to attempt to divert the flow of rural migrants away from such areas, but that on the other hand, it should not attempt to concentrate efforts in those communities least likely, because of location, topography and other limitations, to respond to programs designed to increase economic growth.

Programs to Change Accessibility

It was at this point that research on accessibility and travel behavior came into play. The first step was to use analysis completed at the University of Chicago in 1967 that identified and mapped the 350 principal commuting areas of major urban centers in the United States (Berry, 1967b). (See fig. 1-3) Three sections of the United States were shown to be isolated from these commutation areas: the deserts of the Southwest, areas in the central and northern Rockies, and parts of Appalachia. Of these three regions, Appalachia contained the overwhelming majority of the population so isolated. The areas of Appalachia outside these important commuting fields in which a majority of persons were so isolated were concentrated in the West Virginia, eastern Kentucky, and southwestern Virginia coal fields; southeastern Ohio; north central West Virginia; and the Cumberland River valley area of Tennessee and Kentucky (see figs. 2-1 and 2-2). The corridors of the Development

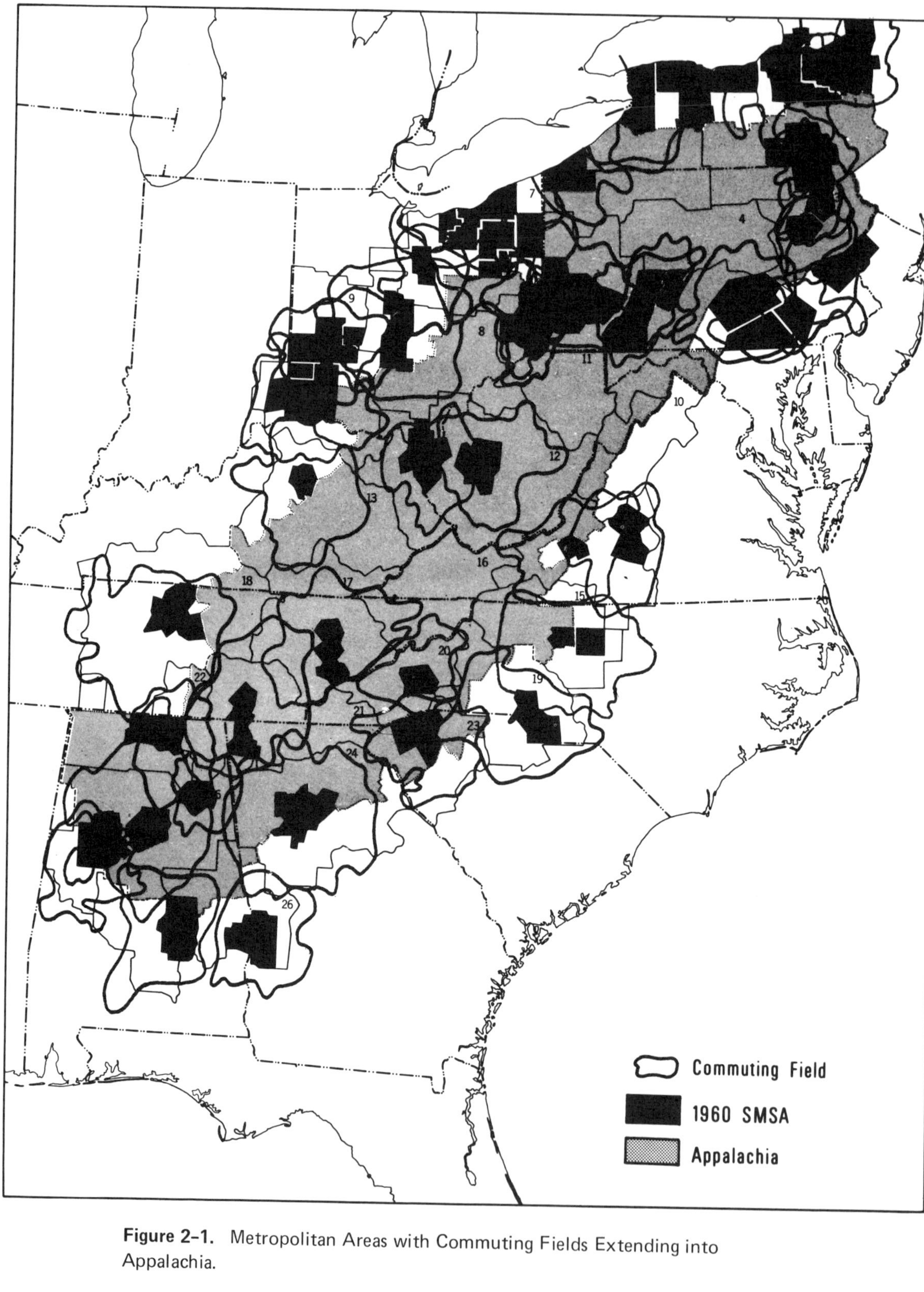

Figure 2-1. Metropolitan Areas with Commuting Fields Extending into Appalachia.

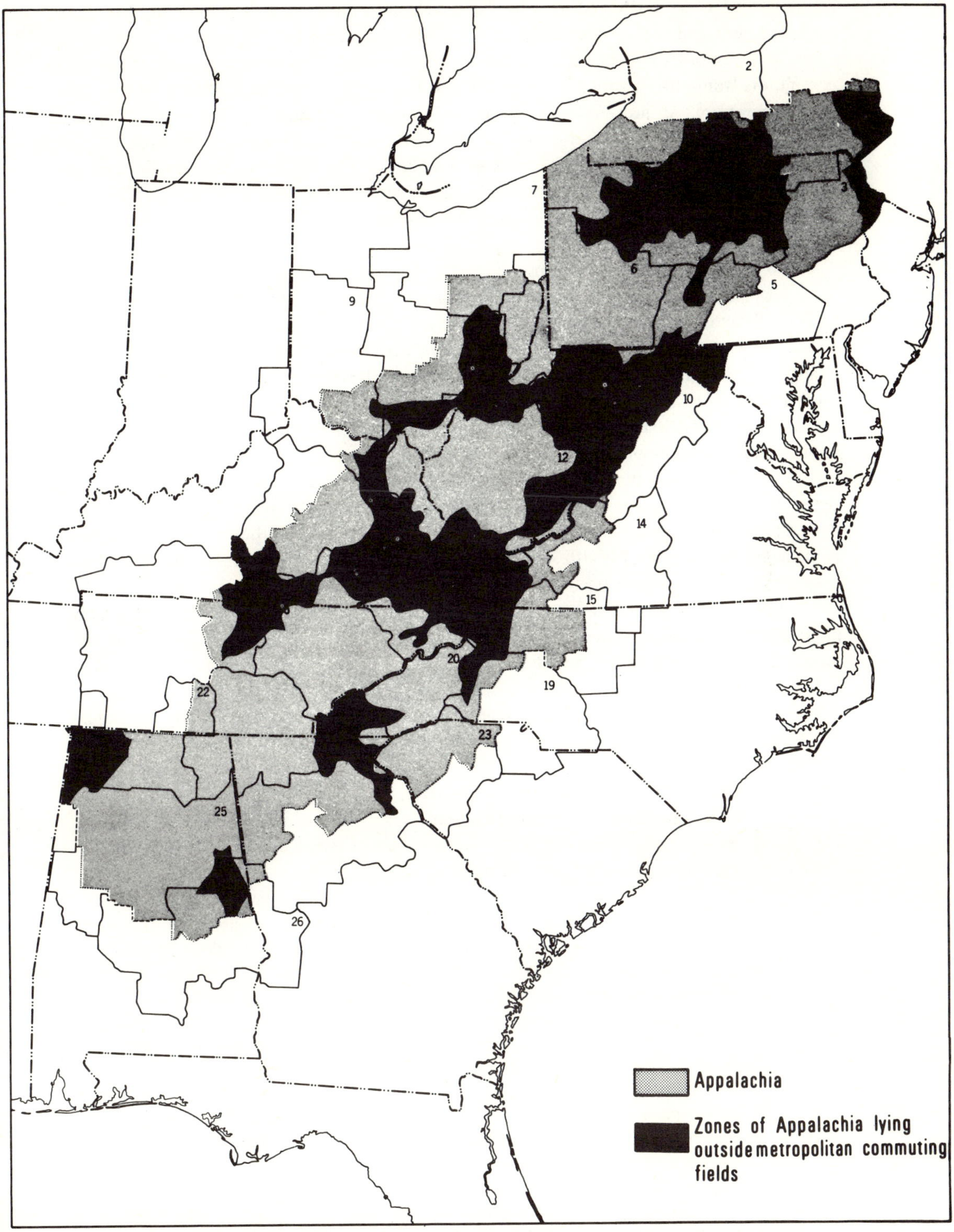

Figure 2-2. Zones of Appalachia Lying Outside Metropolitan Commuting Fields

Highway System were selected so as to incorporate into the surrounding economy the populous but isolated areas identified by the commuting maps (see fig. 2-3).

Among the major centers to which it was hoped that more potential Appalachian commuters from outlying rural areas would find it feasible to commute because of shortened travel times were: Altanta, Asheville, Roanoke, Kingsport, Lexington, Charleston, Cincinnati, Columbus, Huntington-Ashland-Ironton, Parkersburg-Marietta, Pittsburgh, Harrisburg, Williamsport, Elmira, Binghamton, and Erie. Further, it was also hoped that smaller centers of employment would evolve between these major centers as locational advantages for new enterprise are enhanced by construction of the System.

Service Delivery Systems

The Appalachian Development Highway System also was intended to provide the basis for developing new economies of scale for the delivery of social and other governmental services in Appalachia. It was thought that if rural people are to be provided with the same quality of health and educational opportunity as those living in urbanized areas, for example, these services must be provided over areas large enough in population and tax base to be able to support them. This can only be accomplished if people living in the areas to be served can reach them within reasonable travel times.

The model that was contemplated for the service delivery areas is illustrated by figure 2-4. Like the spokes of a wheel, the highways radiate out through each district linking its rural hinterland areas to its center(s) and linking the centers to other centers in or outside Appalachia. In the case of health services, to cite one example, in the center, the specialized area-serving health services are to be located. Further out along the highways in smaller communities, small general hospitals will be found. Finally, in the more remote but heavily populated rural areas, community health centers are being established. All of these will be linked together, according to the model, by transportation and referral systems enabling any individual to be referred and transported to the facility or service appropriate to his case. Similarly, a network of vocational and technical schools is being created equally dependent upon the highway system for efficient transportation of students.

Growth Centers, Development Districts, and a Concentrated Investment Policy

By resolution the Appalachian Regional Commission adopted the following definition of growth centers and growth areas:

> By a "growth center" or "centers" is meant a complex consisting of one or more communities or places which, taken together, provide or are likely to provide a range of cultural, social, employment, trade and service functions for itself and its associated rural hinterland. Though a center may not be fully developed to provide all these functions, it should provide, or potentially provide, some elements of each, and presently provide a sufficient range and magnitude of these functions to be readily identifiable as the logical location for many specialized services to people in the surrounding hinterland. A "growth area" is an extension of the growth center itself. It is the adjoining area likely to experience residential and employment growth because of proximity to a center or location between centers. The hinterlands are surrounding rural which rely upon the growth center and growth area for services and employment. The hinterlands contribute resources and manpower to the overall district economy. Some of the key relationships that should exist between centers and hinterlands include:

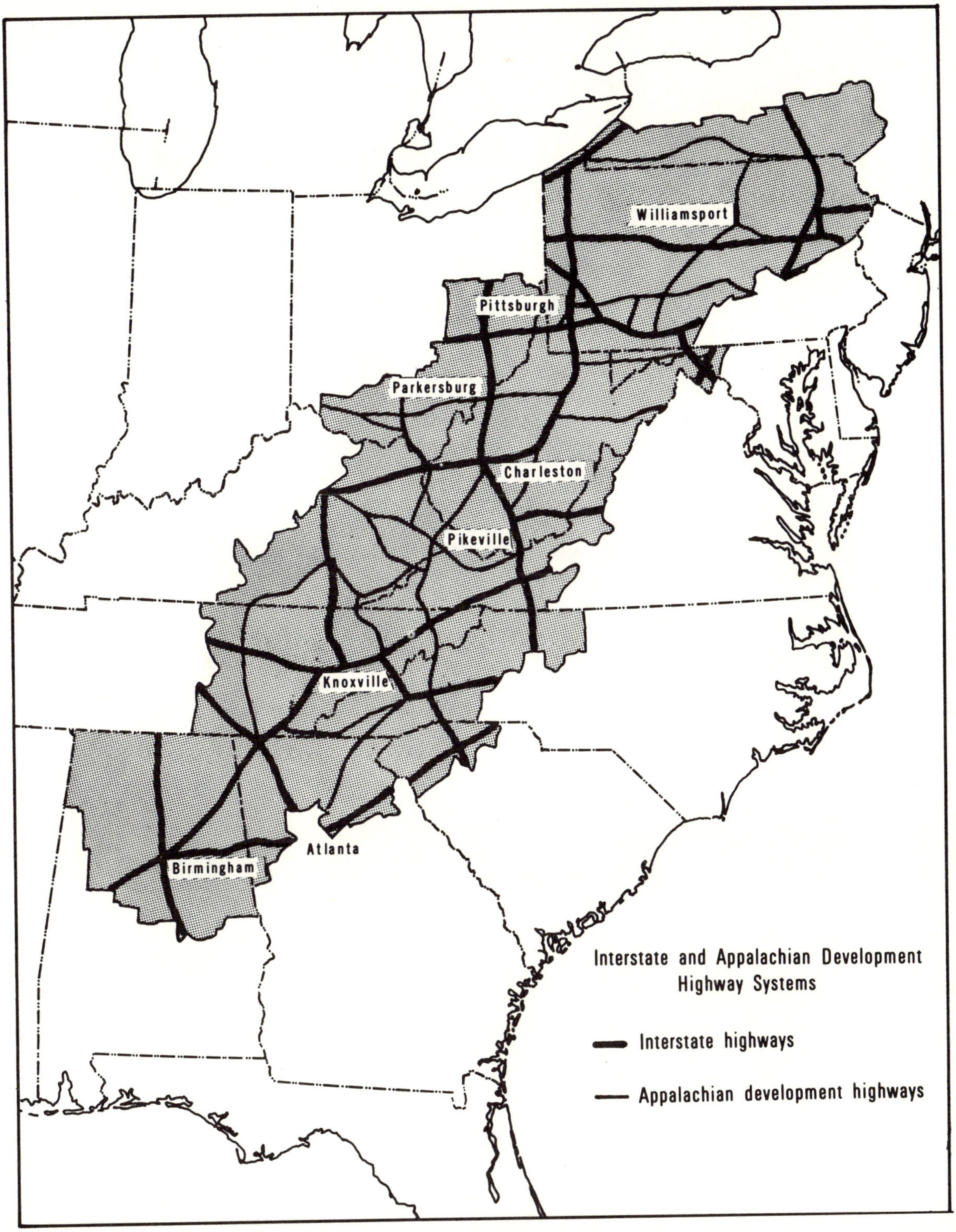

Figure 2-3. The Appalachian Development Highways.

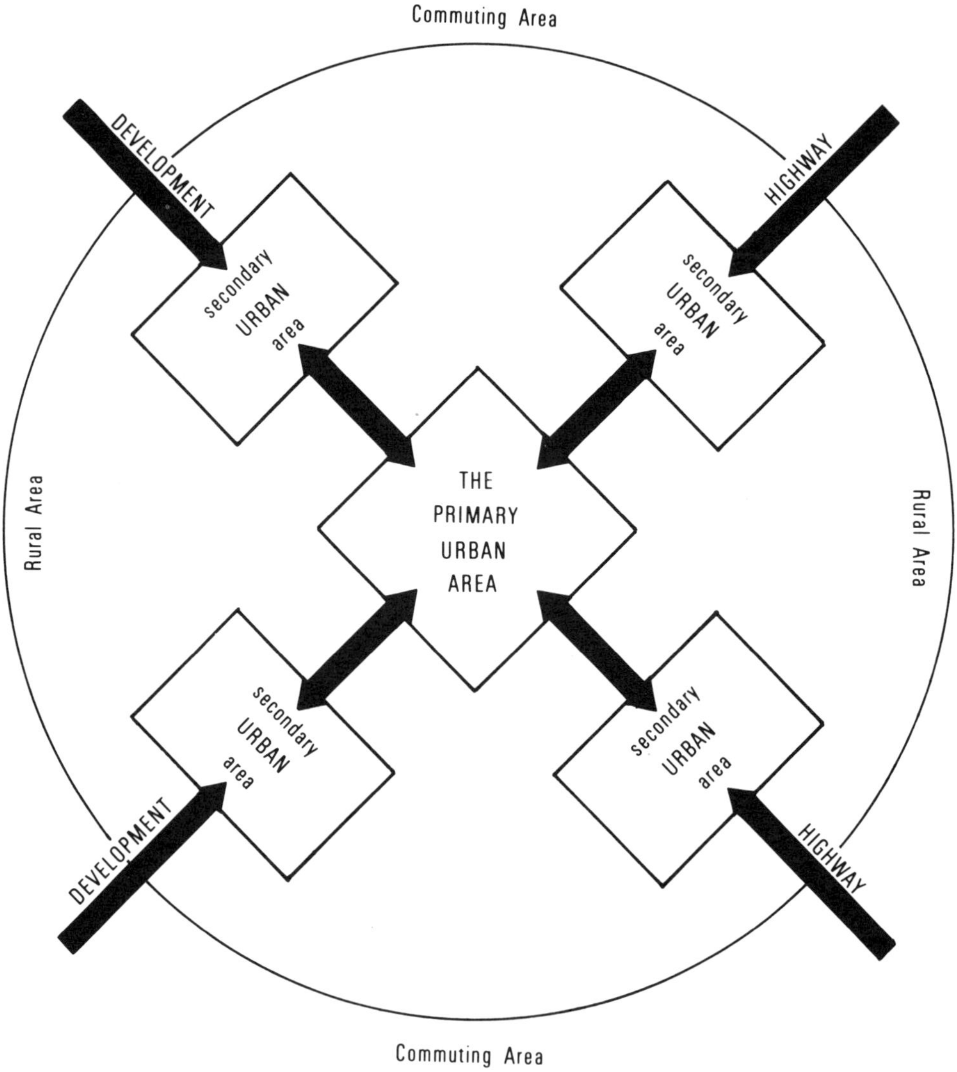

Figure 2-4. Service Delivery System Model.

(1) Commutation patterns
(2) Wholesale and retail trade services
(3) Educational and cultural services
(4) Professional services
(5) Inter-firm and inter-industry trade
(6) Governmental services
(7) Natural resource and topographic considerations
(8) Transportation networks.

Some investments may most appropriately be placed in rural hinterland areas. Most particularly, these investments would be in the fields of health and education, where such services and facilities must be located close to those they are designed to serve. In this way, the labor force of the hinterland can be upgraded to more effectively participate in the growth opportunities occurring in the growth area of the district.

The states first attempted to define the multi-county areas of Appalachia which tended to share common social, political, and economic interests and which tended to embrace common commuting and service areas. For planning and administrative purposes these areas then were designated as "development districts." Sixty such areas were identified, covering the entire Appalachian Region. Of the 60 districts, 37 with a population of 15.0 million encompassed important metropolitan or independent centers; 6 with a population of 750,000 were part of the commutation area of a major city either in or just outside of Appalachia, and 17, with a population of 1.9 million, were outside the commuting fields of major regional or independent centers and were, therefore, dependent upon special approaches to development if their economy was to be made self-sustaining.

The next task was to clearly identify within each of the districts where, in state and local opinion, growth was most likely to occur. To guide this selection, the commission adopted a hierarchical definition of "urban centers" that emphasized the *function* which such centers play within each district and within the region as a whole. While the absolute potential for growth will vary among centers similarly classified from one state to another, their function in the area they serve was to be the same from one part of the region to the next. As defined by the commission:

> *Regional centers* are important metropolitan centers providing specialized services and employment opportunities that extend well beyond the boundaries of the district in which they are located. Investments made in these centers are mainly "region-serving," i.e., they help improve services and employment prospects for a large area of the Appalachian Region embracing several state planning districts.
>
> *Primary centers* are communities or a complex of communities where preliminary analyses indicate a major portion of the future employment base of a district is likely to be located. Investments in these centers will develop their competitive advantages by providing the public facilities and services needed to make the area attractive to increased private investment and growth.
>
> *Secondary centers* are communities from which it is necessary to provide services to a large surrounding rural hinterland if isolated populations are to be given the skills and training they need to compete for opportunities wherever they choose to live and work.

The next task the commission faced was to determine how public investments could be most effectively placed in these areas to permit development and improve the well-being of both the rural and urban communities. It was recognized that by developing an effective transportation network it could make it possible for people living anywhere in the area to commute to new jobs and services, providing they were placed at the right locations.

Those communities most likely to succeed in developing a level of employment growth that could support the surrounding rural populations with rising incomes and improving standards of living were to be chosen. In some cases, those communities might be declining at the present time, but because of highway improvement or other factors, the states might realistically expect them to be important centers of future growth. It was the *potential* for growth, not past growth, in which the commission and the states were interested.

A variety of growth center strategies was envisioned depending upon the character of the area involved. Areas were defined as falling into the following categories (Berry, 1967b):

1. *Areas within the range of influence of major metropolitan areas outside of Appalachia where regional development programs can capitalize on development opportunities pressing outward from those metropolitan areas.* Examples of areas under such influence in Appalachia are the Hagerstown area of Maryland and the extreme eastern part of the Eastern Panhandle in West Virginia close to Washington and Baltimore; the area surrounding Atlanta; a small area in eastern Kentucky near Lexington; those portions of Appalachian Ohio near Cincinnati; portions of New York and Pennsylvania between Buffalo and Cleveland; and portions of eastern Pennsylvania and New York near New York and Philadelphia.
2. *Areas within the orbit of major Appalachian metropolitan centers* such as Pittsburgh, Birmingham, or Charleston, where dual programs must be undertaken to reinforce the service base and employment opportunities in the city while at the same time the surrounding rural area is more effectively integrated and linked to the area economy through improvements in transportation, health, education, and resource development.
3. *Areas unserved by any urban complex large enough to be capable of self-sustaining growth, but where there are many small towns close together.* In these areas the program should help develop complementary services so that together they offer the same service advantages and employment concentration as a middle-sized city. The Pikeville-Prestonsburg-Paintsville or Middleboro-London-Borbin areas of eastern Kentucky or the Dalton-Calhoun area of Georgia are representative of this kind of area.
4. *Large Appalachian cities located in peculiar topographical situations* where a "critical mass" of population and social overhead exists, but where further growth within the city as presently defined is unlikely for lack of available land. Here initial efforts should concentrate on alternative ways for such cities to join with surrounding jurisdictions where growth *will* occur in order to preserve existing overhead in the city and make duplication of those services in the outlying areas unnecessary. Examples of such cities are Johnstown, Pennsylvania; Wheeling, West Virginia; and the central anthracite communities of northeastern Pennsylvania.
5. *Areas with a dense, but rural non-farm, population where there is no viable community and few urban services or urban centers.* A combination of two approaches may be required in these areas; one may be similar to the third strategy above; the other is a "new community" approach in which an urban center is consciously induced based on analysis that indicates that access, market, and demographic conditions are such that a viable urban center can be created.
6. *Areas that are sparsely populated but which have had conferred upon them unusual access and resource advantages which make it probable that development and emigration of population will occur.* In such areas a planned "new community" approach may be indicated. A number of sites were identified where practically no community currently exists but where for many reasons the State believes a "new community" can be successfully created. Examples are the Midland new town site on Interstate Highway 64 near Morehead, Kentucky; the Lucasville, Ohio new town site near Portsmouth, Ohio; the Fairdale new town site near Beckley, West Virginia, as well as a number of others still being studied in Pennsylvania and Georgia. In addition, a number of large employment complexes are being planned in areas along the development highways where no

community currently exists, ample is the so-called Duffield industrial site in southwestern Virginia.

A final step in the growth center strategy was to select from among the 22 regional and 78 primary centers that had been defined those growth areas where investments were to be concentrated early in the program. Thirty places were selected, with the criteria for selection varying among the four major subregions of Appalachia:

> *Northern Appalachia* which covers parts of New York, Pennsylvania, Maryland, West Virginia, and Ohio, consists of many older industrial cities with problems of obsolescence and blight. Primary employment is in manufacturing. In Northern Appalachia, the states placed greatest emphasis on the strength of growth areas as centers of retail trade and employment with lesser emphasis on past population growth. The role of the community as a future service center with good sites for developing employment on the main transportation network was taken into account.
>
> *Central Appalachia* covering parts of Kentucky, West Virginia, Virginia and Tennessee, is far different from Northern Appalachia. Here the dominant employment is coal mining. The 1.5 million persons who live in this area are widely dispersed up the creeks and hollows near the mine heads. Topographically, it is the most rugged section of Appalachia in terms of developable sites. The states assigned greatest weight in Central Appalachia, therefore, to the role of communities as centers of retail trade and professional, educational, and cultural services, as well as to their location on the Appalachian Development Highway System and the availability of sites nearby for industrial expansion.
>
> *Southern Appalachia* covers the valleys and plateaus of parts of Virginia, Tennessee, North Carolina, South Carolina, Georgia, Alabama, and Mississippi. This area is now making a rapid transition from an agricultural to an industrial and service economy. The states, in identifying the potential future centers of growth, gave primary weight to recent population and employment growth and in-commutation, as well as location on the Interstate or Appalachian Development Highway System.
>
> The final sub-region of Appalachia is the *Appalachian Highlands,* a sparsely populated, highly scenic recreation and resource region stretching from north Georgia to the Catskills of New York. There are relatively few growth centers in the Highlands. Instead, concentration was upon developing recreation complexes to serve the metropolitan markets to the south, east, and west in which local people will work. Those growth centers which have been designated are the centers of educational, health and retail services or which have major potential as centers for serving the resort industry.

In addition to these more formal factors, the states also took into account more intangible ones such as the capability of local leadership to direct a successful program. Where such leadership exists, the probability of success is much higher.

Some Early Results of the Concentrated Investment Program

Are there any observable results of the growth center strategies at this time? Fuller (1970) provides some insights into what has been happening in the region. The qualities of places which apparently produced growth after they had been given concentrated doses of public investment, Fuller concluded, appear to include the following: (1) a labor force of sufficient size, diversity, and skill to attract new activities; (2) a surplus of developable sites for location and expansion of economic activities; (3) an attractive living environment which includes competitive levels of community services and facilities; (4) accessibility to a sufficient size market and resource base to support a growing economy; (5) proximity to a major metropolis which can supply at some minimum level of effort, cultural and other services to local residents and businesses nor normally available in a center of its size; and (6) a modern governmental and financial structure.

The additional financial support provided by the Appalachian Regional Commission to the growth centers permitted them to broaden their public improvement programs, leading them to reallocate local fiscal resources to projects including those for which nonlocal assistance either was not available to all or was unattainable at the time.

The projects supported specifically by Appalachian Regional Commission grants in the selected growth centers were generally addressed to their more critical service deficiencies. Increased financial participation of the localities in community modernization stimulated in part by the Appalachian Program placed definite strains on local treasuries. But such participation stimulated additional local efforts to expand revenue sources. Some centers were more successful than others in gaining non-local support for local programs. However, all the communities showed good knowledge of available funding sources and little hesitation in seeking such assistance from a wide range of programs. Those communities appearing to be most successful in their improvement efforts combined nonlocal and local financial sources in a variety of ways to best utilize all available resources.

The programs of community improvement given impetus by the Appalachian Program stimulated both improvement to and expansion of existing private facilities in those centers as well as being a significant force in attracting new private investment to these localities. The public improvement efforts helped to reestablish local confidence in these centers and contributed to making them attractive to new commercial and industrial ventures. The composite effect of these public improvement programs was to stimulate what was in many cases an apathetic and very conservative private sector into becoming active and progressive.

The positive attitude being developed within the private sector is evidenced in the constructive leadership being provided by some of the centers' banks. Bankers interviewed by Fuller were almost unanimous in their estimates with regard to local economic recovery. No hesitancy was suggested regarding the banks' support of local businesses in their remodeling and self-improvement efforts. Generally, the banks seemed to be leading the improvement movement in the private sector.

The suddenness and magnitude of improvement programs initiated in these centers has been in sharp contrast to the inactivity formerly characterizing them. The leadership guiding these programs has been largely elected public officials with some support coming from influential businessmen. With signs of progress and change in economic climate, greater numbers of businessmen are becoming involved in local improvement efforts, often through Chamber of Commerce-type organizations. The changing community image and developing pride found to be related directly to specific improvements in which the Appalachian Regional Commission participated (the more visible—hospitals, voc-ed schools and libraries—generating the most interest) has brought an awareness among businessmen of their responsibilities to these communities and the potential opportunities associated with their renewed economic growth.

Existing industrial firms have demonstrated their renewed confidence in these centers by reaffirming their support of the communities through greater involvement in local affairs, expansion of operations, and in some cases, with monetary gifts for selected facilities.

There are numerous examples of plant expansions occurring in these centers. Entirely new industries are also evident in many of these communities and their surrounding areas. Whether these can be tied directly to Appalachian Regional Commission projects (some probably can) is not important. That these new locations and expansions are occurring is the significant factor. The creation of a combination of conditions which successfully promotes economic growth in these locations is indication that these centers have achieved the forward motion for which the Appalachian Program had been aiming.

Individually, public improvement projects have stimulated a wide range of effects within the communities in which they have been located and throughout the area they are intended to serve. In addition to direct impacts such as job and income generation and the alleviation of a specific service deficiency, the projects have had a wide range of additional effects. These have included improvement of related services, strengthening of local leadership, intensification of modernization programs, institutionalization of the planning process, generation of citizen involvement, development of a sense of pride in the community, and emulation by other nearby communities. While expectations with regard to these public improvements have been guarded in many cases, experience has shown increasing local enthusiasm following project completion. Visual impact has resulted in unexpected verbal approval of some facilities. In several cases, the contrast between these new facilities and the unattractiveness of the communities in general has heightened citizen approval and interest in them and has resulted in these becoming community landmarks to be shown to out-of-town visitors as being representative of the "new look" in that city.

The provision of more sophisticated services in centers capable of serving a large attendant area has attracted a substantial non-local clientele. This is evidenced in the high rates of utilization associated with services intended to be area-serving such as health and education facilities.

Much of the indirect impact accruing to the centers from these public investments can be associated with the fact that a visible change has occurred and that this change has involved several projects. The fact that improvements have been made, transcending the specific nature of the investments, constitutes a substantial source of impact. The more visible and concentrated this investment has been, the greater the impetus it has had towards encouraging other local public and private efforts. Consequently, an investment package which effects improvements on a broad front while serving to alleviate specific and essential local deficiencies appears to have the greatest composite impact with respect to creating the preconditions most likely to generate self-sustaining growth. And in this sense, early readings suggest that the Appalachian growth center strategy is working.

GROWTH CENTERS FOR THE UPPER GREAT LAKES REGION

The Appalachian experience indicated the necessity of providing a fine-grained understanding of local spatial organization as the backdrop against which a hierarchically-structured set of growth prospects might be developed. In the Upper Great Lakes Region, attention was turned to development of a consistent methodology for regionwide growth center identification (Berry, 1969).

The problem was again that of a declining resource-oriented hinterland region. In the Upper Great Lakes, initial regional growth stemmed from exploitation of its agricultural, timber, and mineral resources, and these activities provided a base for growth of anciliary activities: railroads, processing of natural resource products, and related services. But agriculture, mining, timber, railroads and their associated manufacturing sectors are declining in terms of employment opportunities, as we saw in Chapter 1. Demand for natural-resource-tied outputs continues to grow, but slowly. Productivity growth is more rapid than demand growth in most of these sectors. Hence, their employment levels have been falling over time. These changes are nationwide and are not unique to the Upper Great Lakes Region. However, the Upper Great Lakes Region is relatively specialized in activities tied to natural resources and consequently the region has made adjustments far beyond those suggested by the national averages. Whereas national employment increased at 1.09 percent per year and the population at 1.85 percent annually between 1950 and 1960, the labor force of the Upper Great Lakes Region declined and the decadal population increase was only 3.6 percent in that period. Population growth followed national patterns—urban populations grew, the rural non-farm population increased modestly, and the rural farm population declined. Farm earnings in the Duluth-Superior economic region, to cite one example, were 19.1 millions in 1929 (0.26 of one percent of the nation's farm earnings). By 1966 they have shrivelled to 3.87 millions (.02 of one percent of the nation).

Declining employment in mining, the railroads, and natural-resource tied manufacturing were and still are reflected in limited opportunities for new entrants to the labor force and relatively high unemployment rates among those already committed to these sectors in the Region. National unemployment was 3.9 percent in March, 1966; in the Upper Great Lakes Region it was 7.1 percent. To this must be added the effects of transition in agriculture, where unemployment rates are low but there is serious underemployment and commensurate low income levels, particularly where opportunities for off-farm employment are meager.

Between 1950 and 1960 some of the nation's other peripheries—those of western and southern fringes—grew rapidly as new amenity resources became significant locational factors, as we saw in Chapter 1. But the northern fringe, comprising the 119 counties and 2,700,000 people of the Upper Great Lakes Region was unable to benefit from this most recent reevaluation of the nation's resources, for as it experienced depletion of its highest quality mineral resources and the problems of lack of economic diversity, its remoteness and severe climates repelled rather than attracted new growth (Henderson and Krueger, 1965).

The Upper Great Lakes Regional Commission was established to do something about this situation. Central to the commission's strategy for development became identification of potential growth centers and specification of investment needs and opportunities in them. Growth centers were defined by the commission as those places likely to attract private investment and be locations of significant employment opportunities in the future (UGLRC, 1968).

Initial UGLRC Attempts to Define Growth Areas

A preliminary attempt was made by the Upper Great Lake Regional Commission to define its growth areas before the systematic research summarized in the following pages was commissioned. In addition, a set of Development Districts was established, consistent with Economic Development Administration practice (Bird, 1968). (see fig. 2-5) Many questions arose concerning these initial efforts, including whether an adequate job of research had been done, whether their areas of influence were adequately defined by the Development Districts, and whether, therefore, the initial proposals represented an adequate base for making decisions about investment priorities.

The Economic Development Administration has described the Development District program as one of *community* development. The development process is seen as one of institution-building, rather than economic development, *sensu stricto* (EDA, 1967).

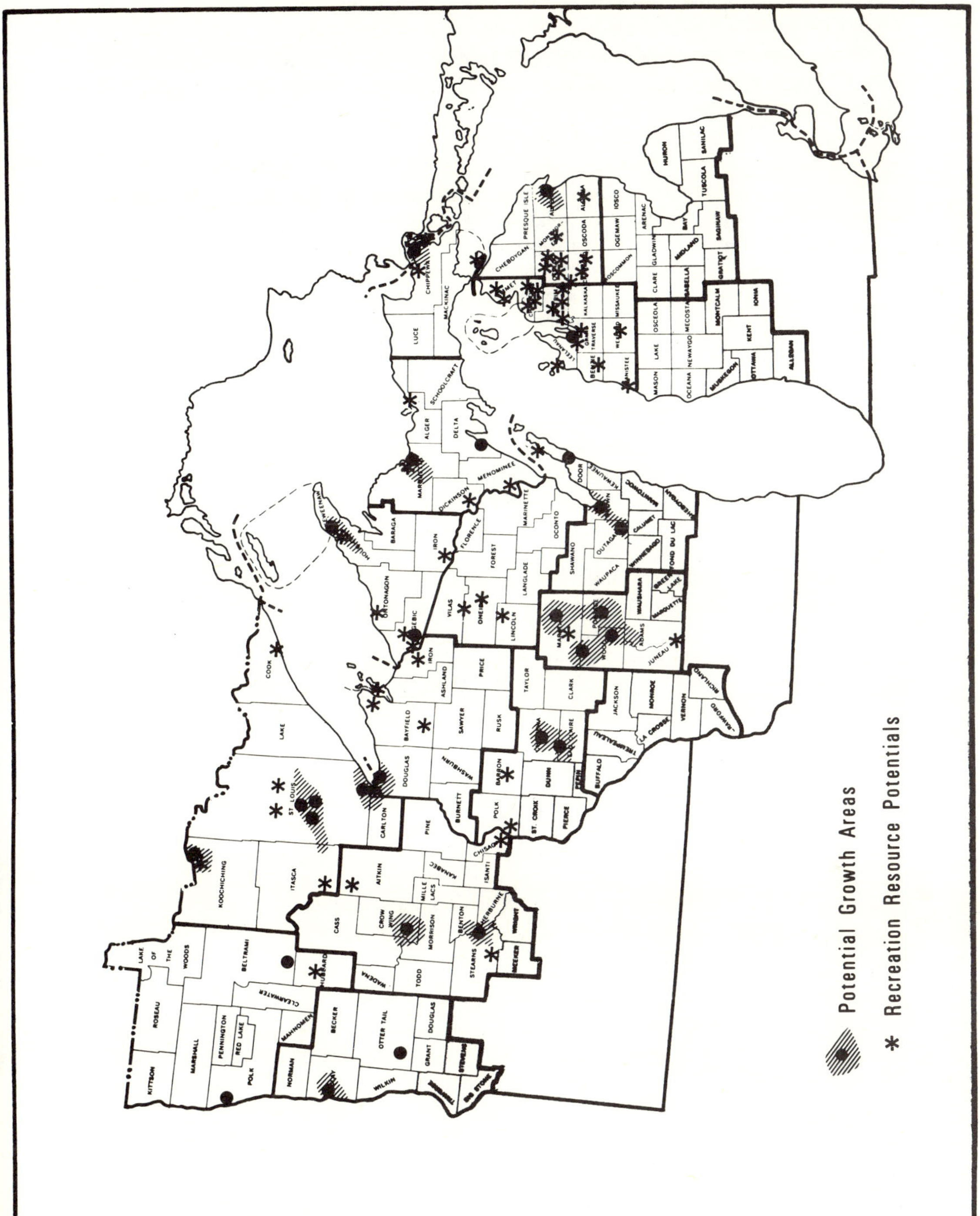

Figure 2-5. Initial UGLRC Proposals for Growth Areas.

Community development was seen by EDA as a process of social action whereby the community organizes itself for planning and action, on the thesis that jobs may be created in development centers but that they will only help unemployed and low-income populations in redevelopment areas with organization and with creation of matching facilities for investment funding.

Ideally, according to EDA, districts:

1. Should be economic communities—trade areas sharing economic interests
2. Should contain two redevelopment areas
3. Should contain a growth center of sufficient size and potential to foster economic growth (generally, greater than 10,000 population, but less than 250,000), and geographically and economically related to the district in such a way that its economic growth can be expected to contribute to alleviation of distress in the redevelopment areas of the district
4. Should be of sufficient size to contain the necessary resources for economic development (generally, of population 100,000 to 1,000,000)
5. Should have a history of multi-county cooperation
6. Should have redevelopment area populations amounting to at least 25 percent of the population of the district, an income 70 percent or less of the national average, or 35 percent of the population below the poverty criterion
7. Should have State participation in the design and designation (EDA, 1967).

Criteria (5) and (7) appeared to have prevailed in preliminary definition of the Upper Great Lakes Development Districts (Bird, 1968), although the bases of prior cooperative activity in the states may certainly have involved shared economic interests (criterion 1). Thus, the Development Districts did appear to have the necessary foundations for further institutional development.

The definitional bases for deriving the preliminary set of proposed growth areas shown in figure 2-5 were:

1. That urban-industrial growth areas should have major potential for attracting productive residents through a wide range of development activities of benefit to the Nation, the States and the Region—specific criteria involve:
   (i) minimum population generally 7,500;
   (ii) generally the largest population in the Region;
   (iii) with a significant population increase;
   (iv) advantageous locations;
   (v) access to higher educational facilities;
   (vi) adequacy of fuel, power, water supplies.
2. That tourist-recreation growth areas should have the capability of attracting a cluster or concentration of tourist-oriented investments sufficiently sizeable to provide for a good sized population—specifically including:
   (i) desirability and uniqueness of the tourist attraction;
   (ii) transport accessibility to potential users; possibilities for expansion and diversification through other than tourist activities.
3. That resource-growth areas should contain a resource available for a long period, requiring processing and other associated activity, and giving rise to substantial investment and growth.
4. That service areas are smaller centers without significant growth potentials, but performing necessary functions for a permanent population to maintain adequate living standards and to prepare elements of the population for successful integration to higher order growth areas (Bird, 1968).

The proposed growth areas were apparently defined independently of the Development Districts, and "service centers or district capitals" (Bird, 1968) were then added to each district in the belief that

> these centers . . . permit meaningful decentralization of essential services . . . provide a minimum guarantee that every citizen in the Region will be able to realize his potential . . . are prime sites for location of enabling staff . . . to serve local people more effectively . . . every center having ready access to other centers, to the relevant state capital and to major U.S. and Canadian cities of likely significance to the upgrading of regional trade and commerce and the enabling public services and facilities . . . reasonably accessible to all citizens of its development district . . . with evidence of commitment to improved education and related activities . . . with ready access to technical services . . . a reasonable range of retail shopping facilities" (Bird, 1968).

The problem was that the growth areas as defined, bore little relationship to the urban systems fabric of the region. Nor were relationships specified between the resident population and areas of growth potentials. Interconnections among the centers that can benefit from external sources of growth and the urban network serving the region's population were not charted in these preliminary efforts. This was in spite of the fact that the commission's charge called for identification of a hierarchy of growth areas into:

1. Primary urban-industrial growth areas (regional centers)
2. Secondary urban-industrial growth areas influencing smaller tributary areas
3. Service centers, which may or may not have significant growth potentials, but perform important functions for a local population.

Therefore, to serve the economic development needs of a growth center policy it became necessary to develop a clear understanding of the structure of the economic space of the Upper Great Lakes Region. Such an understanding permitted redefinition of a comprehensive and consistent hierarchy of growth centers for the region, an understanding of the likely impact and areas of influence of such growth centers, and an analysis of the growth centers' potentials.

Bases of the Hierarchical Definitions

Borchert and Adams (1963) had already conducted an exhaustive study of urbanization in the Upper Midwest in the early 1960s when I responded to the Upper Great Lakes Commission's charge. One outcome of their work was the definition of an urban hierarchy of the following levels:

Metropolis
Primary Wholesale-Retail Center
Secondary Wholesale Center
Complete Shopping Center
Partial Shopping Center
Full Convenience Center
Minimum Convenience Center
Hamlet.

They developed an elaborate set of definitional criteria, based upon the functions performed by the centers and classified all centers in the Upper Midwest into their proper hierarchical position using these criteria. This classification included all centers in the Upper Great Lakes Region except those located in mid-Wisconsin and lower Michigan.

The Borchert-Adams criteria were checked against two other sources, first a series of comparative studies of urban hierarchies completed in the early 1960s by Berry (1967a) and second, the output of a series of elaborate multivariate factorial studies of all American cities with populations exceeding 10,000 (Berry, 1972). The results of these studies were consistent, and so the multivariate criterion of "functional size" or total "economic power" developed in the latter study, representing the synthesis of 97 separate criteria, was used to extend the Borchert classification to the balance of the Upper Great Lakes Region for *all* centers exceeding 10,000 in population. For smaller centers, the Borchert-Adams-Berry hierarchy based upon population was applied. Because there were only two centers of secondary wholesale-retail level in the Upper Great Lakes Region, the primary and secondary levels of the Borchert system were combined for purposes of analysis. Further, because Borchert had shown elsewhere that the minimum convenience centers and hamlets of the region were no longer viable parts of the urban system (table 2–1), a finding independently confirmed by others (Berry, 1967a), these two lowest categories were eliminated from consideration. The result was a five-level urban hierarchy:

Metropolis
Wholesale-retail center
Complete shopping center
Partial shopping center
Convenience center (town)

The Urban Hierarchy of the Upper Great Lakes Region

Table 2–2 classifies every center of the Upper Great Lakes Region falling within the top three echelons of the hierarchy derived in the above manner. Note that the network of growth centers previously proposed by the Upper Great Lakes Regional Commission picked up some but not all of the metropolitan and wholesale-retail level centers with areas of influence extending into the region (see disucssion below), and then extended to an incomplete sampling of those complete shopping centers that either form "clusters" with other nearby centers, or which might conceivably function as the service centers of the Development Districts (as defined by prior work on community development needs) remaining unserved by an "urban-industrial" growth center.

Table 2–1. Growth Characteristics of Places in the Borchert-Adams Hierarchy

Level	*Percentage Declining*	*Median Population*
Metropolis*	0	1,400,000
Primary Wholesale-Retail	14	55,000
Secondary Wholesale-Retail	10	32,000
Complete shopping	12	9,500
Partial shopping	20	2,500
Full convenience	21	1,500
Partial convenience	42	800
Hamlet	77	200

*The Twin Cities Metropolis accounts for 90 percent of the net growth of the Upper Midwest. John R. Borchert, *Upper Midwest Urban Change in the 1960's,* Upper Midwest Research and Development Council, 1965.

Table 2-2. Hierarchical Position of Urban Centers in the Upper Great Lakes Region

State	City	Population, 1960 SMSA	Population, 1960 City	Upper Great Lakes Prelim. Growth Centers	Factor Score (Economic Power or Functional Size: Berry "Latent Structure")
	Metropolitan Centers				*Scores Over +2.0*
Ill.	*Chicago	6,794,000	3,550,000		5.40
Mich.	*Detroit	3,762,000	1,670,000		4.45
Minn.	*Minneapolis	1,482,000	482,000		3.35
	*St. Paul		313,000		2.79
Wisc.	*Milwaukee	1,194,000	741,000		3.65
Mich.	*Grand Rapids	295,000	177,000	S	2.22
	Wholesale-Retail Centers				*Scores 0.25 to +2.0*
Minn.-Wisc.	Duluth-Superior		135,000	UI, S (M-Lake Co.)	1.79, 0.48
Wisc.	Green Bay		85,000	UI, S	1.31
Wisc.	Eau Claire-Chippewa Falls		50,000	UI, S	0.65, –0.75
Minn.	St. Cloud		38,000	UI, S	0.30
Wisc.	Appleton		54,000	UI, S (with Oshkosh)	0.83
Wisc.	Wausau		32,000	UI, S	0.49
N.D.	*Fargo-Moorhead		69,000	UI, S	1.06
Wisc.	*La Crosse		47,000	UI, S	0.83
Wisc.	*Madison		126,000		1.81
Mich.	*Bay City-Saginaw		150,000	S	1.00, 1.33
N.D.	*Grand Forks		35,000		0.55
Mich.	*Muskegon		46,000		0.56
	Complete Shopping Centers				
Minn.	Virginia		14,034		–0.76
	Hibbing		17,331	S	–0.47
	Grand Rapids		7,265		–
	Bemidji		9,958	S	–
	International Falls		6,778	S	–
	Thief River Falls		7,151	S	–
	Crookston		8,546		–
	Detroit Lakes		5,978		–
	Wadena		4,381		–
	Fergus Falls		13,733	S	–0.67
	Alexandria		6,713		–
	Brainerd		12,898	T, S	–0.38

(continued)

Table 2-2. (continued)

State	City	Population, 1960 SMSA	Population, 1960 City	Upper Great Lakes Prelim. Growth Centers	Factor Score (Economic Power or Functional Size: Berry "Latent Structure")
	Little Falls		7,551		–
	Cloquet		9,013		–
Wisc.	Rhinelander		8,790	T, S	–
	Merrill		9,451		–
	Ashland		10,132	S	–0.83
	Rice Lake		7,303		–
	De Pere		10,045		–0.96
	Kaukau		10,096		-1.20
	Marinette		13,329	UI	–0.62
	Marshfield		14,153	UI, S (with Wausau)	–0.45
	Steven Point		17,837	UI, S	–0.17
	Wisconsin Rapids		15,042	UI, S	–0.58
	Anitgo		9,691		–
	Kimberley		5,322		–
	Little Chute		5,099		–
	New London		5,228		–
	Oconto		4,805		–
	Shawano		6,103		–
	Sturgeon Bay		7,353		–
Mich.	Sault Ste. Marie		18,722	UI, S	–0.34
	Calumet-Larium		4,187		–
	Manistique		4,875		–
	Houghton-Hancock		8,415	UI, S	–
	Escanaba		15,391	UI, S	–0.19
	Ishpeming-Negaunee		14,983		–
	Menominee		11,289	UI	–0.84
	Iron River		3,754		–
	Marquette		19,824	UI, S	–0.40
	Ironwood-Hurley (Hurley is in Wisc.)		12,928	UI, S	-1.05 (Ironwood)
	Alpena		14,682	UI, S	–0.50
	Cadillac		10,112	S	–0.65
	Traverse City		18,432	T, S	–0.33

Note: Includes major metropolitan and wholesale-retail centers serving the region but located outside it, identified by an *. If the place is a preliminary designated growth center by Upper Great Lakes Region Commission, the UGL sub-category is noted, viz: UI, urban industrial; M, mining; T, tourist-recreation; S, service center.

Figure 2-6 maps the hierarchy, and figures 2-8 and 2-9 show trade areas for centers of the top three levels, as defined by Borchert and Adams for the Upper Midwest portion of the Upper Great Lakes Region. For comparison, figure 2-7 shows the hierarchical levels and economic specialization of centers as published in the widely used Rand McNally *City Rating Guide*, and figures 2-10 and 2-11 reproduce the "major" and "basic" trade areas as defined in the Rand McNally *Marketing and Commercial Atlas.*

The comparison is of some significance, because the Rand McNally system has been relied upon by the Economic Development Administration in evaluating Development District and growth center proposals. Figures 2-6, 2-8, and 2-9 are realistic representations of the urban system of the Upper Great Lakes Region. The Rand McNally classification of market areas diverges in significant ways from this representation by mixing centers of the wholesale-retail and complete shopping levels. This misture is a product of the non-systematic and untrustworthy process used by Rand McNally in defining an urban hierarchy, and the lack of any clear conceptual basis in their marketing studies.

What is missing in Rand McNally's approach is systematic understanding of the implications of the idea of an urban hierarchy, so ably demonstrated in the Upper Midwest by Borchert and Adams. A hierarchy has two principal features:

a. An arrangement of the system of cities into "levels" according to functional size and complexity.
b. "Dependence" of lower-level centers upon those of higher level, in that the market areas of centers of each lower level "nest" within those of centers of the next higher level.

Figure 2-6 shows the hierarchy of centers. Figure 2-12 shows the network of areas of influence of centers of the top three hierarchical levels—all metropolitan, wholesale-retail and complete shopping centers are represented at the shopping level of market areas; centers of the top two levels have market areas at the wholesale-retail level. This is not to say that there are not other kinds of interdependency—figure 2-13 for example, shows the region's three-digit zip-code areas and the Post Office's district centers. But figure 2-12 does show the main areas of urban-centered economic interdependency and interaction in the Upper Great Lakes Region. It is this network of interdependence that patterns processes of change in the Upper Great Lakes Region.

Labor Markets, Spread Effects, and Gradients of Urban Influence

The interdependencies mapped in figure 2-12 are further expressed by the shape and extent of the region's labor markets. Figure 2-14 shows the intensity of commuting from surrounding areas to the central cities of the Standard Metropolitan Statistical Areas in and around the region in 1960 (Berry, 1968). Clearly, wide areas of the Upper Great Lakes Region lay beyond the daily influence of the nation's metropolitan centers in that year. Figure 2-15 adds the commuting fields of non-metropolitan centers serving as employment centers by the population of the Upper Great Lakes Region; unreached gaps are still evident. Table 2-3 records the populations residing within the metropolitan and non-metropolitan labor markets.

Change was found to move into the Upper Great Lakes Region through these urban centers, spreading outwards from them in succeeding waves. A definite sequence is involved.

a. First, impulses of change "filter" *down* the urban hierarchy.
b. Once a particular development impulse has reached a center, it spreads *outward* from it into its hinterland, with the closest population influenced earliest.

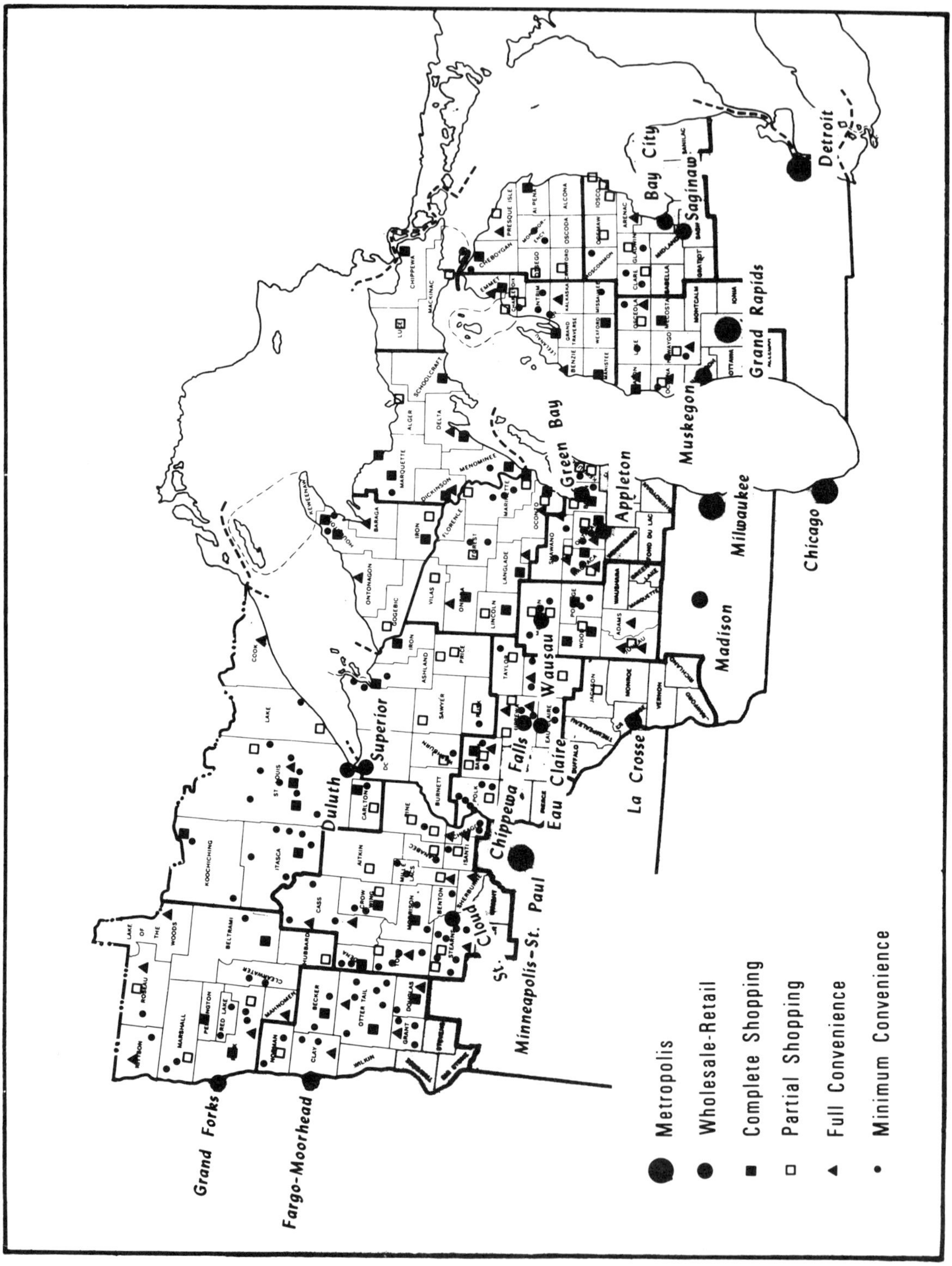

Figure 2-6. The Urban Hierarchy of the Upper Great Lakes Region.

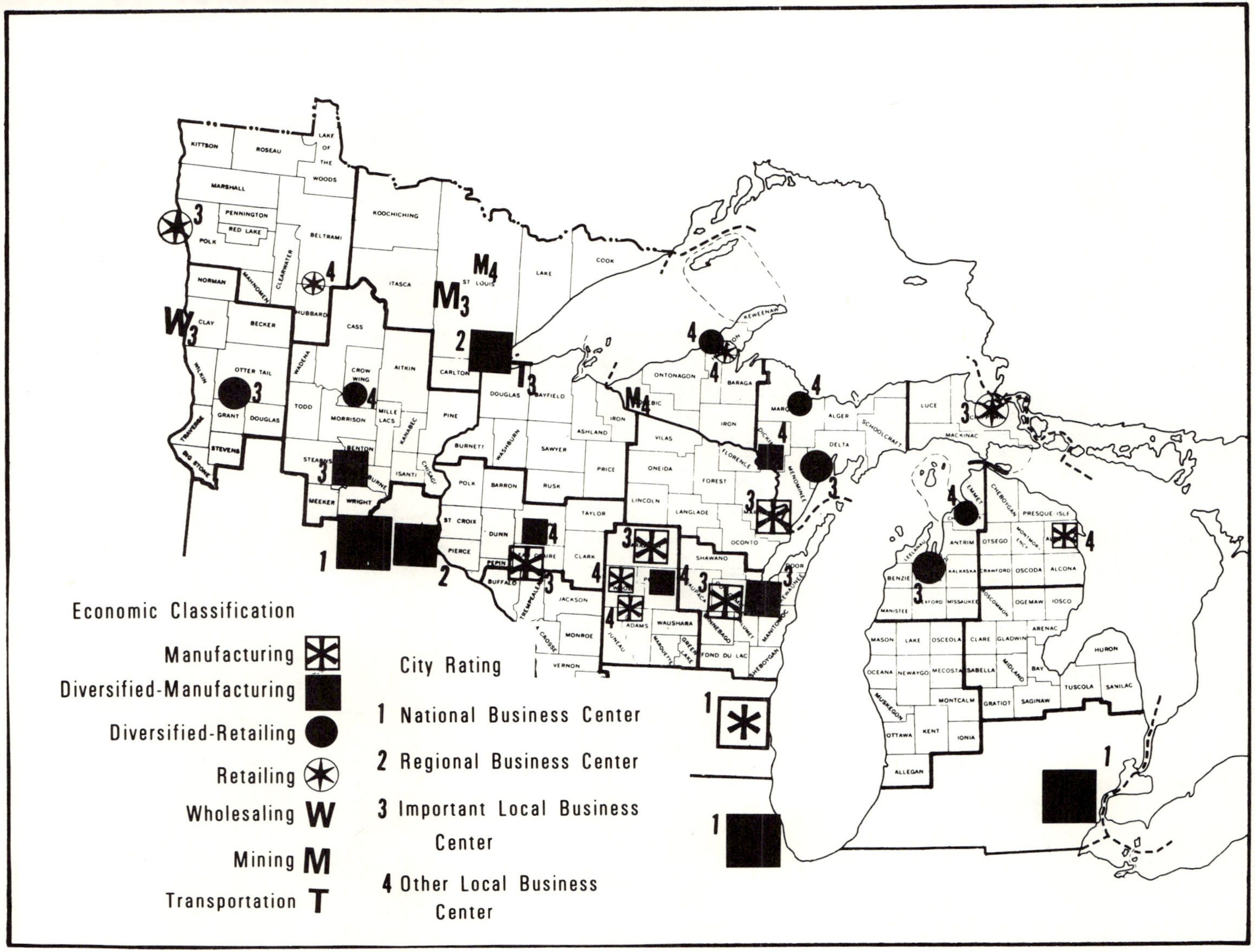

Figure 2–7. Rand McNally City Ratings and Economic Classification.

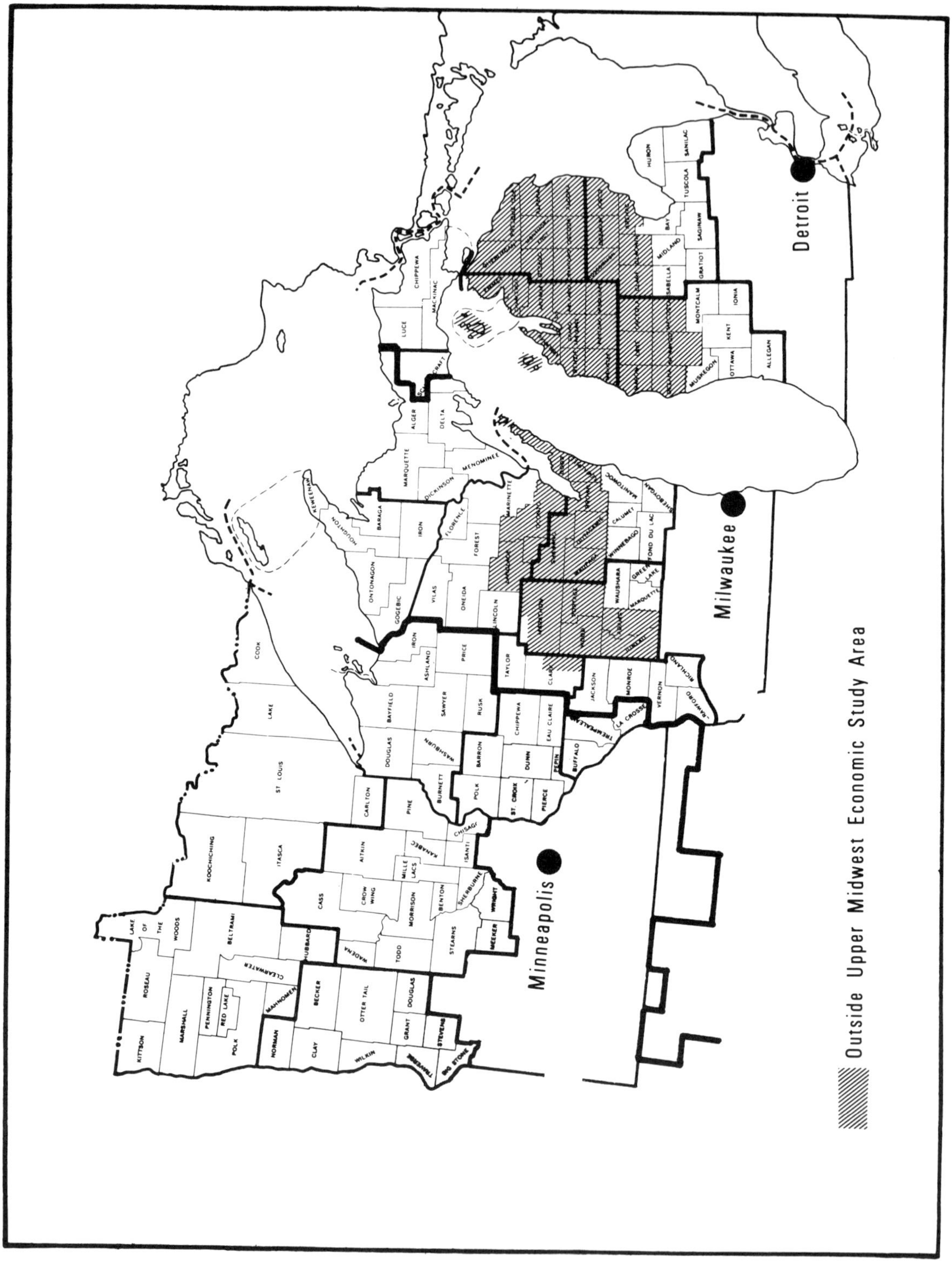
Detroit
Milwaukee
Minneapolis
Outside Upper Midwest Economic Study Area

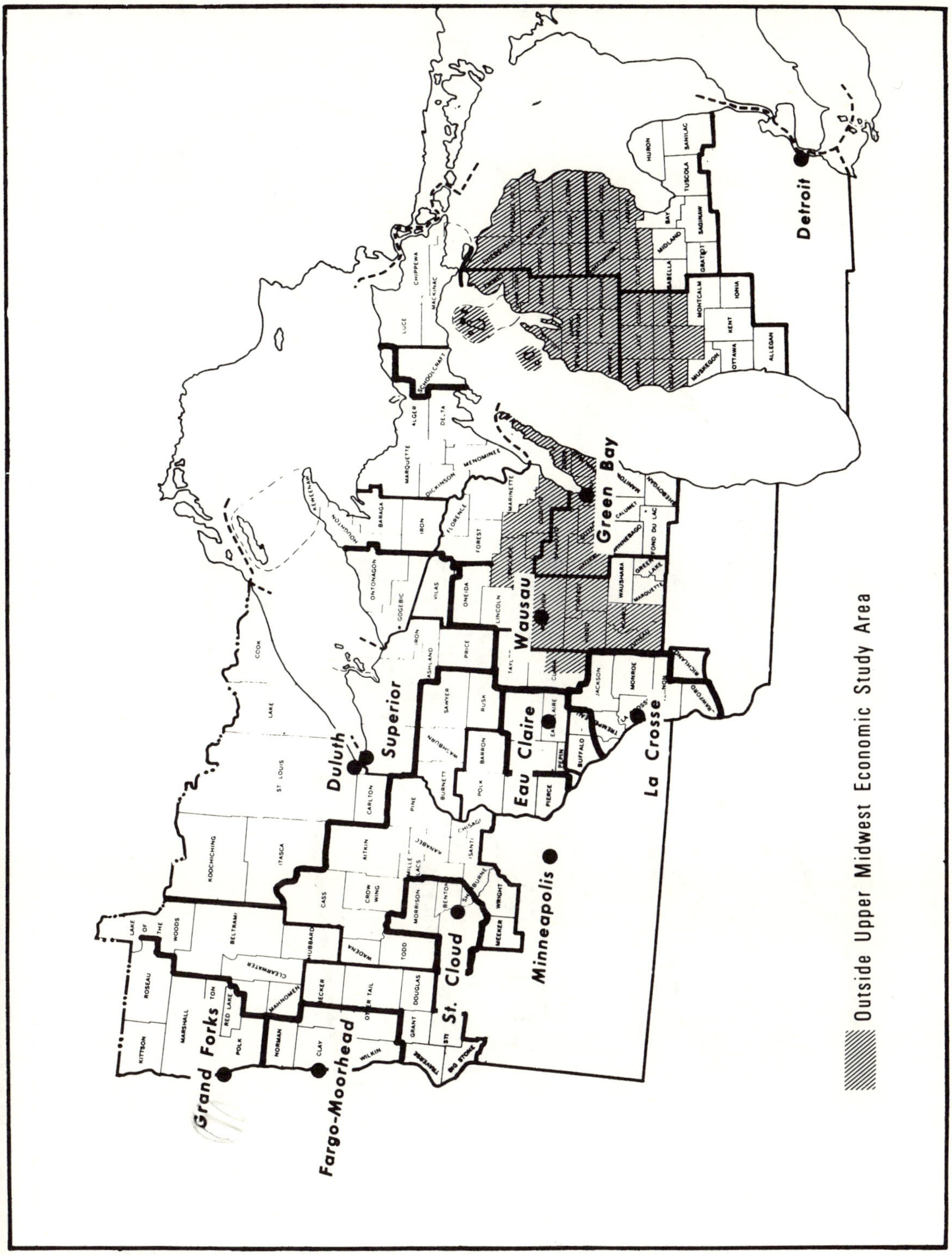

Figure 2–9. Wholesale-Retail Trade and Service Areas (after Borchert).

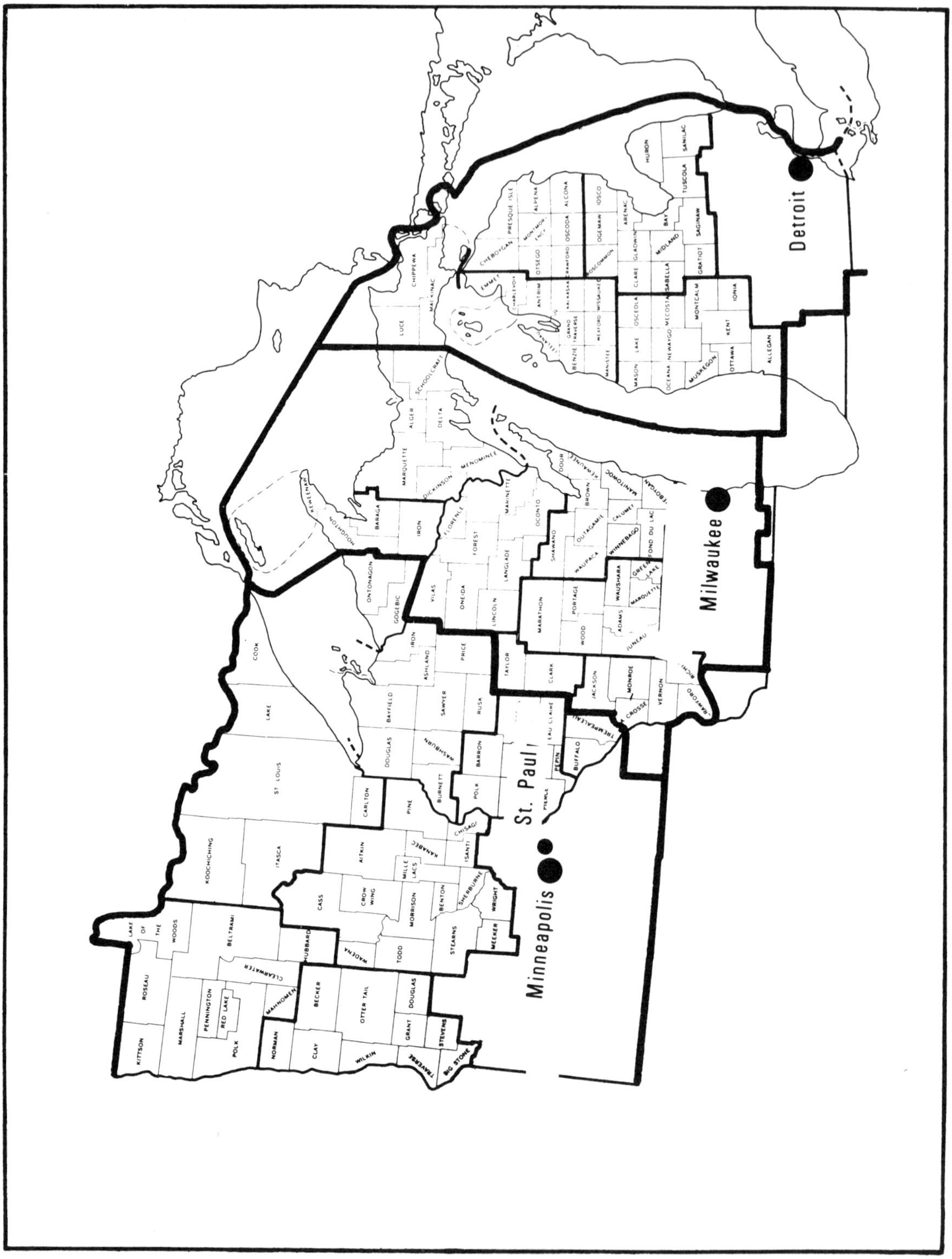
Detroit
Milwaukee
St. Paul
Minneapolis

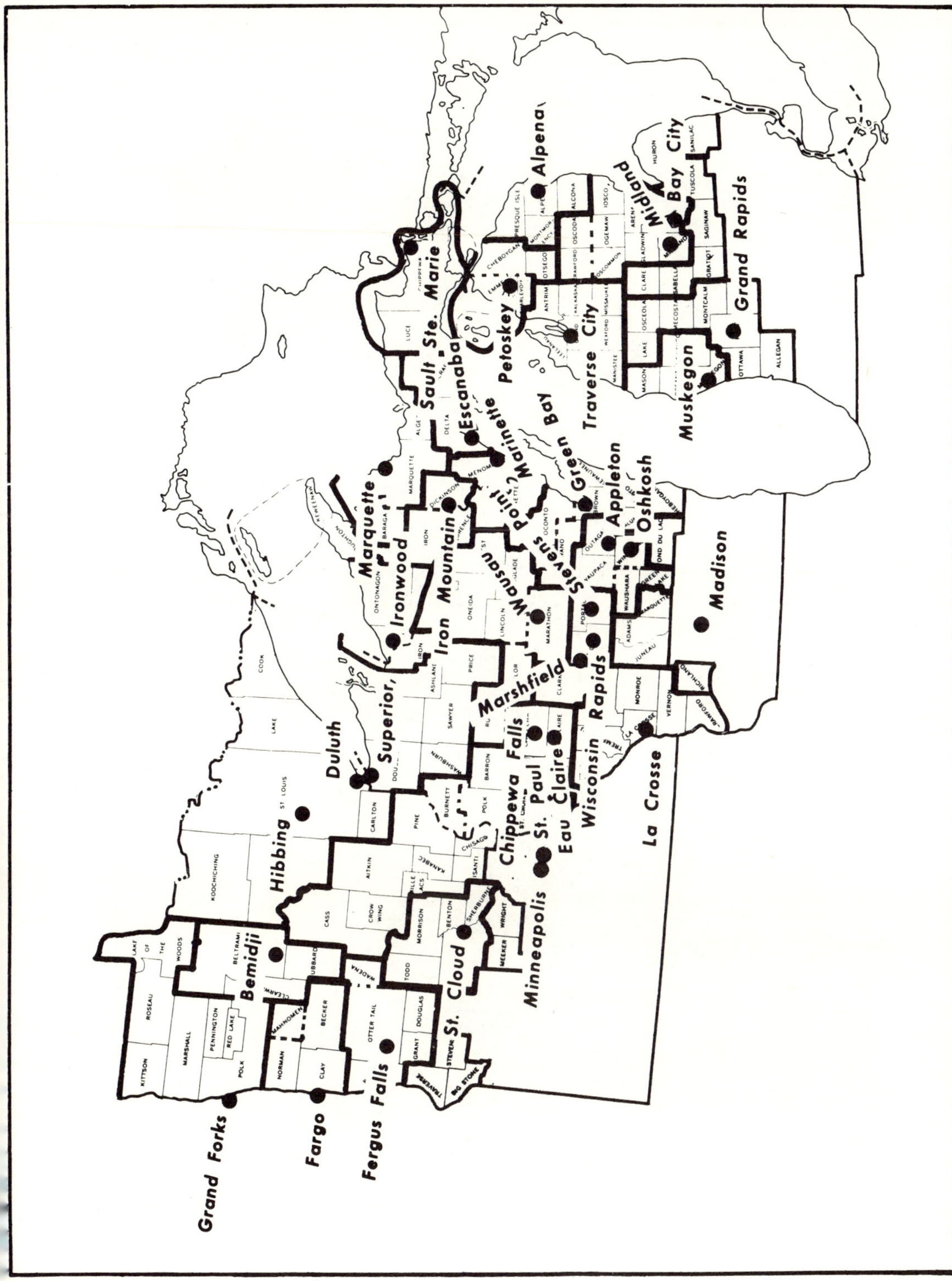

Figure 2-11. Rand McNally Basic Trade Areas.

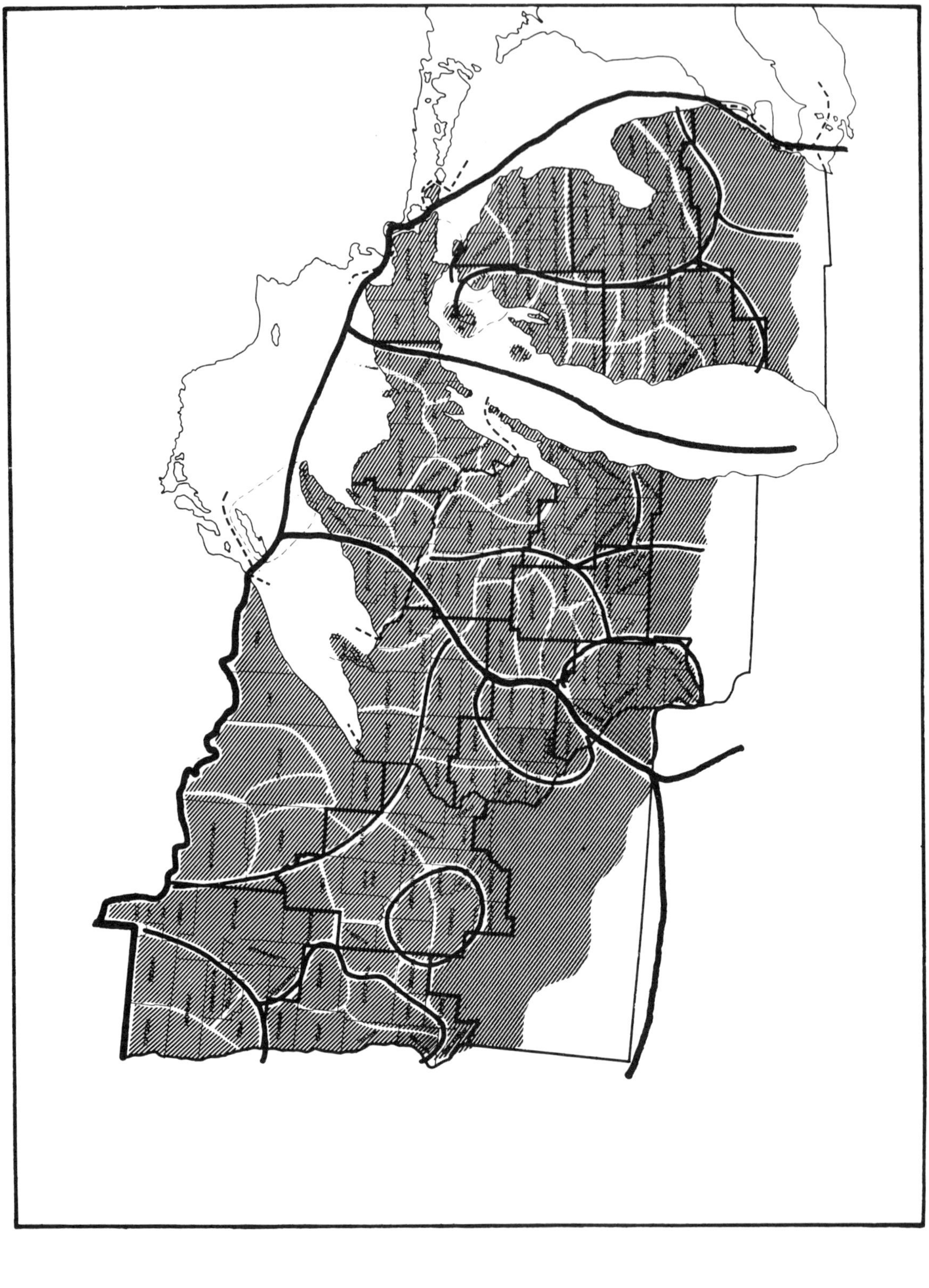

[illegible] the Three Top Levels of the Urban System.

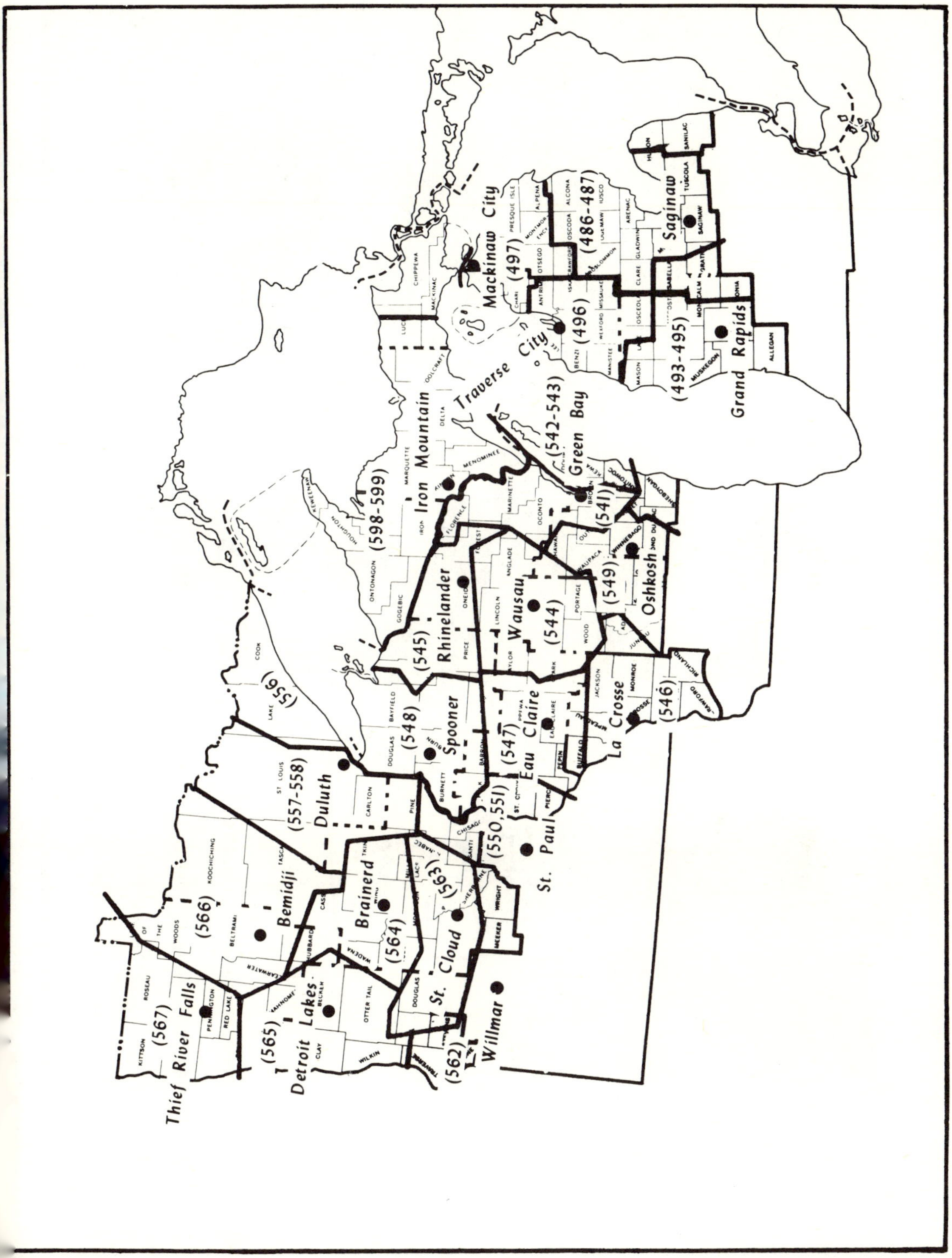

Figure 2-13. Three-digit Zip-Code Areas and Sectional Center Cities.

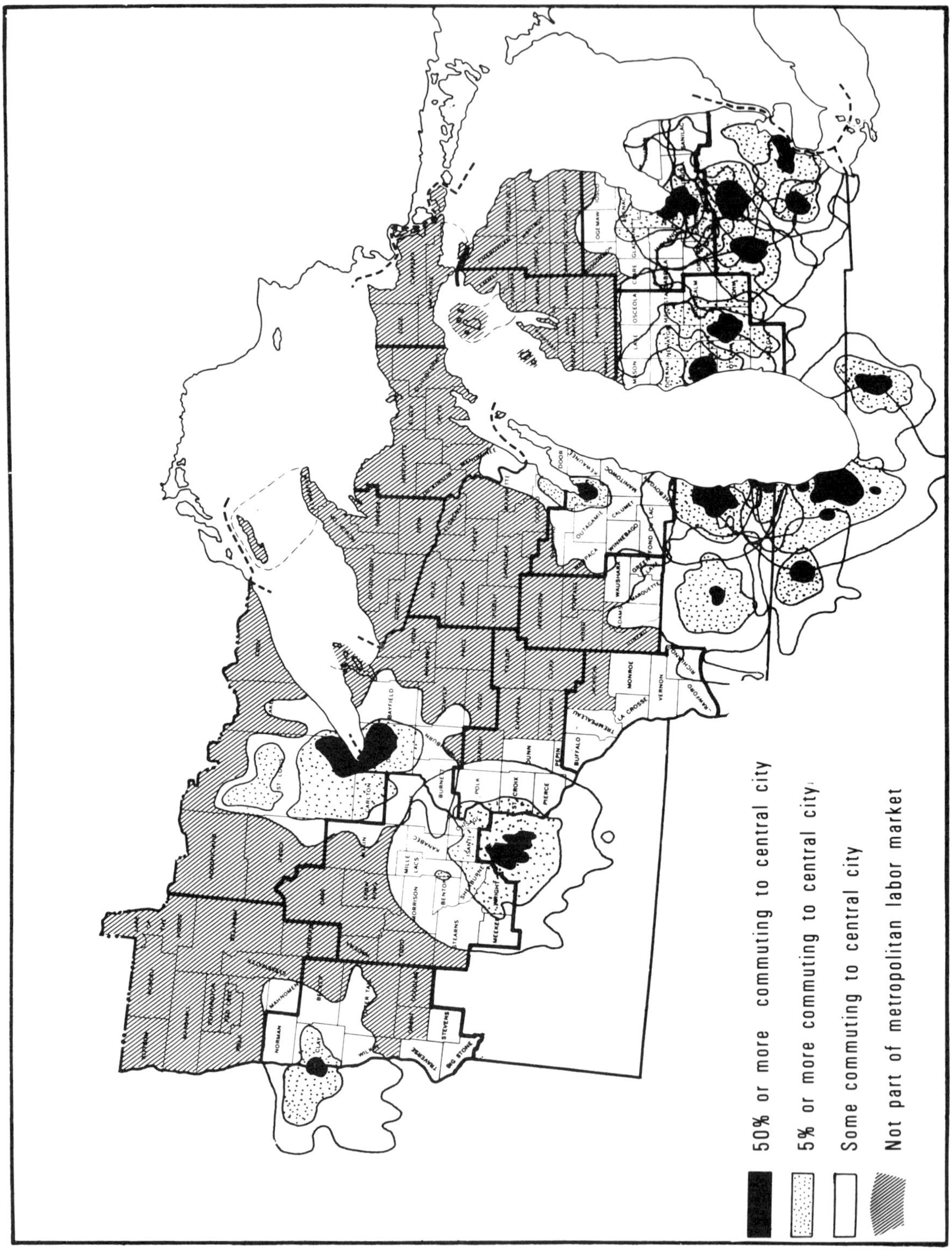
50% or more commuting to central city
5% or more commuting to central city
Some commuting to central city
Not part of metropolitan labor market

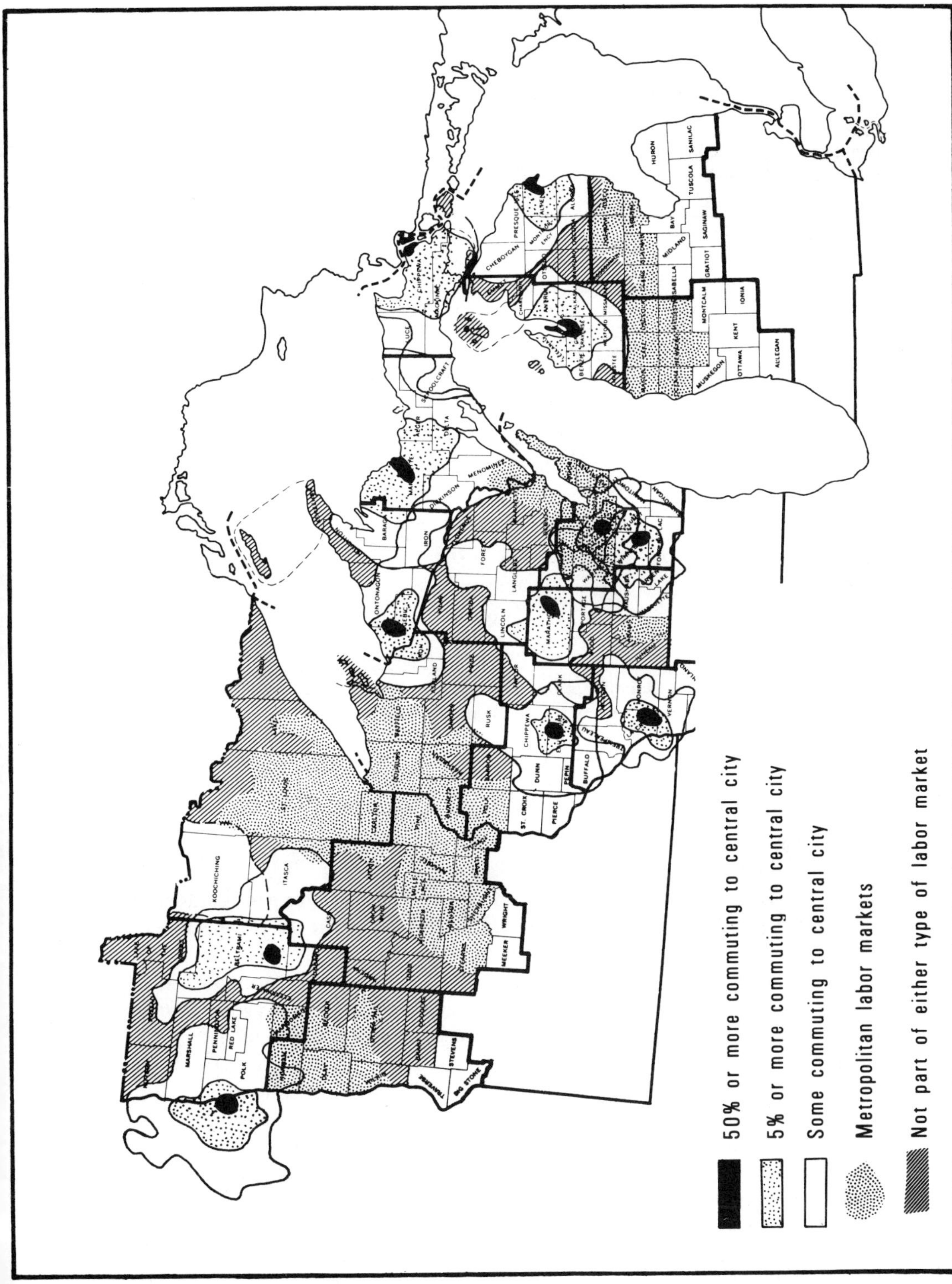

Figure 2-15. Labor Markets of Non-Metropolitan Centers.

Table 2-3. Labor Market Populations, 1960

Metropolitan Centers	*Population (in thousands)*
Chicago-Gary-Milwaukee Urban Region	8,857
Detroit-Ann Arbor	4,080
Minneapolis-St. Paul	2,009
Flint-Saginaw Bay City Urban Region	1,059
Muskegon-Grand Rapids	883
Wholesale-Retail Centers	
Madison	389
Duluth-Superior	350
Green Bay	346
Fargo-Moorhead	258
Appleton	206[a]
Wausaw	190[a]
La Crosse	185[a]
Grand Forks	176[a]
Eau Claire	152[b]
Complete Shopping Centers	
Marquette-Ishpeming	184[a]
Traverse City	110[c]
Bemidji	97[d]
Alpena	75[e]
Ironwood-Bessemer	60[e]
Sault Ste. Marie	52[e]
Brainerd	44[e]
International Falls	18[e]

(Source: Metropolitan Area Definition, op. cit., and the classification of centers in table 5)

[a]Not SMSA—but exceeds population of labor markets of following SMSAs, for example: St. Joseph, Lawton, Ogden, Odessa, Decatur.

[b]Not SMSA—but still greater in population than labor markets of Great Falls, Las Vegas, or Billings.

[c]Likewise, exceeds Reno.

[d]Likewise, still bigger than Laredo and San Angelo labor markets.

[e]Not SMSA, labor markets smaller than these of smallest SMSA.

Documentation of this process had been difficult in the past because relevant series of spatio-temporal data have been unavailable. However, it was possible to obtain indicative evidence for a few postwar phenomena, and the spread of television communications was selected an illustrative case in point. The example serves two purposes—first, to confirm that hierarchical filtering and spread effects are operating; and second, to suggest those segments of the Upper Great Lakes Region most closely bound into national processes of change and those least affected by them, coming last in a sequence of lagged emulation.

Figure 2-16 graphs size of city against date on which a television station was opened in that city. The downward-sloping scatter results from the hierarchical filtering process. Generally, urban centers of a given size-class located within the nation's heartland (points in the upper left of the scatter) installed facilities sooner than centers of comparable size located in one of the peripheries (points on the lower right). Thus, the Duluth-Superior market was the last of its size-class to be served by television communications. Figure 2-17 shows the television industry's market areas in 1968, as defined by the Nielson Company, together with the date at which the city serving the market first opened its stations.

The opening of a station provides the supply. For supply to enter the household, a television receiver must be purchased. Figures 2-18–2-22 map the percentage of families

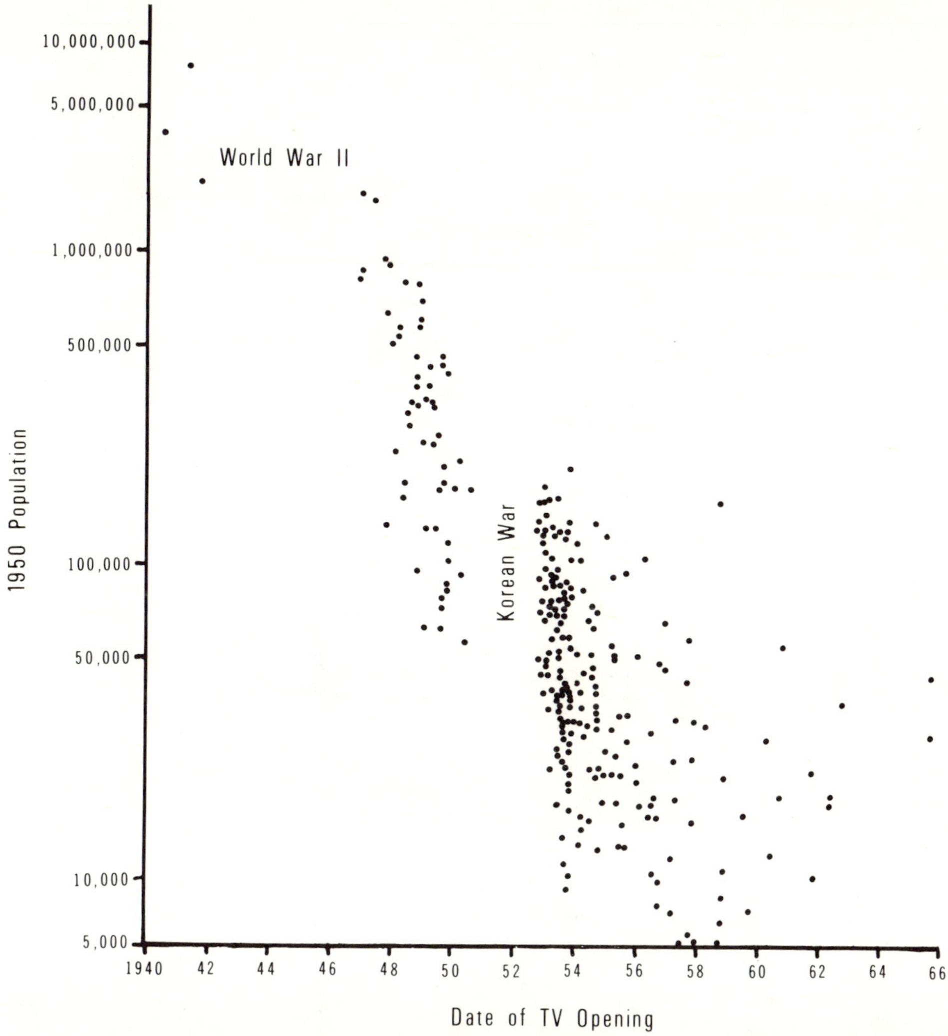

Figure 2-16. Hierarchical Diffusion of TV Stations.

with television sets in the years 1953, 1956, 1959, 1962 and 1965 (percentages were calculated by counties by the Nielson Company). In 1953, only the southern counties lying within the labor markets of the great metropolitan centers to the south were served. Only these areas were linked visually into communications about international, domestic, and regional affairs. The degree of penetration diminished with distance. By 1956 all counties had some coverage, as stations opened in the wholesale-retail centers serving the region. Again, penetration dropped off with distance from the centers, and most of the people within metropolitan labor markets were served. The principal inter-urban peripheries can be traced out in 1956, and again in 1959. By 1962 the effects had spread almost to completion, although in that year and again in 1965, a "hold-out" periphery in the northwest was evident.

Very few processes filter and spread as quickly or as completely as television, but for other changes the patterns and channels of diffusion are the same, and the effects are the same: a structuring of population and economic characteristics according to location within urban fields and rank of the center of the field within the urban hierarchy.

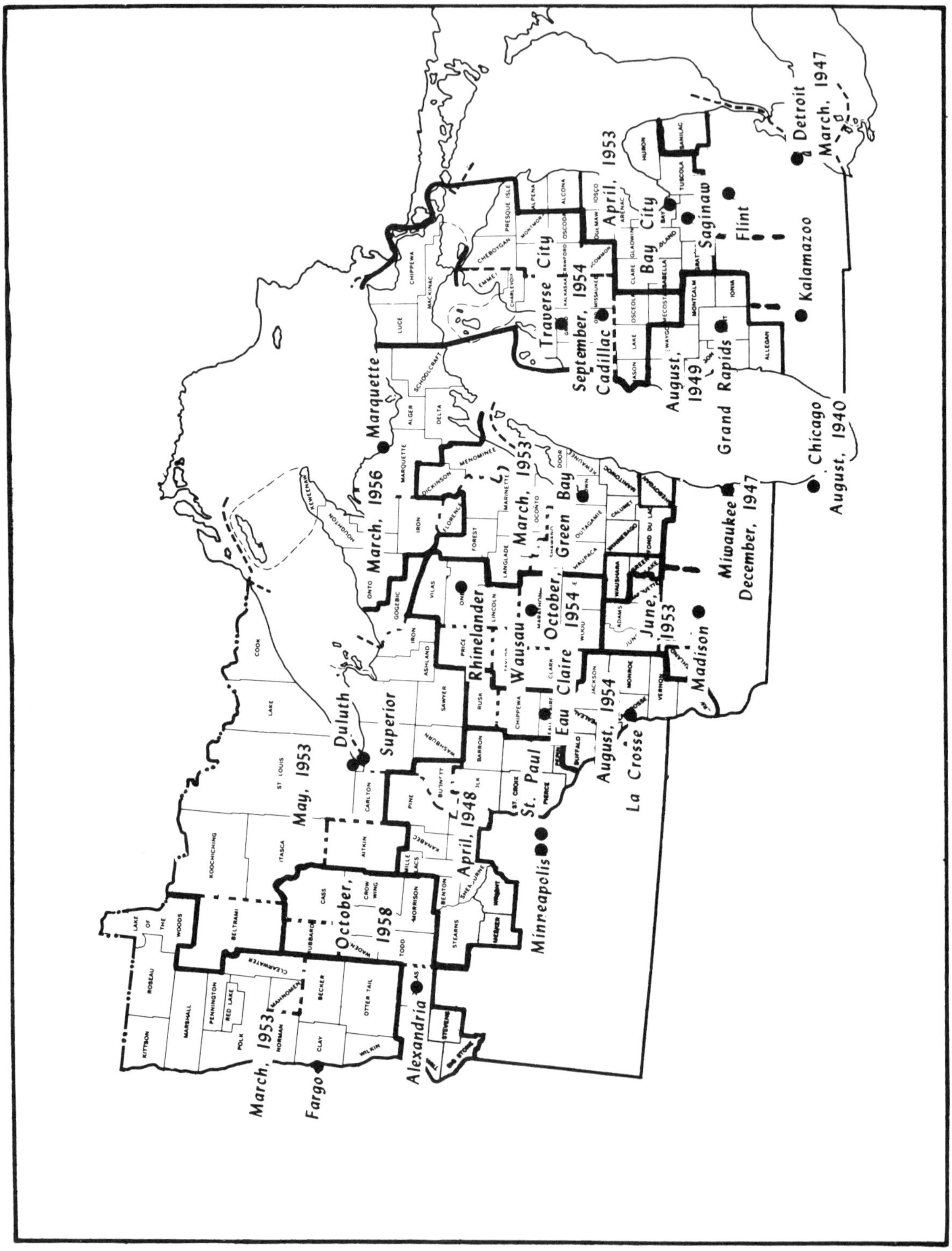
Detroit
March, 1947
Flint
Saginaw
Bay City
April, 1953
Kalamazoo
Grand Rapids
August, 1949
Traverse City
September, 1954
Cadillac
Chicago
August, 1940
Milwaukee
December, 1947
Madison
June, 1953
Green Bay
March, 1953
Marquette
March, 1956
Rhinelander
Wausau
October, 1954
Eau Claire
August, 1954
La Crosse
Duluth
Superior
May, 1953
St. Paul
Minneapolis
April, 1948
October, 1958
Alexandria
Fargo
March, 1953

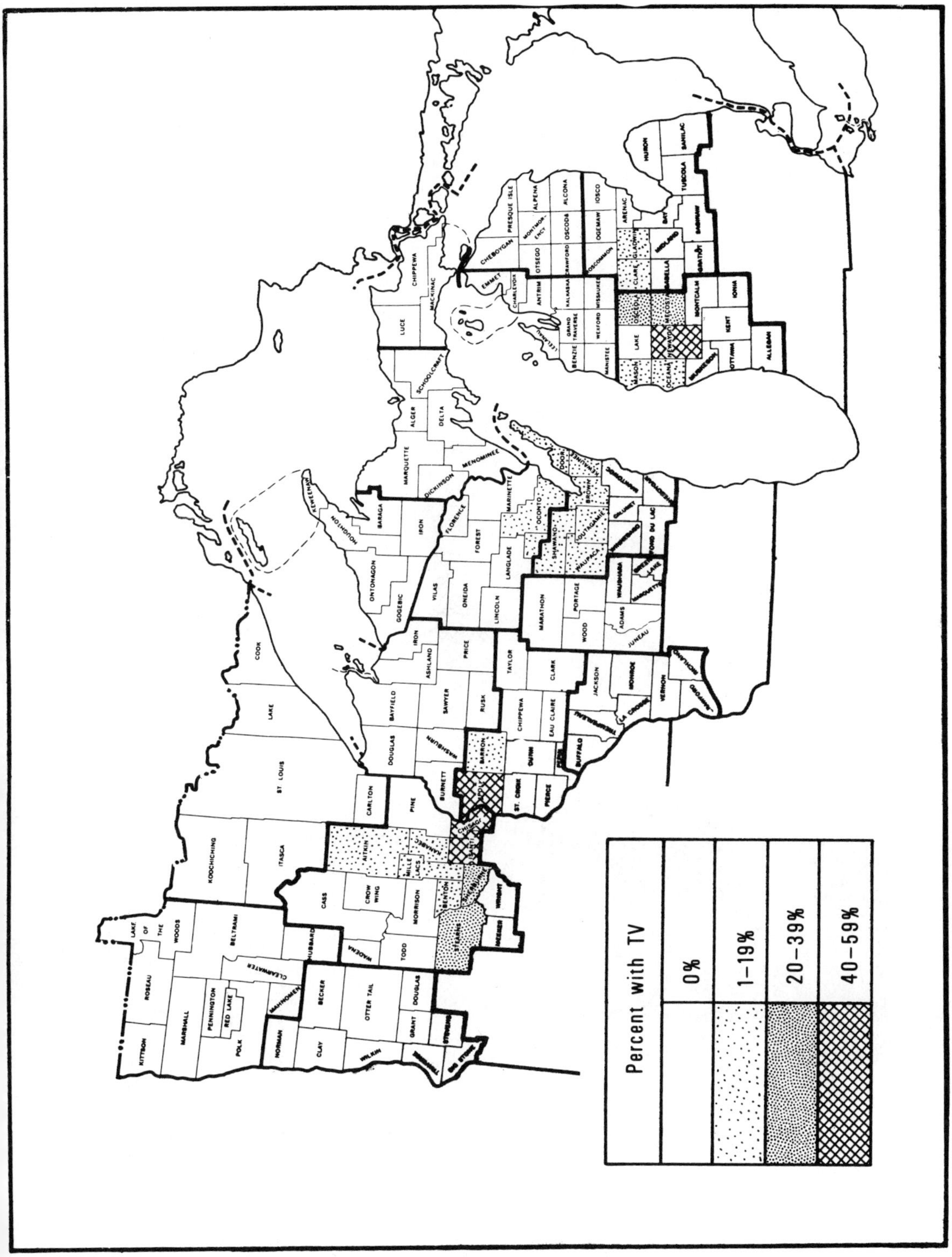

Figure 2-18. TV Market Penetration in 1953.

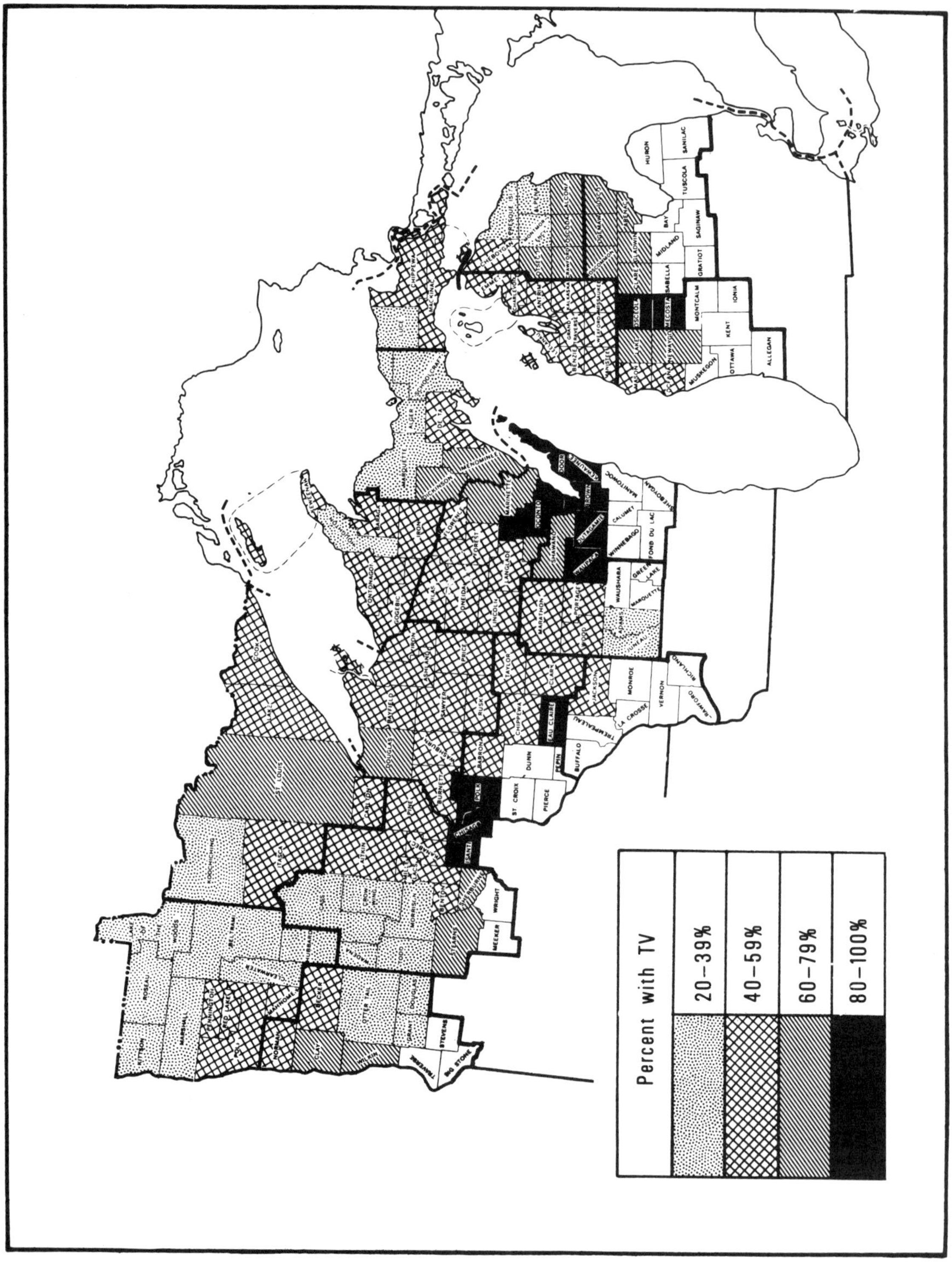

Figure 2-19. TV Market Penetration in 1956.

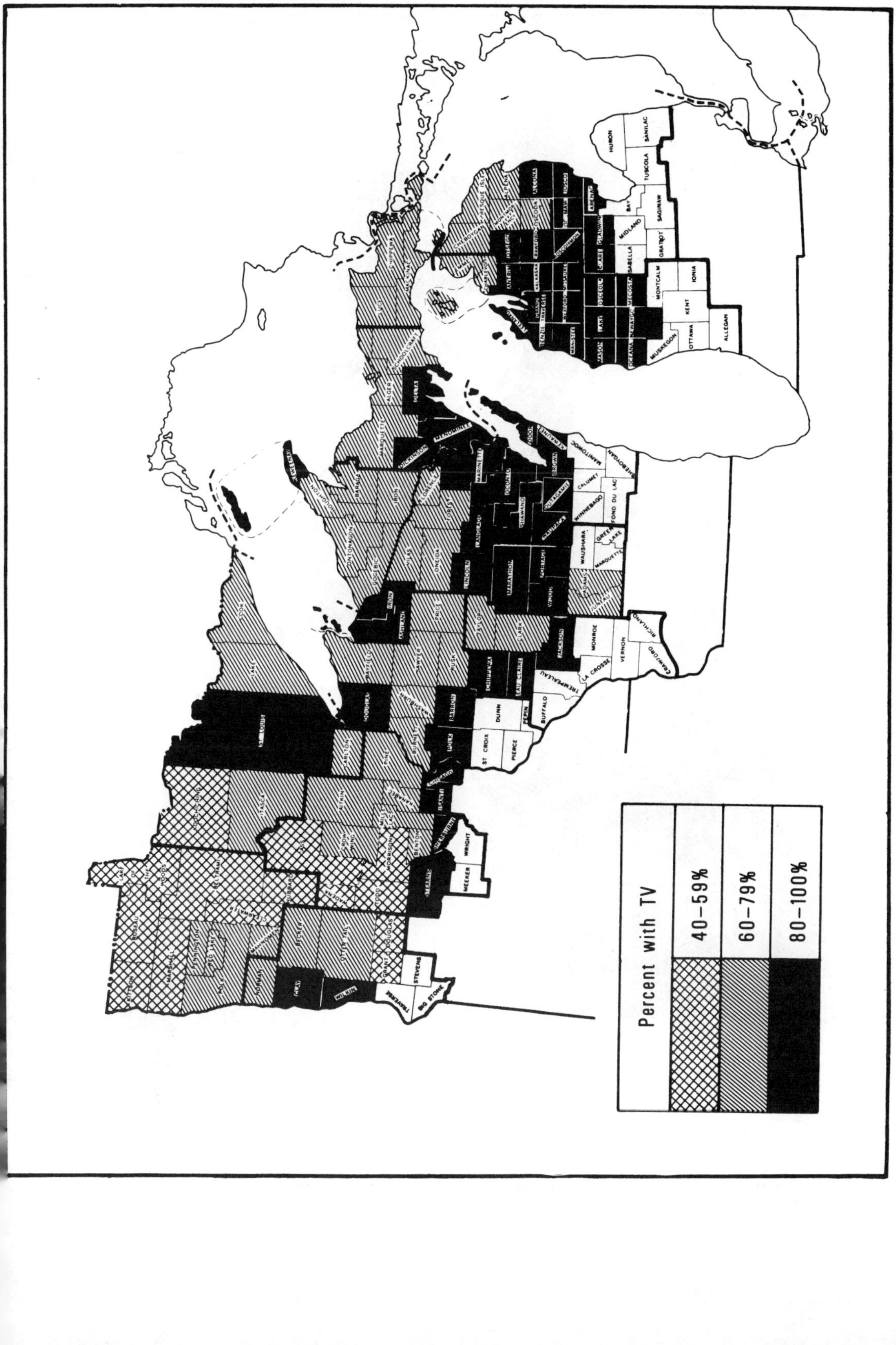

Figure 2-20. TV Market Penetration in 1959.

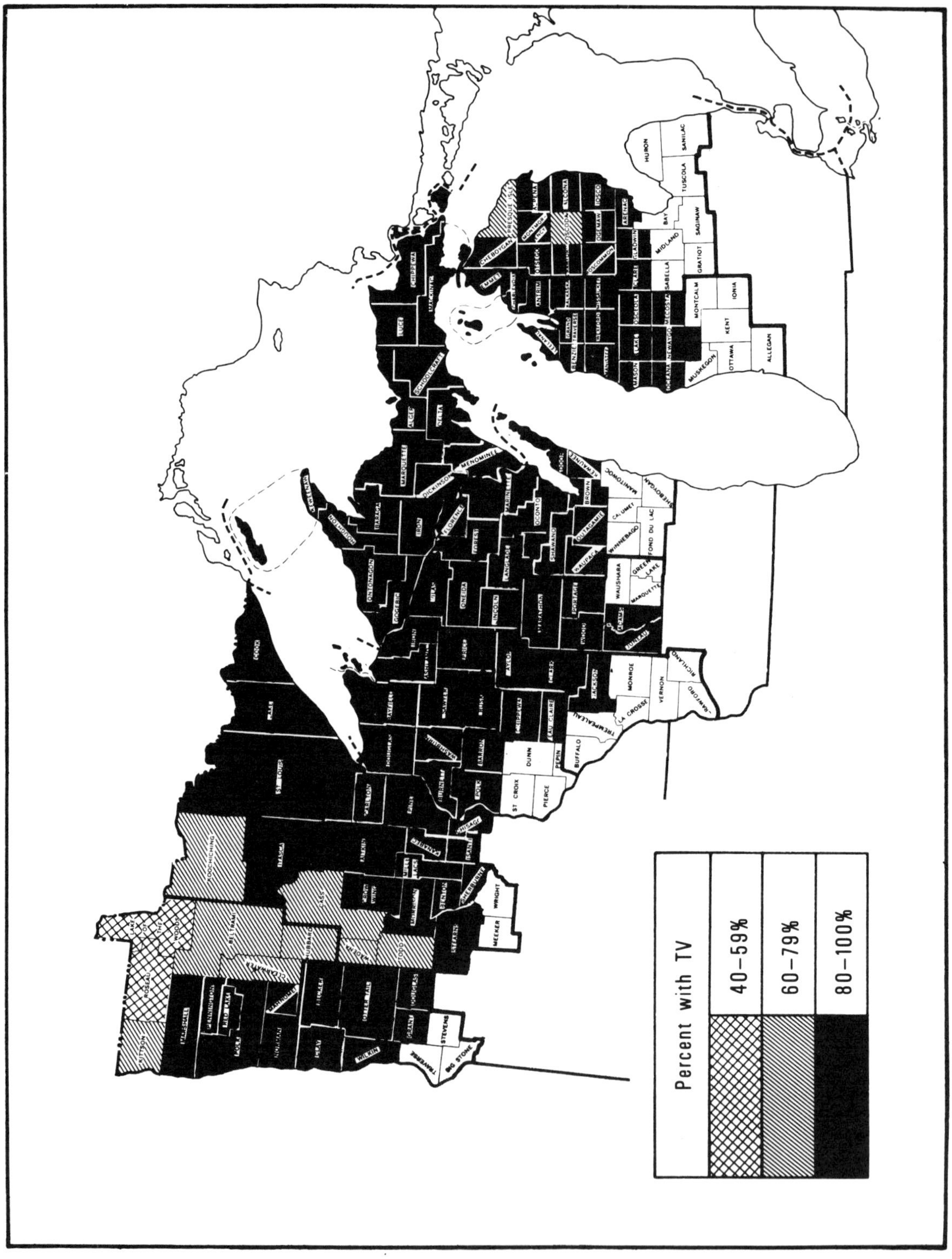

Figure 2-21. TV Market Penetration in 1962.

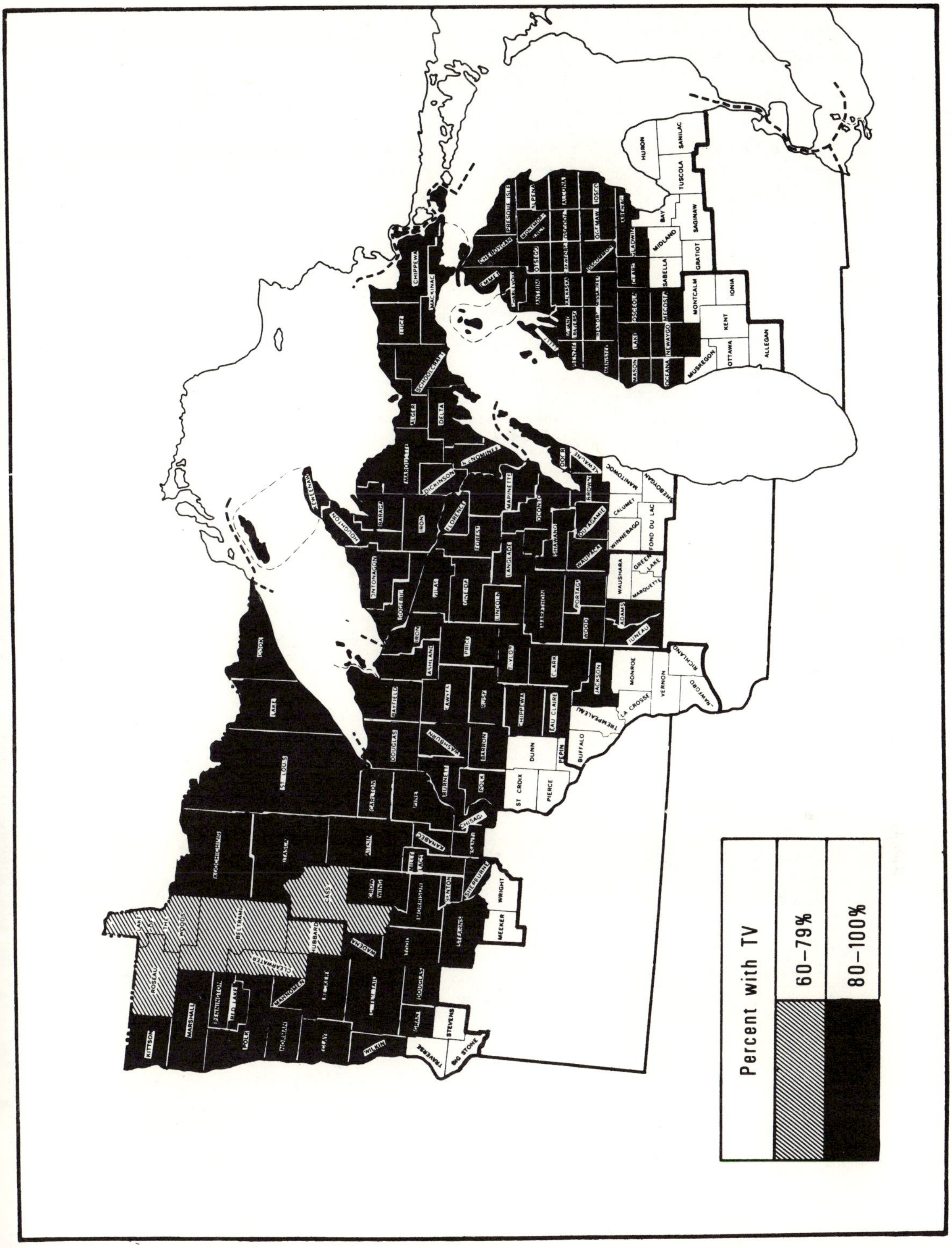

Figure 2-22. TV Market Penetration in 1965.

This structuring was also revealed with dramatic clarity in figures 2-23-2-31 which graph a series of gradients of urban influence. Each figure includes twelve graphs, showing the levels of key variables of economic welfare or performance in 1960, or key rates of change 1950-1960, along traverses between major cities.

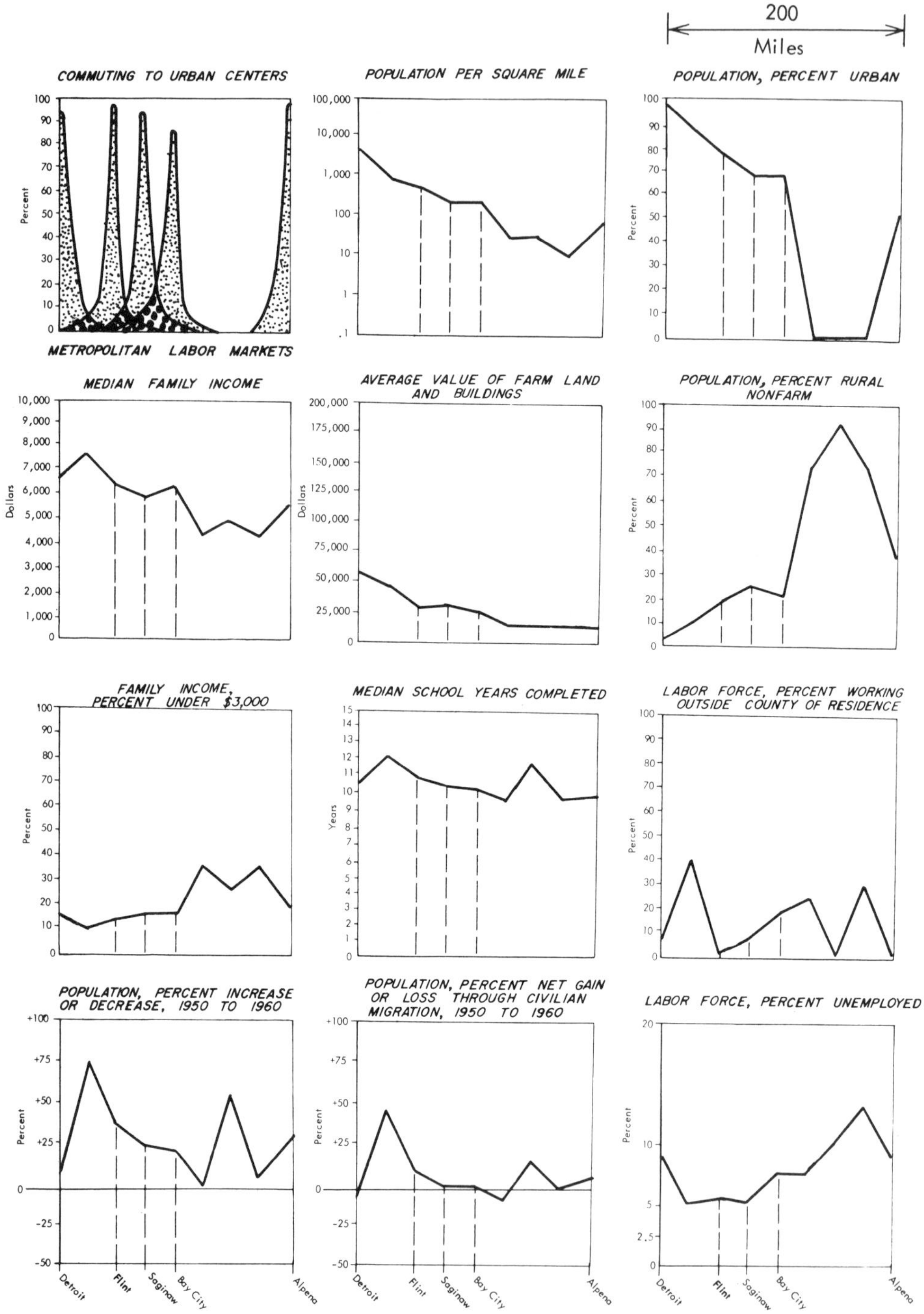

Figure 2-23. Detroit-Alpena Gradients.

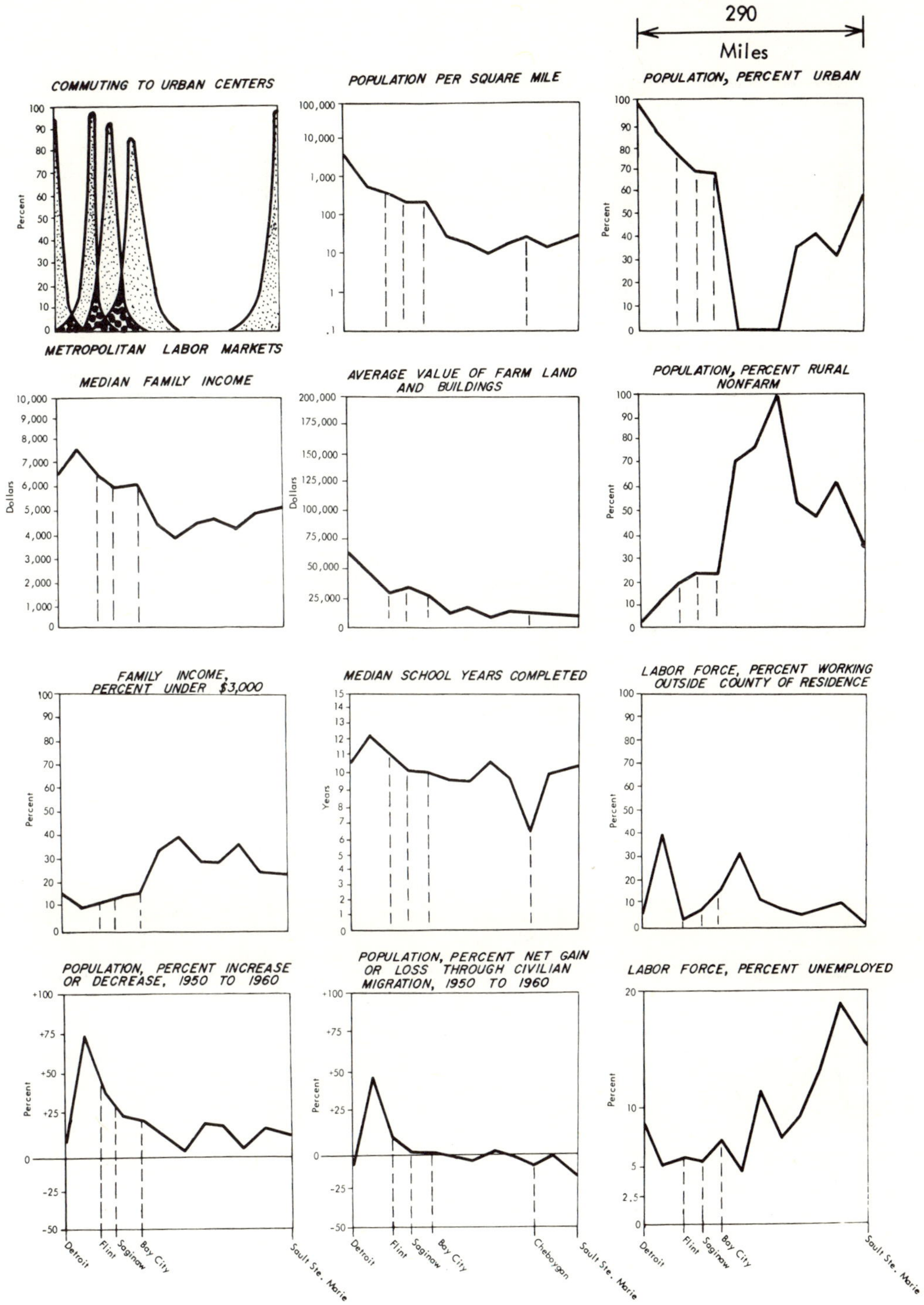

Figure 2-24. Detroit-Sault Ste. Marie Gradients.

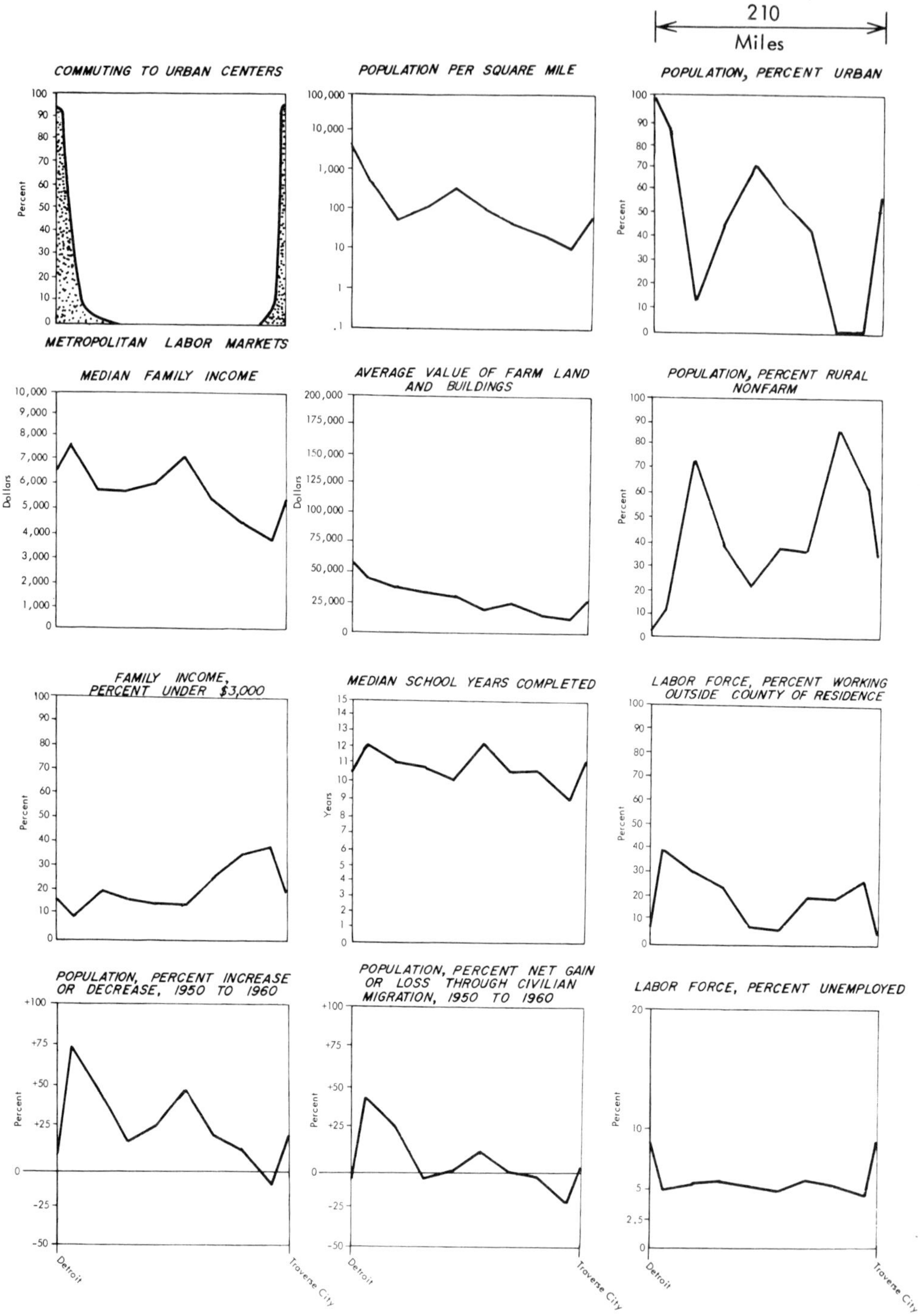

Figure 2–25. Detroit-Traverse City Gradients.

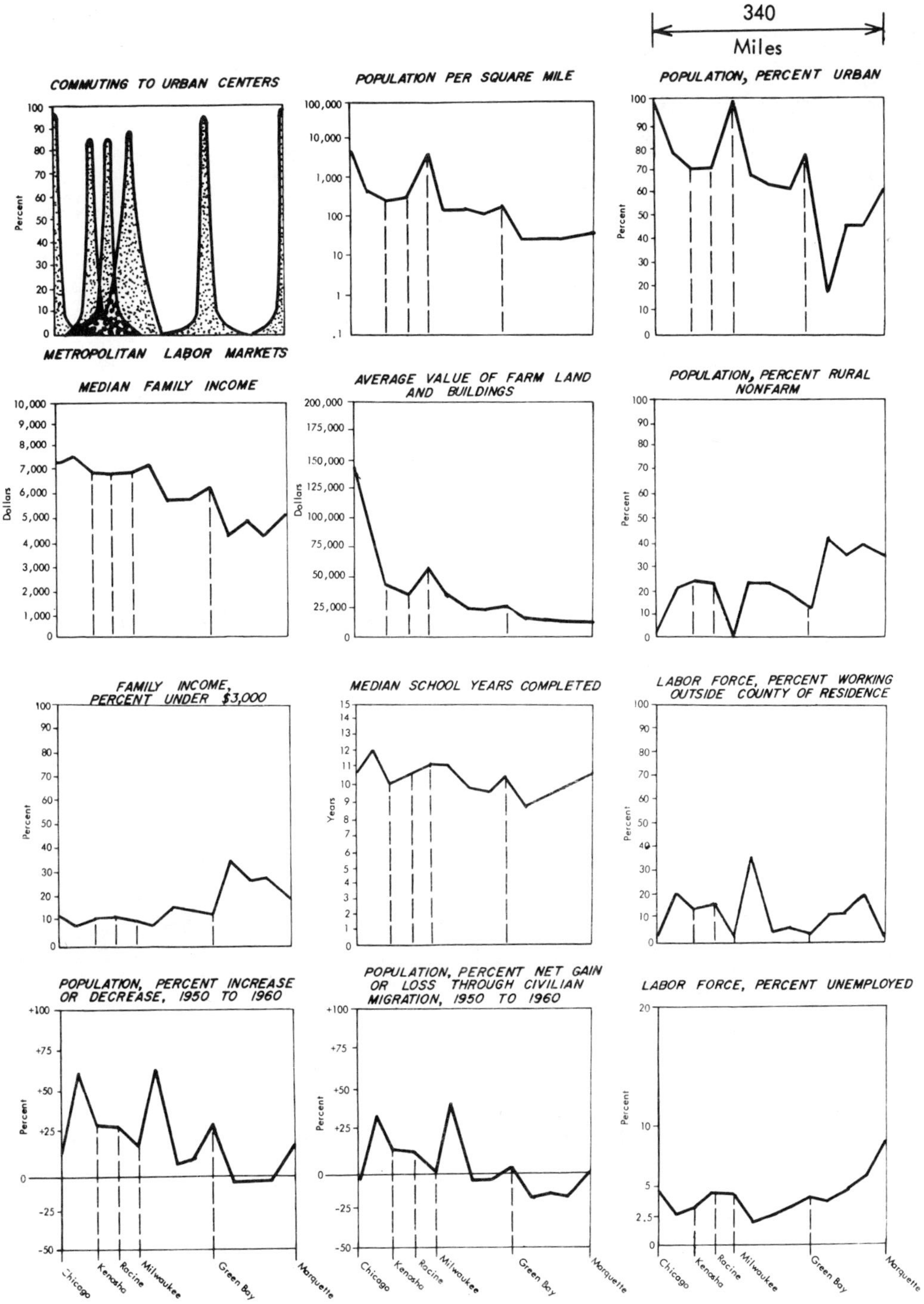

Figure 2-26. Chicago-Marquette Gradients.

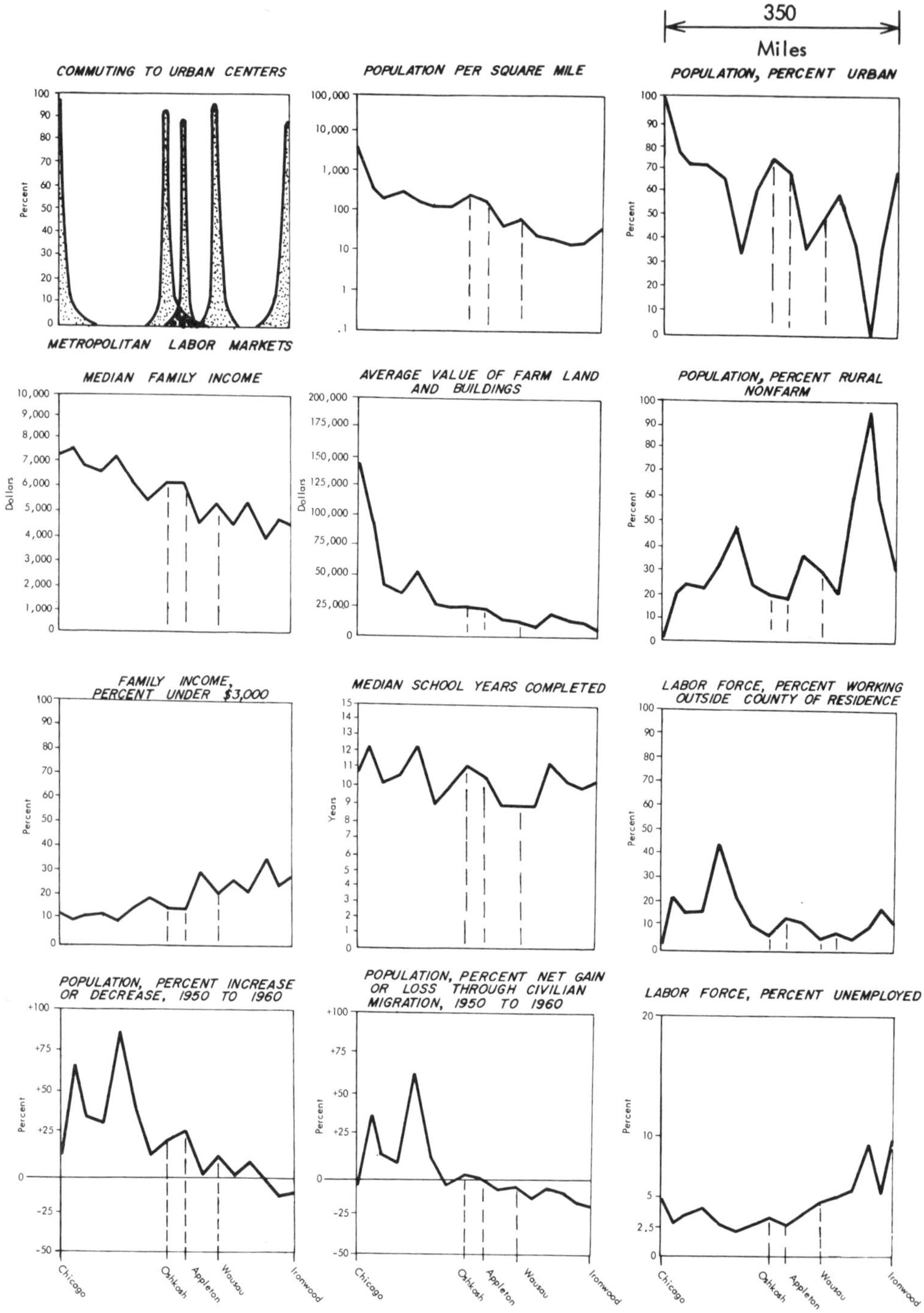

Figure 2–27. Chicago-Ironwood Gradients.

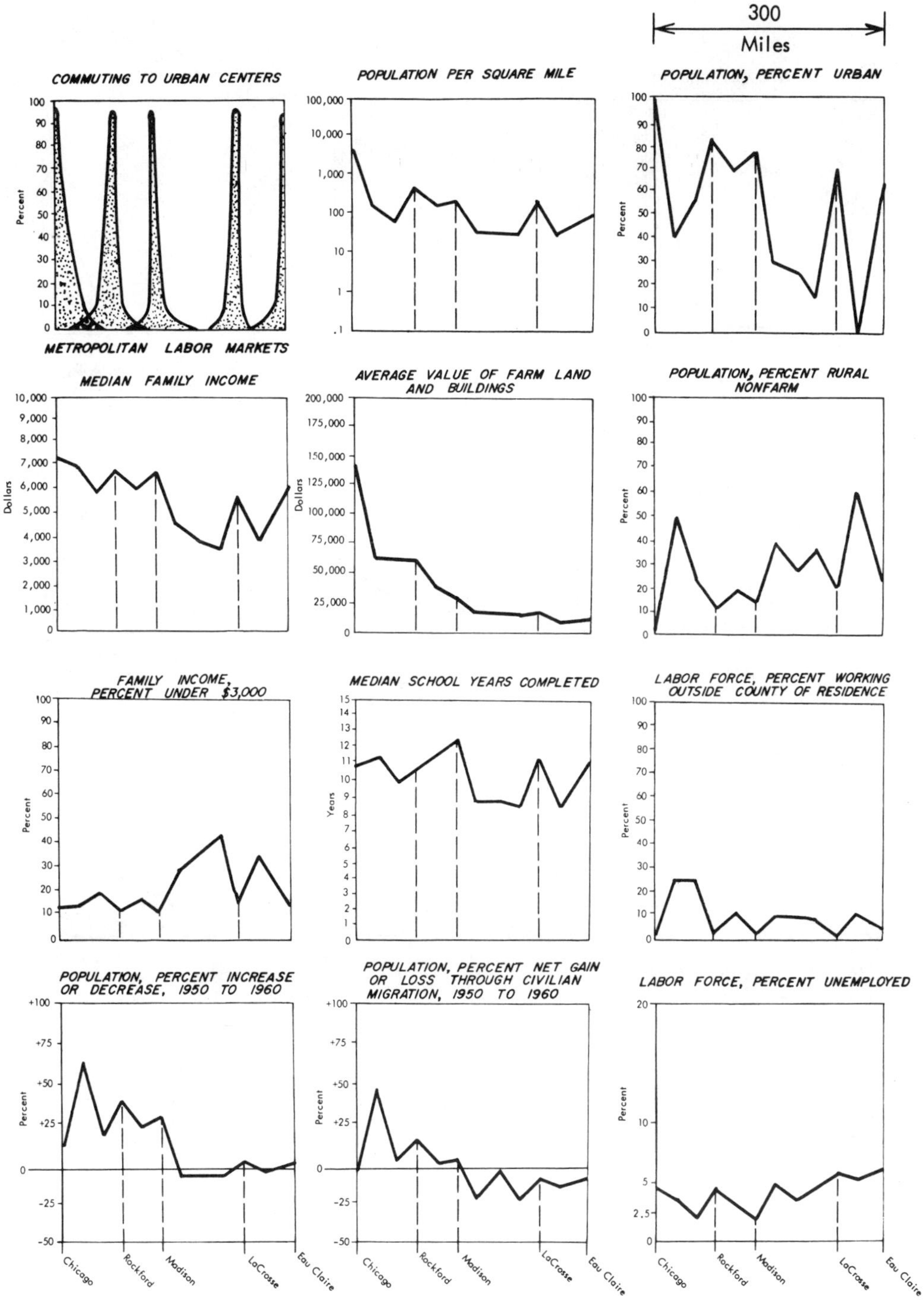

Figure 2-28. Chicago-Eau Claire Gradients.

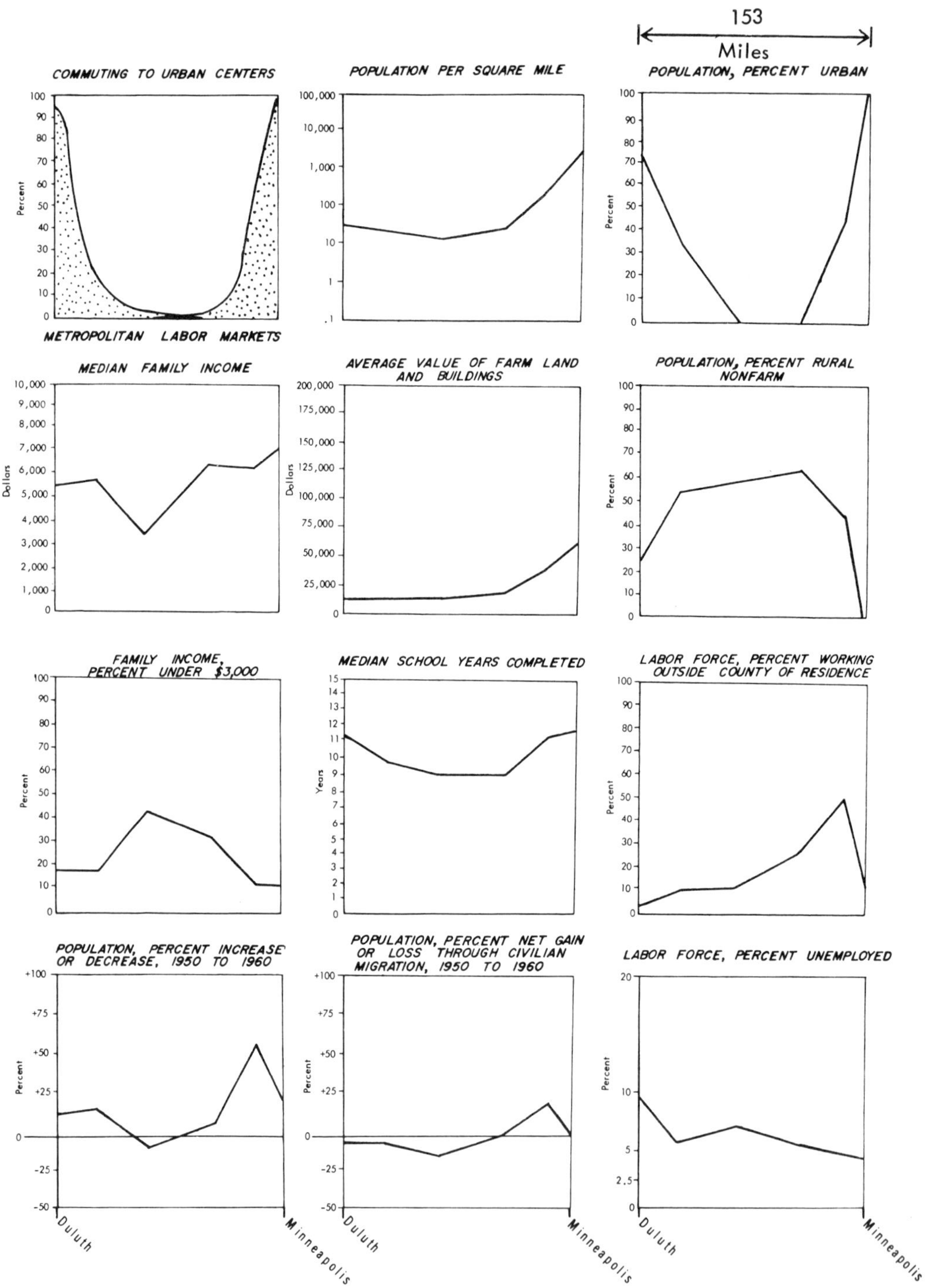

Figure 2-29. Minneapolis-Duluth Gradients.

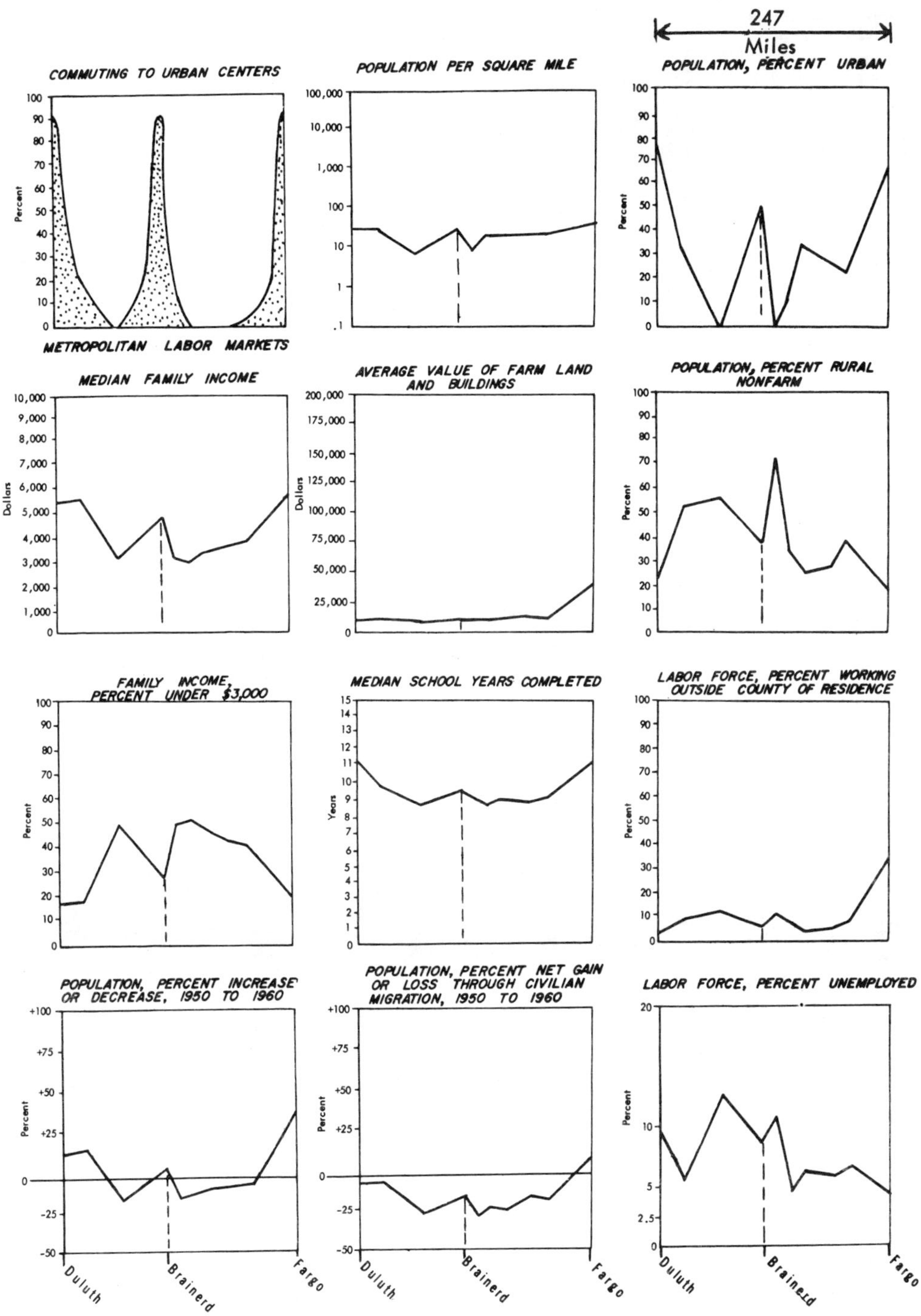

Figure 2-30. Fargo-Duluth Gradients.

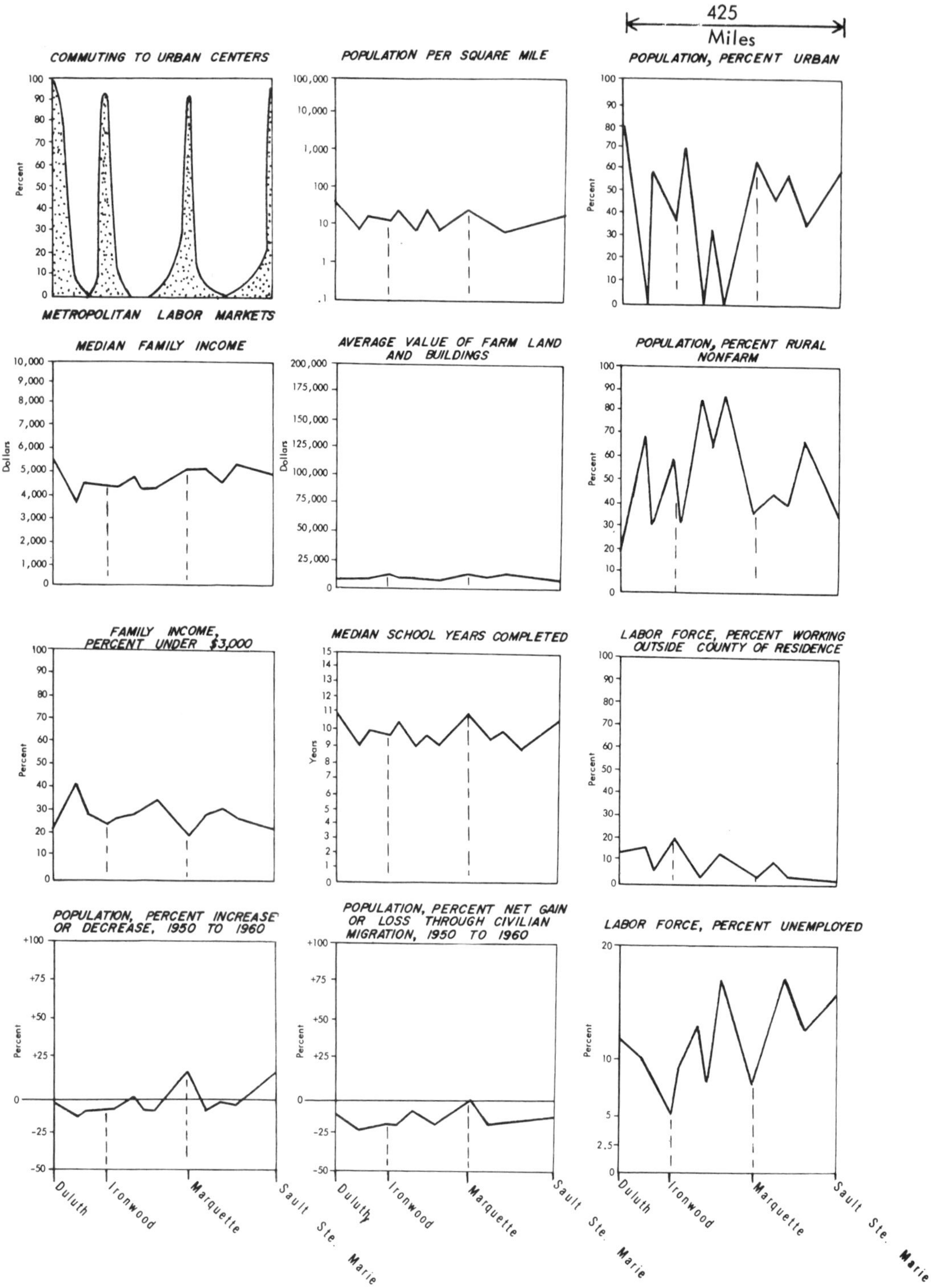

Figure 2-31. Duluth-Saulte Ste. Marie Gradients.

See, for example, figure 2–23, which depicts gradients along the Detroit-Flint-Saginaw-Bay City-Alpena traverse. The top left hand graph provides an important referent, revealing the declining degree of labor-market participation of residents with increasing distance from urban centers. Incomes, densities, educational levels and agricultural productivity are all high within the complex urban region stretching from Detroit to Bay City. Poverty levels and employment are greatest, educational levels lowest, and agriculture weakest in the intervening area between Bay City and Alpena. The graphs show a rhythmic variation of indicators of economic welfare and performance, highly correlated with degree of participation in the urban labor markets. The peaks of the gradients, in turn, are related to rank of centers in the hierarchy. Comparison of the illustrations shows, also, the dramatic downward displacement of the gradients northwards.

Patterns of Change

Careful study of figures 2–23–2–31 suggested much about the network of interdependencies in the Upper Great Lakes Region. Clearly, regional levels of welfare were controlled by the urban system. The figures also provided insights into the response of the population to these welfare differentials. Examination of the first two graphs on the bottom row of each figure showed rates of population growth to be positive in the urban centers and low or negative along the peripheries, for example. They were greatest in the complex urban regions of southern Michigan and the Chicago-Milwaukee corridor, and dropped northward from there, with the greatest rates of decrease in the interurban-peripheries between the smaller northern towns. The rate of change in smaller urban centers also dropped with distance from larger centers, as suggested in figure 2–32. Only the largest centers and urban regions were growing due to net in-migration; elsewhere the dominant direction of migrants was outwards and southwards (fig. 2–33).

Clearly, the population was responding to the sub-regional differences in welfare. Such a response, because it drains off many of the most skilled and qualified individuals in the active age-groups, has been found throughout the nation to be one of the principal contributors to the cumulative disadvantages of the peripheries.

This broad response, but also some more limited positive aspects of change, were revealed very clearly in the related results of a factorial study of the changes that took place in sixty-one variables in the 1950–1960 decade. This study was completed for all 3,102 counties of the United States, and sought to identify the principal dimensions of change in the nation (Berry, 1971). Included in the results of the study were "scores" of every county in the country on each of these dimensions.

The scores were mapped for the Upper Great Lakes Region. They showed broad areas of the region to have rates of labor force expansion and population growth inferior to that of the nation (fig. 2–34). Many of these areas (and, indeed, one or two counties with growing populations and labor force) showed increases in unemployment and in the proportion of their populations in the disadvantaged category (fig. 2–35). The population of many areas also aged perceptibly in the decade (fig. 2–36). Of interest is the fact that some of the peripheral counties in the first two categories nonetheless showed above-average growth in incomes and educational levels in the period (fig. 2–37).

Most counties declined agriculturally. A few showed positive shifts however (fig. 2–38). In the case of Juneau County, Wisconsin, to cite one example, this reflects growth in specialty cropping for the canning and freezing industry (fig. 2–39).

Expansion of manufacturing employment was, however, most rapid in Michigan counties closest to the core of the manufacturing belt (fig. 2–40). The growth of manufacturing payrolls and value added was similar (fig. 2–41). Nonetheless, from very low starting-

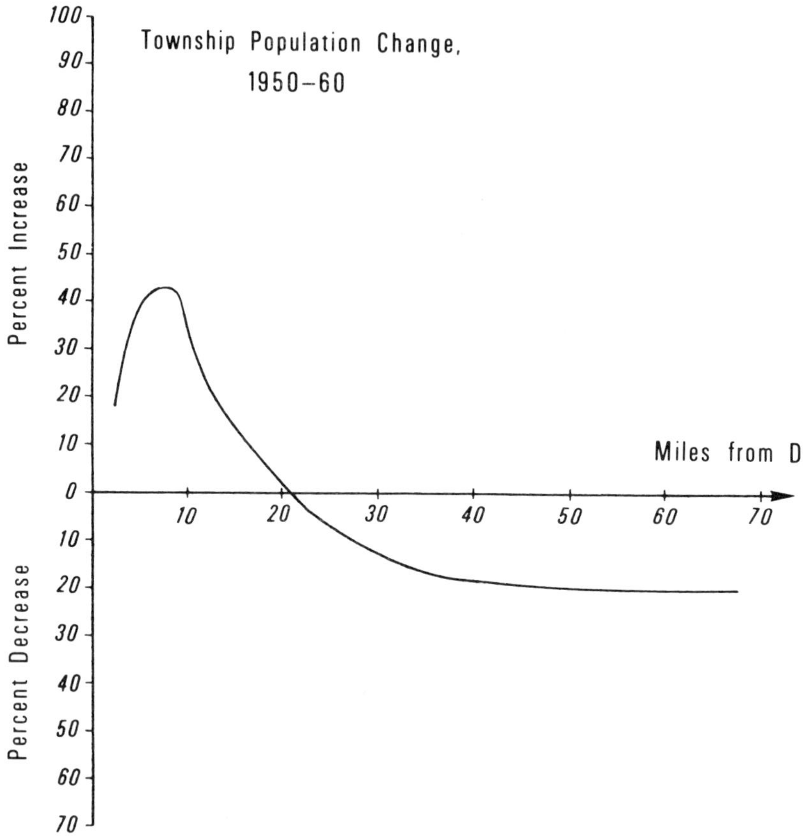

Figure 2–32. Rate of Population Change of Smaller Urban Centers Related to Distance from Deluth.

points, counties elsewhere in the region did experience growth in numbers of manufacturing establishments (fig. 2–42). And commensurate with growth in manufacturing employment, Michigan's counties showed the greatest growth in wholesaling (fig. 2–43).

Other maps prepared by the Upper Great Lakes Regional Commission showed related aspects of structure and change in the Region. Further details were provided in a variety of publications, for example the *Urban Reports* of the Upper Midwest Economic Development of the State of Wisconsin, of the Department of Resource Development of that state, and the State Resource Planning Program of the Michigan Department of Commerce.

These reports were rich with local insight and enabled many facets of the factorial study to be given contextual interpretation. In Wisconsin, they suggested the strong gradients of urban influence on everyday life, and migration patterns focusing intraregionally on the state's wholesale-retail level centers and interregionally drifting southeastwards among these centers. Four growth regions could thus be identified: the southeast Wisconsin part of the Chicago-Milwaukee urban region; the Chicago-Twin cities Interstate corridor; the Fox Valley from Fond-du-Lac through Oshkosh and Appleton to Green Bay; and the central axis from Wausau through Stevens Point to Sauk and Jackson Counties and La Crosse. Commensurate with the substantial gradients in wage-rates some dispersion of the

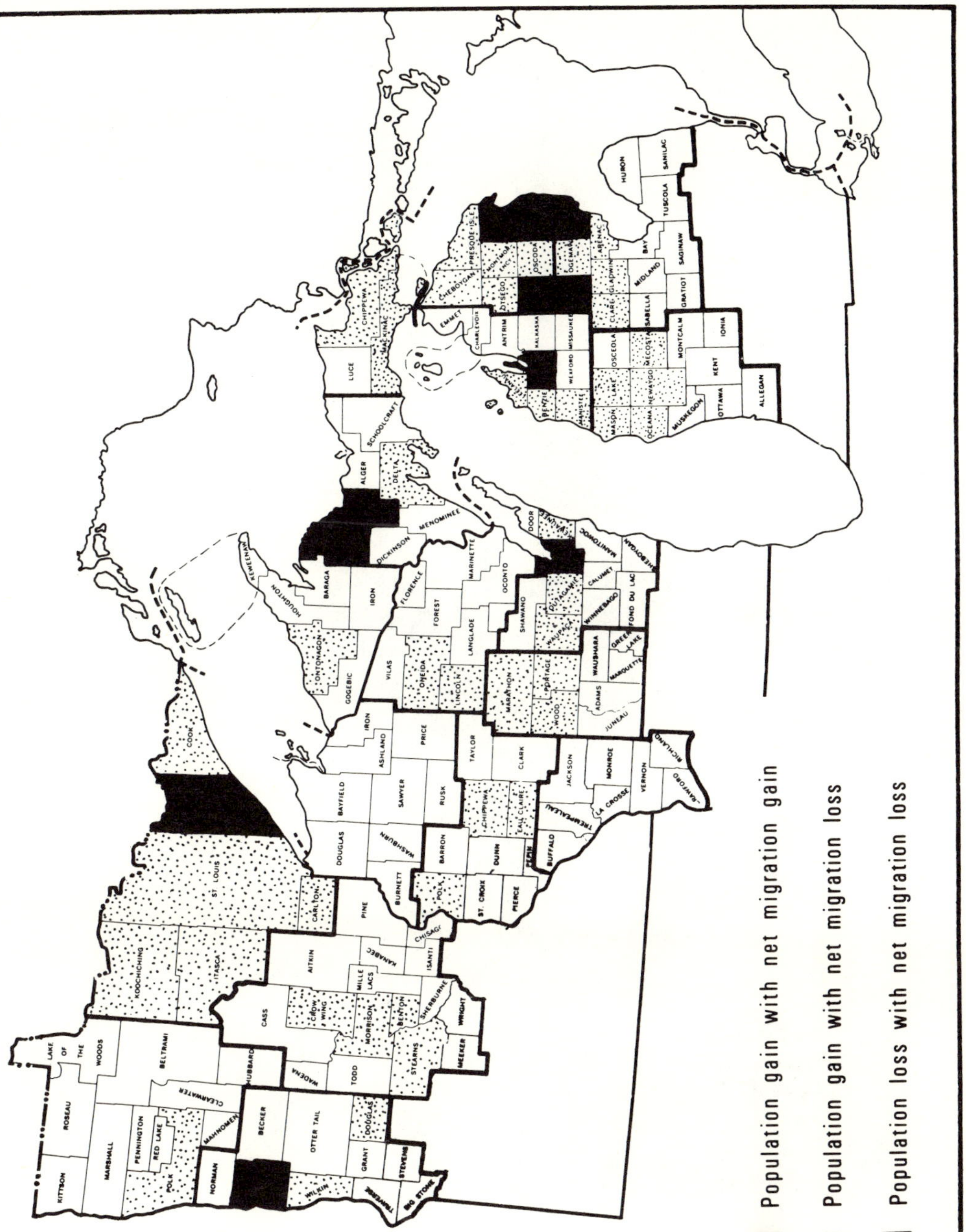

Figure 2–33. Population Change and Migration Rates Compared.

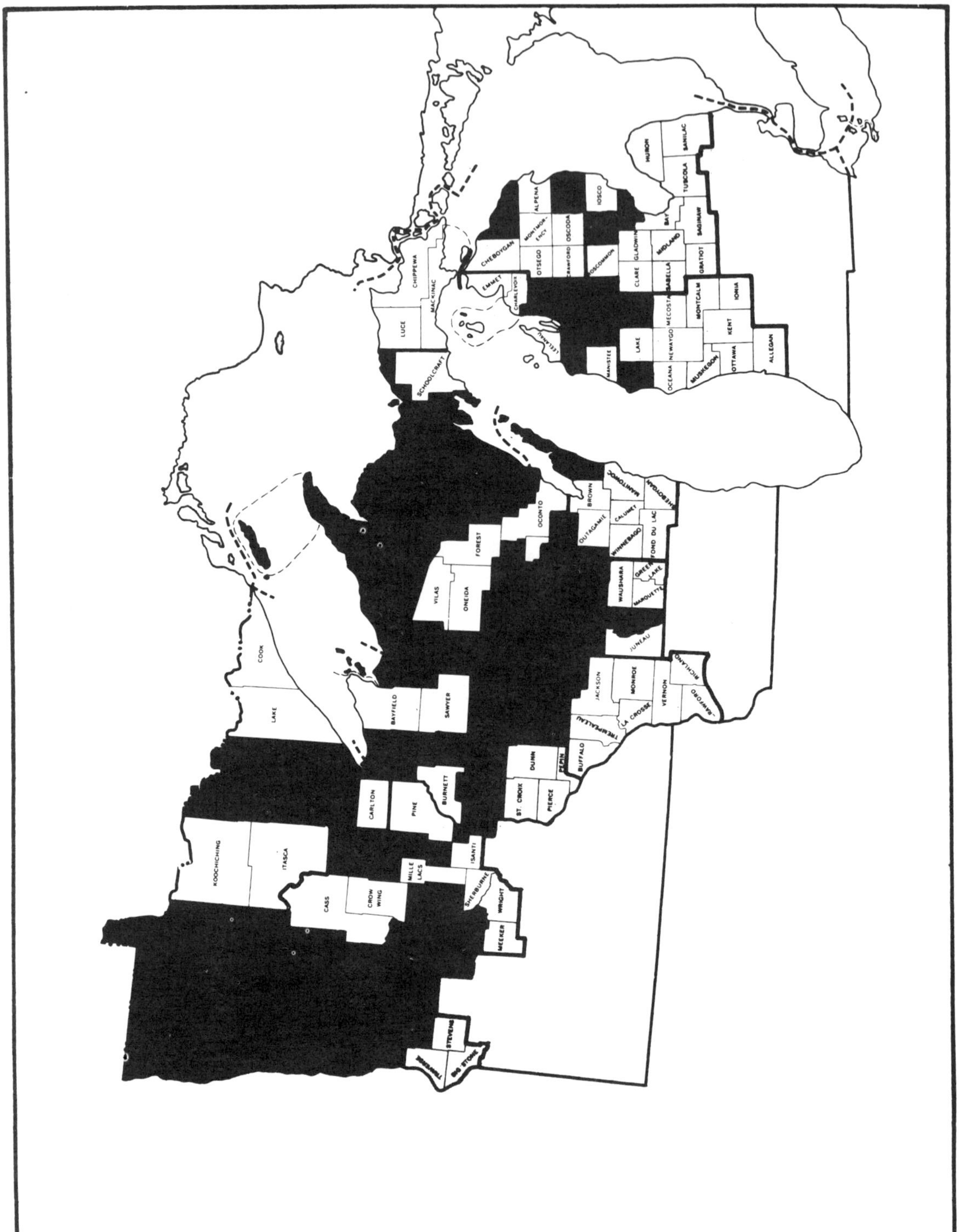

Figure 2-34. Counties with Lagging Population and Labor Force.

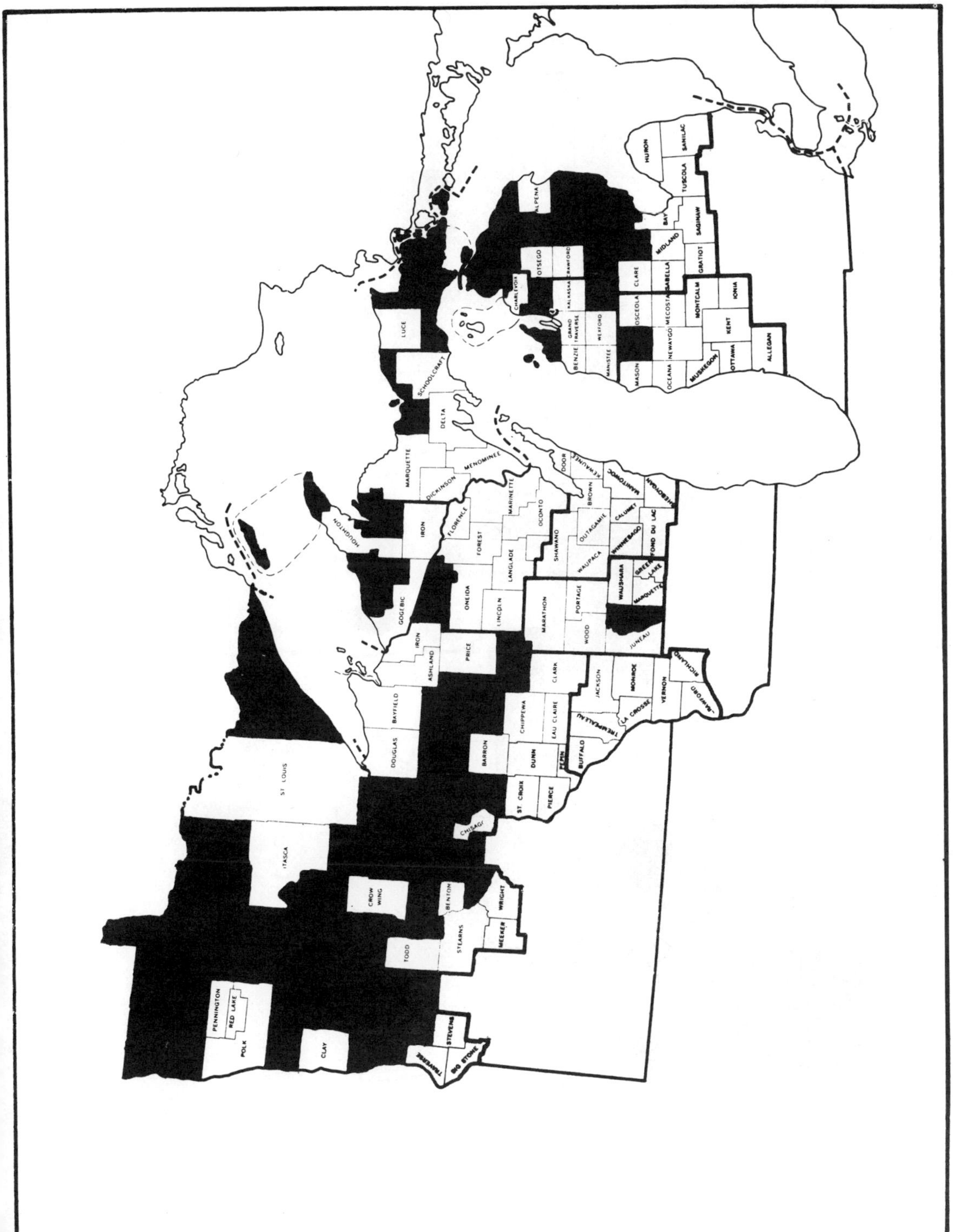

Figure 2–35. Counties with Growing Disadvantaged Population.

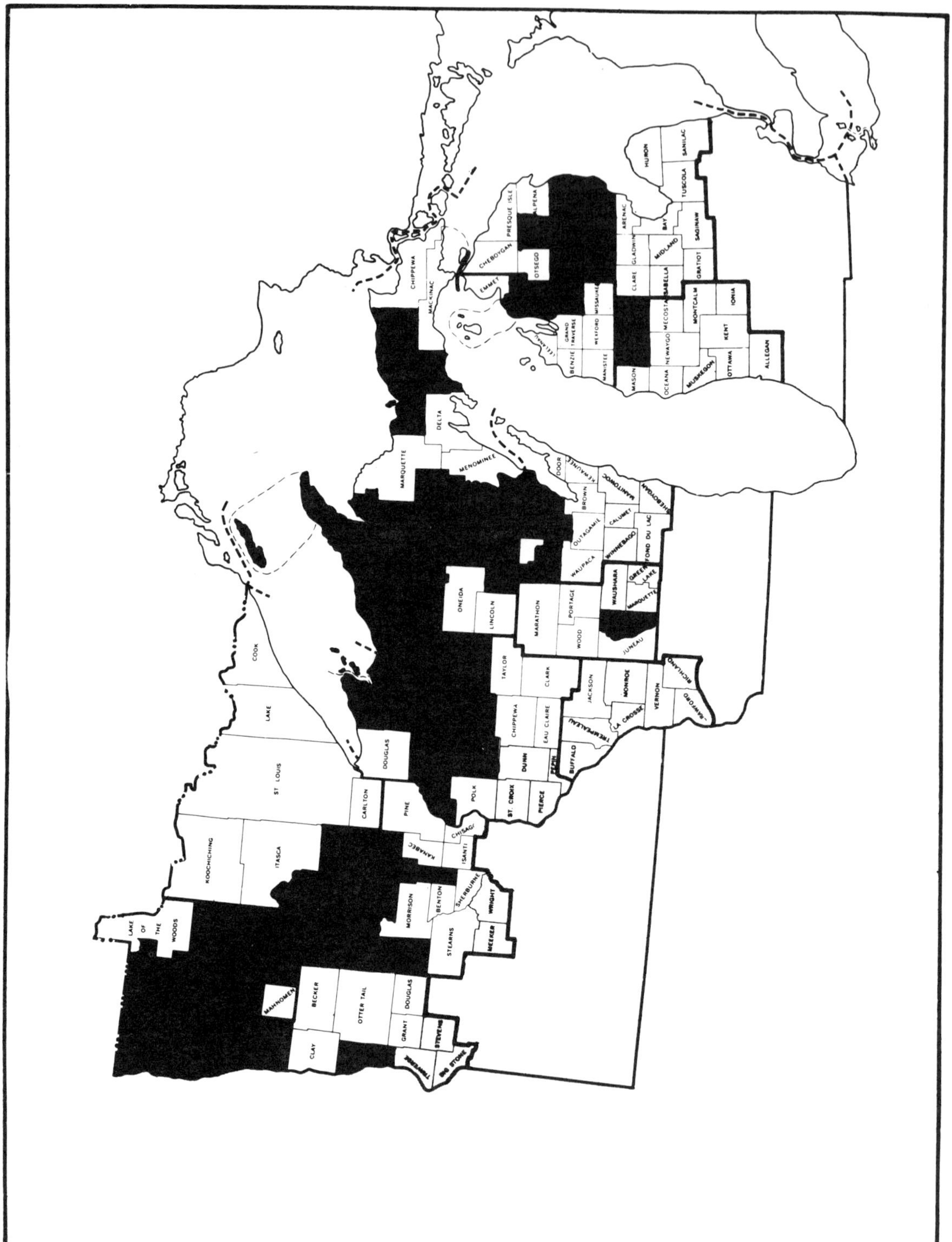

Figure 2–36. Counties with an Aging Population.

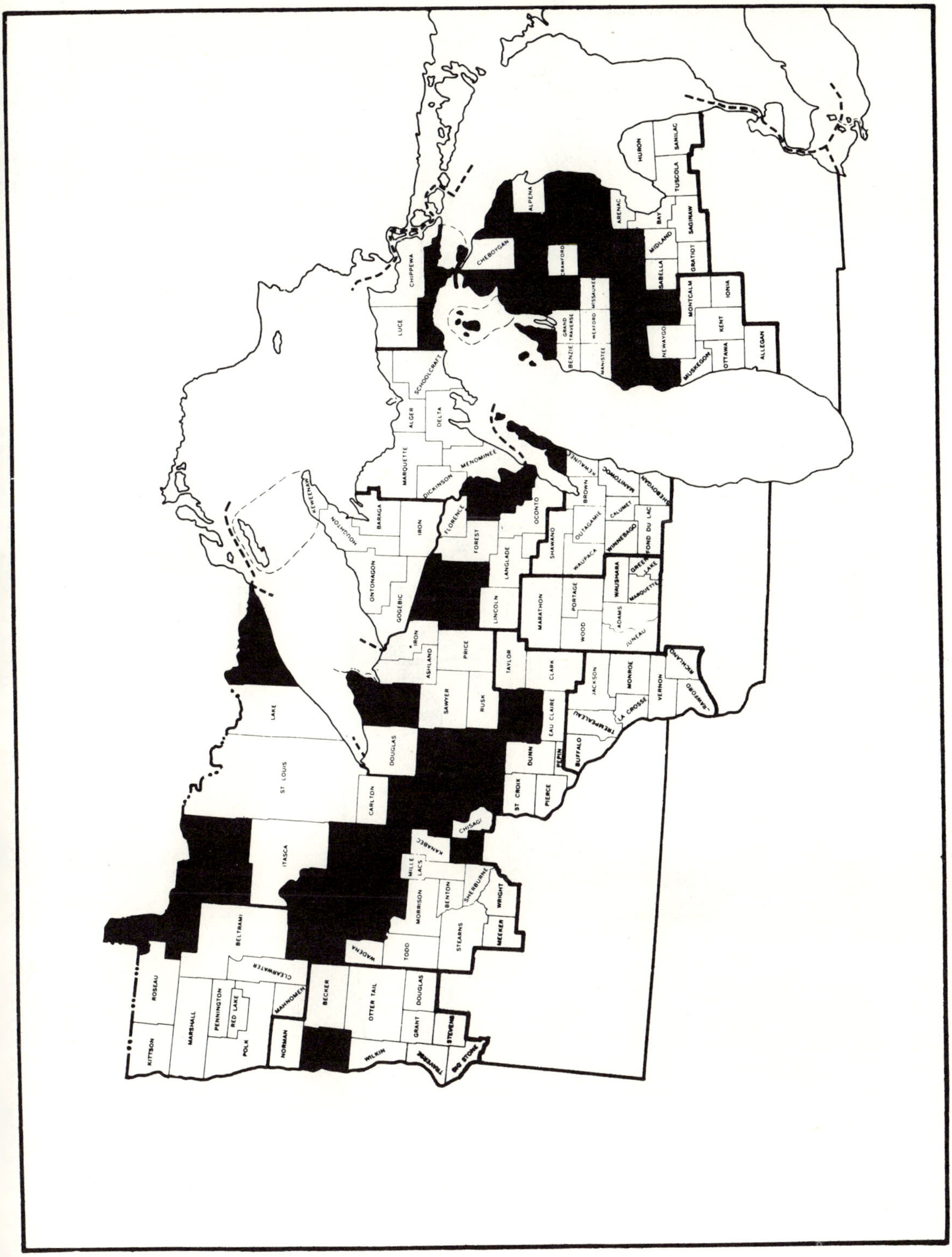

Figure 2-37. Counties with Above-Average Income Growth.

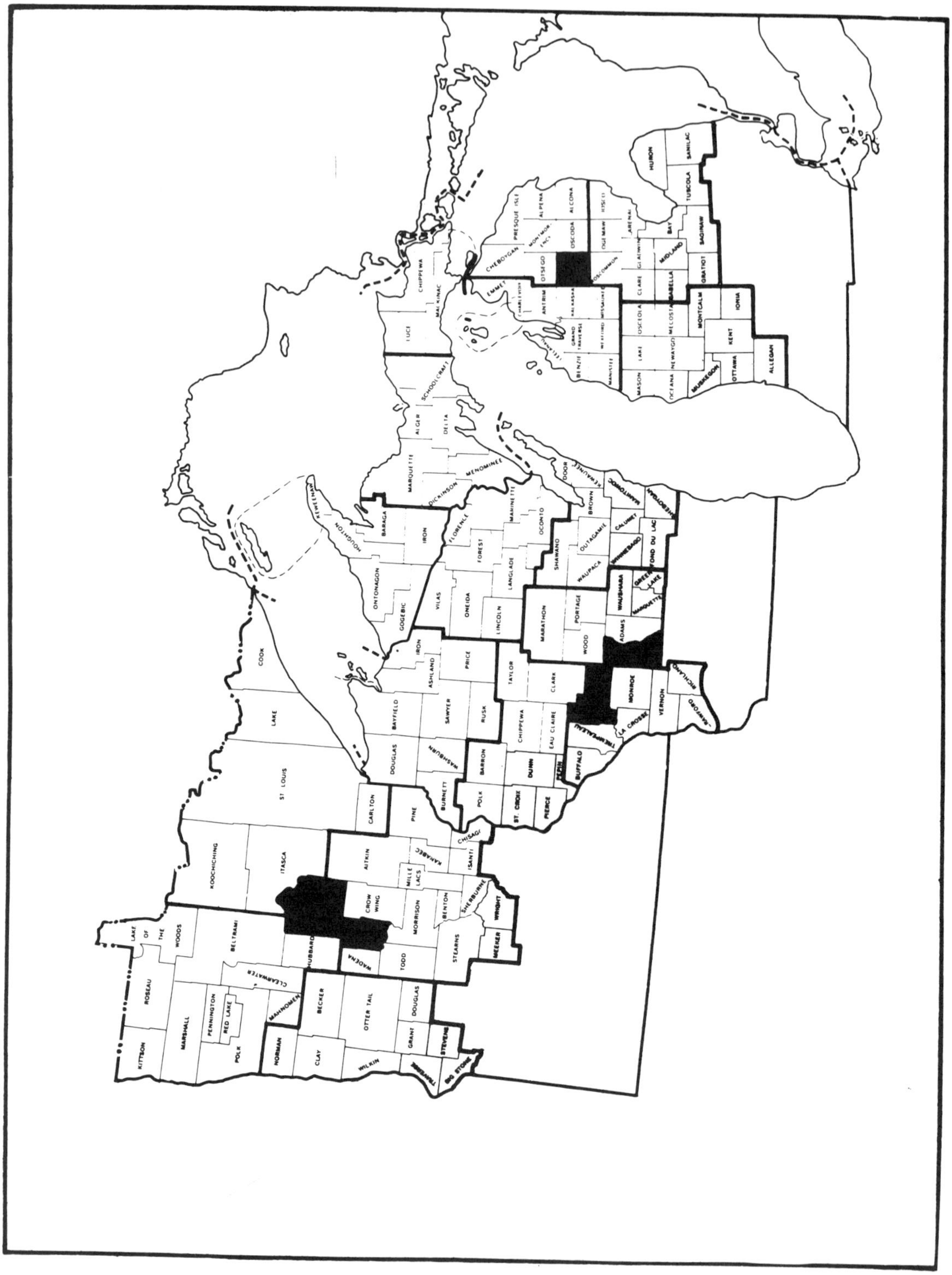

Figure 2–38. Counties with Positive Agricultural Change.

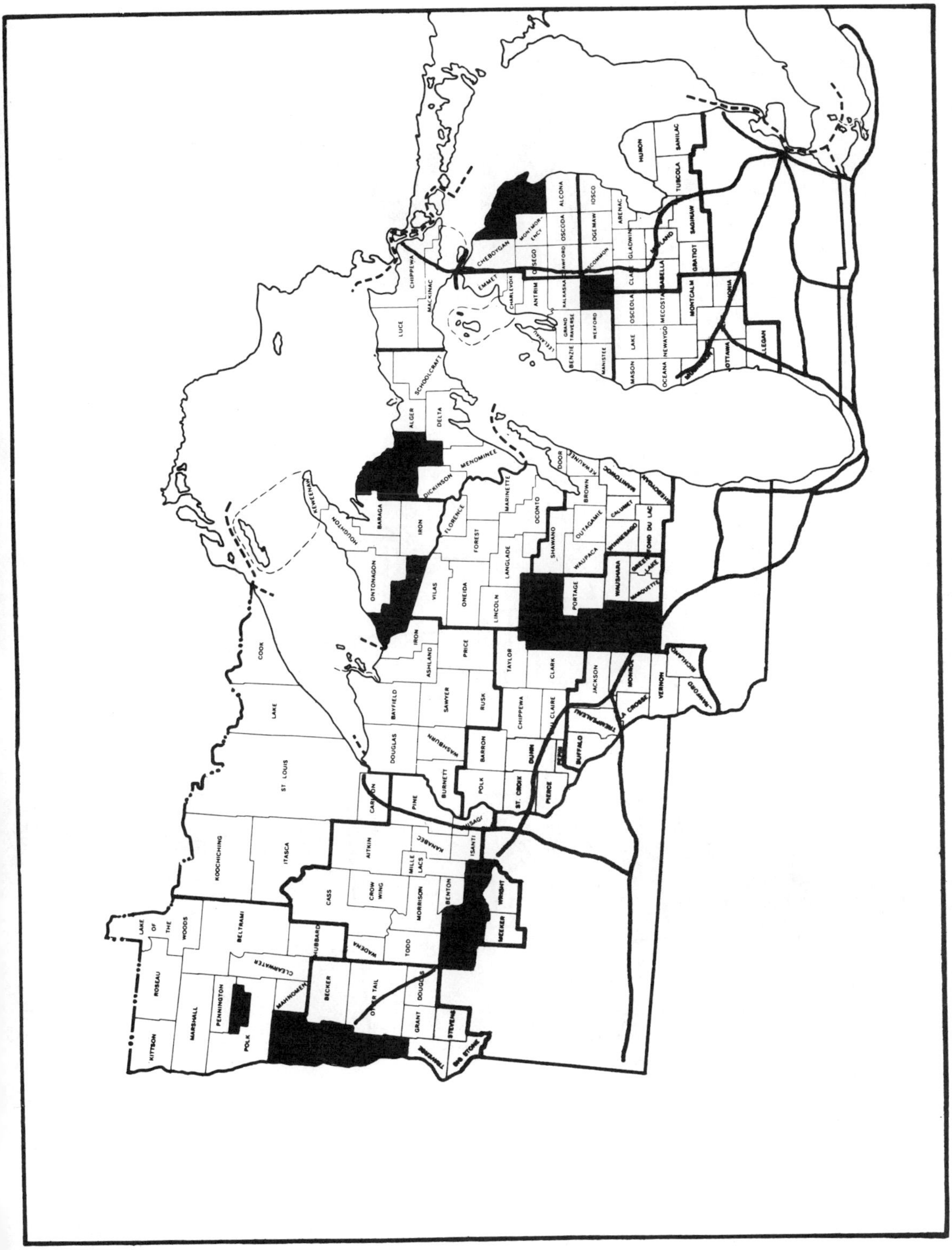

Figure 2–39. Counties with Expanding Service and Transport Functions, and Related Residential Growth.

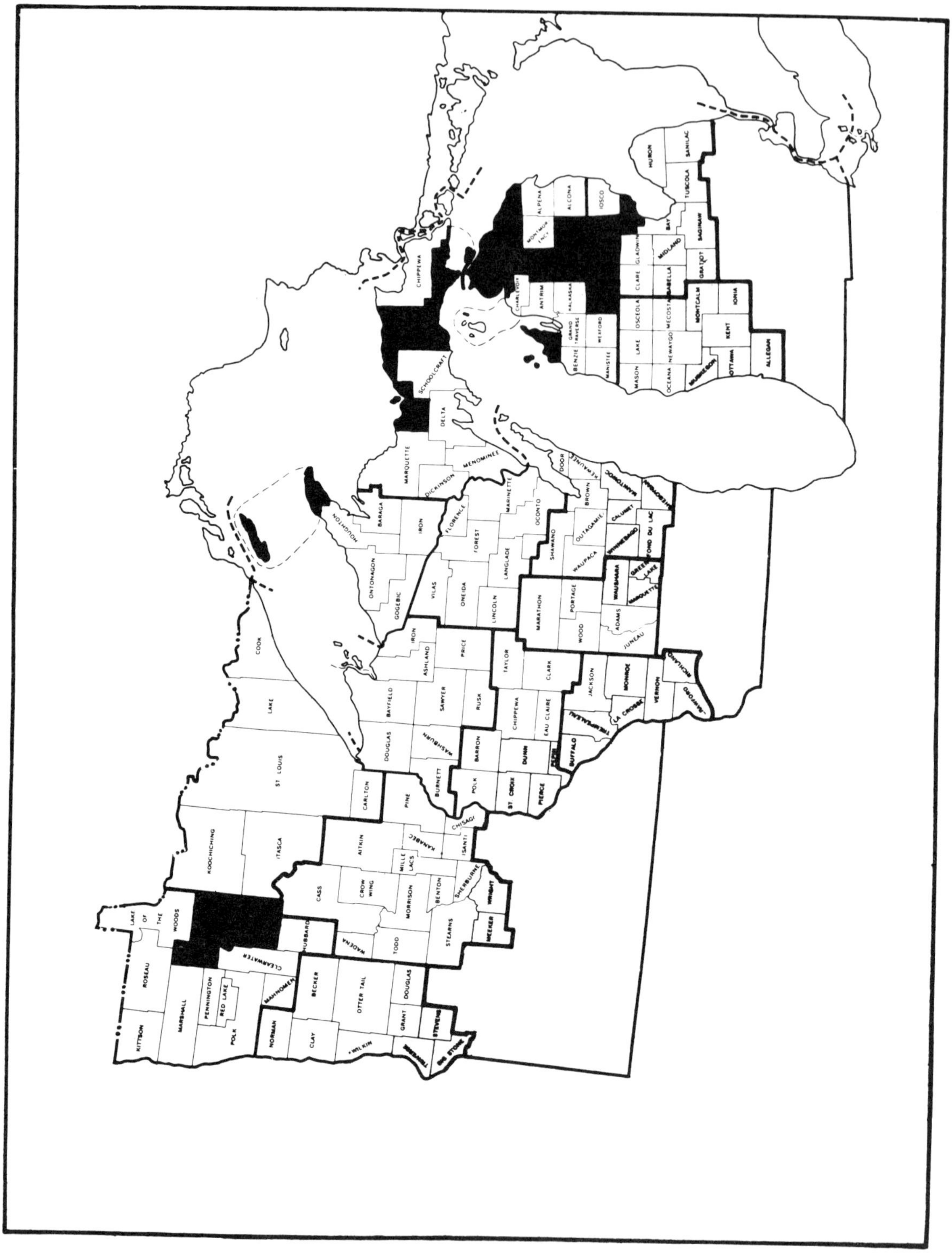

Figure 2–40. Counties with Greatest Manufacturing Employment Growth.

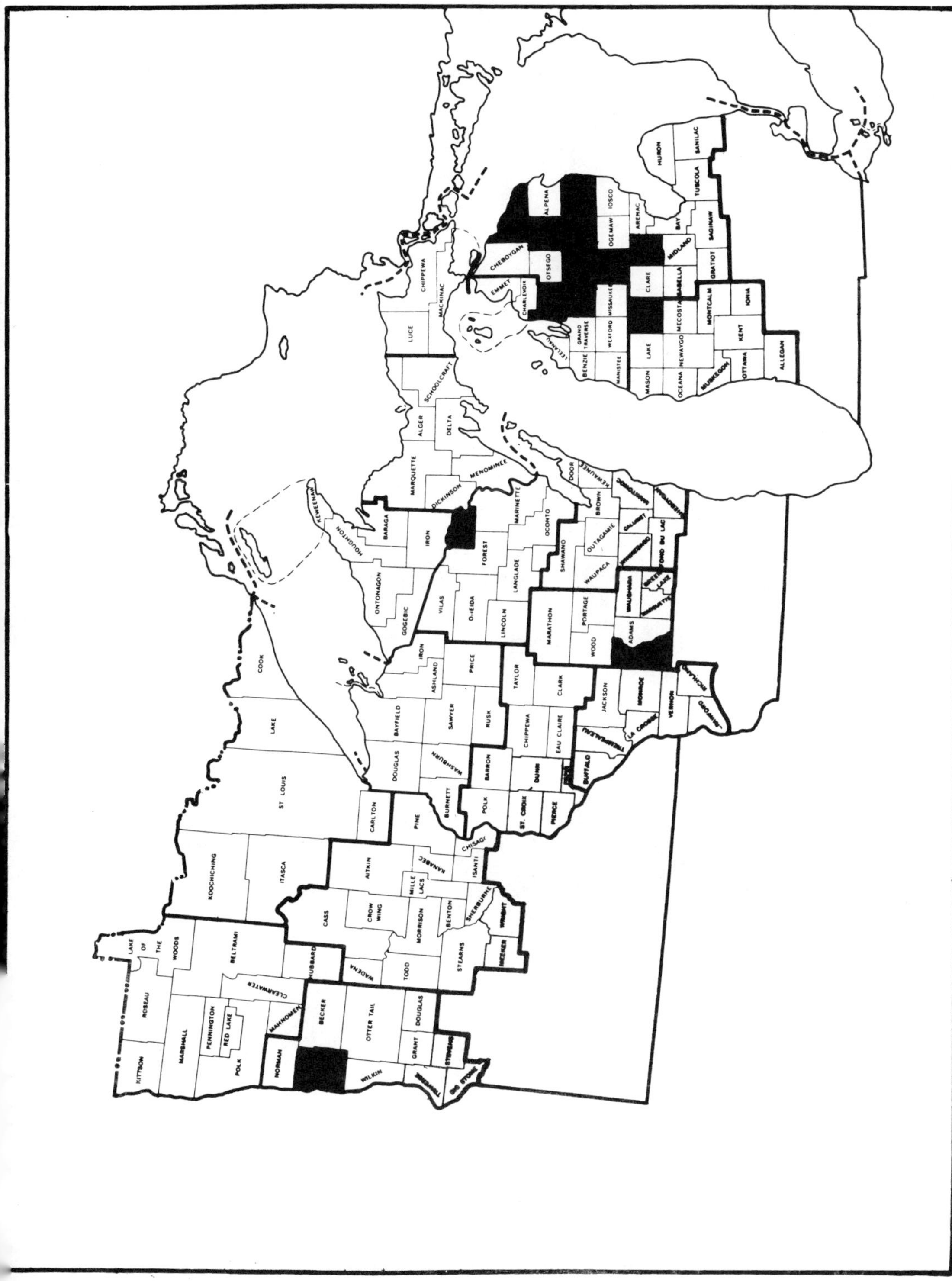

Figure 2–41. Counties with Growing Manufacturing Payrolls and Value Added.

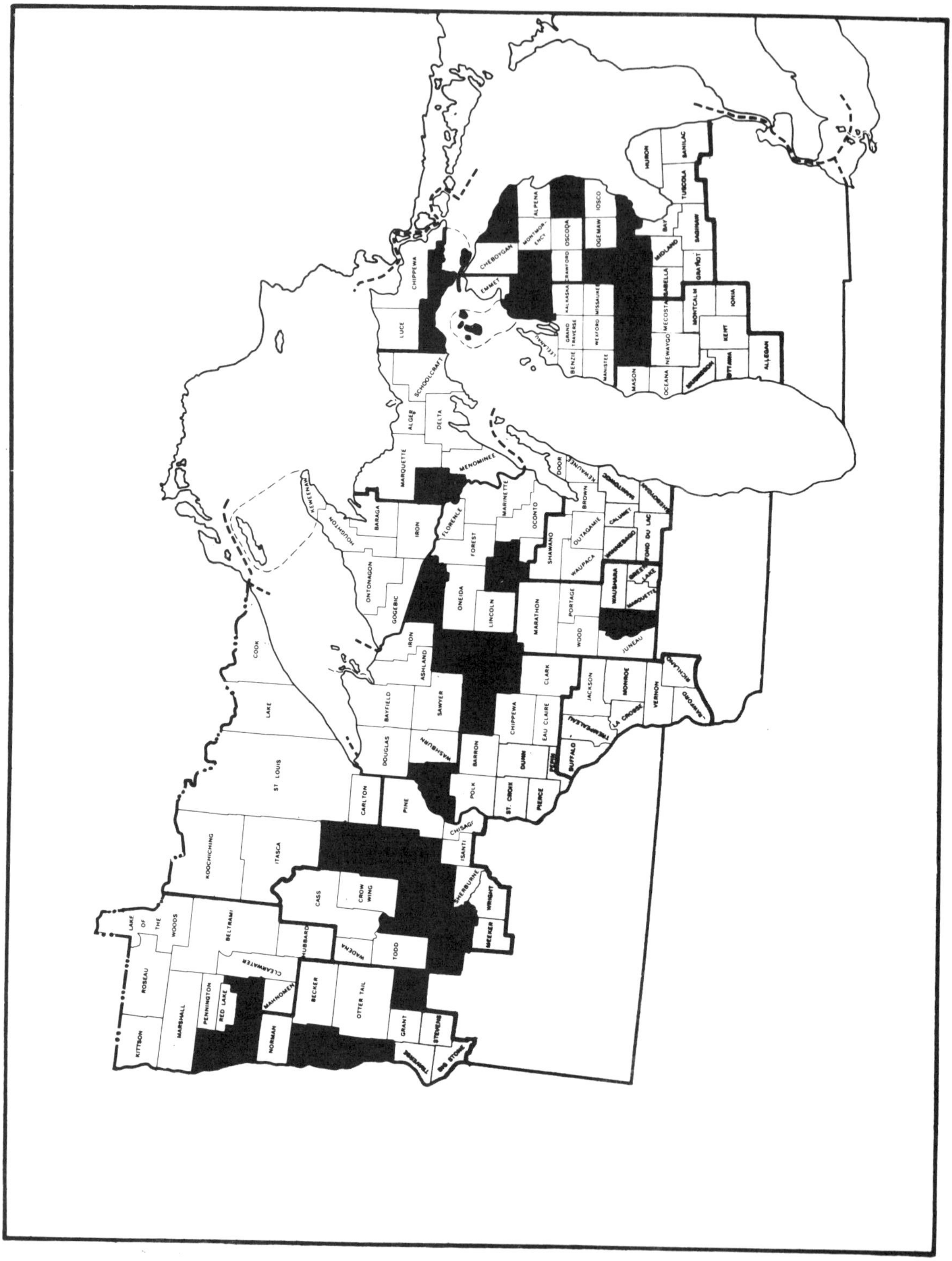

Figure 2-42. Counties with Greatest Changes in Manufacturing Establishments.

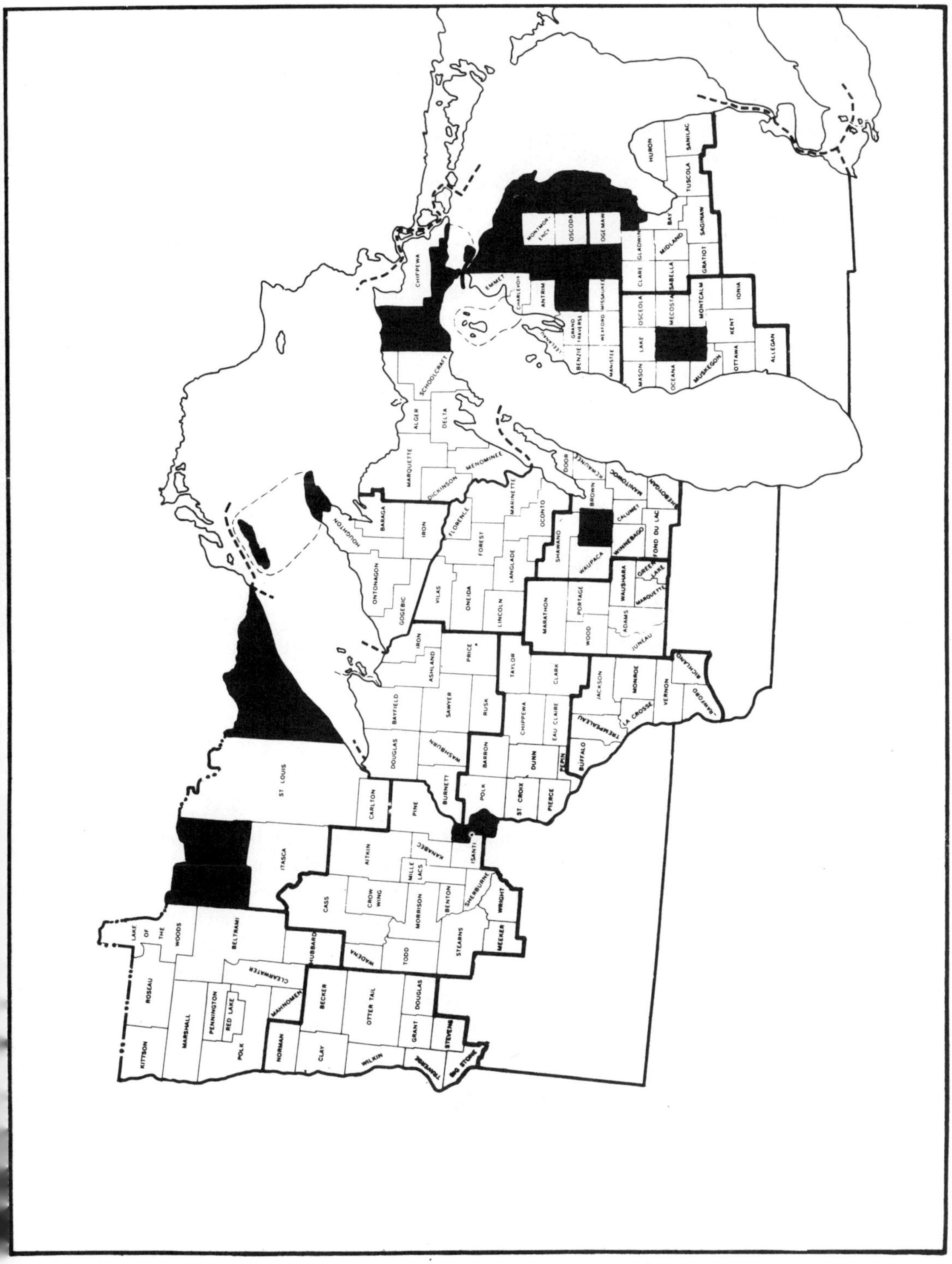

Figure 2–43. Counties with Greatest Changes in Wholesale Employment.

clothing industry was also revealed (for example, Munsingwear in Ashland), consistent with the filtering hypothesis.[a] Similar variations in the proportion of farm incomes derived from a declining agriculture further verified the urban-centered nature of life in the region (fig. 2–45).

A similar story was revealed by local Michigan reports, many of which were based upon industry mix-competitive shift analysis of existing industries. Rapid continued growth was seen in the Midland-Bay City-Saginaw region based upon a superior competitive position in the chemicals and miscellaneous manufacturing industries. Similarly, the Grand Rapids-Muskegon area was expected to continue to grow rapidly because of its favorable industry mix in electrical, machinery and miscellaneous manufacturing, and in related wholesaling, retailing and services. On the other hand, an unfavorable industry mix and competitive position for rapid growth was indicated in Alpena, as it is in Traverse City-Cadillac. Here, too, the great seasonal variation in the essentially summer recreation industry was noted. The Eastern Upper Peninsula likewise had both an unfavorable industry mix and competitive position for growth. On the other hand, the Western Upper Peninsula had an unfavorable industry mix, but an improved competitive position in the mining industry. Projected employment increases were only 25 percent in the Upper Peninsula, and increased southwards to 34 percent in the Grand Rapids and Bay City-Saginaw regions. Part of this projected growth was based on favorable locational conditions for expansion of apparel industries into the lower-wage northern areas, along with expansion of service industries—tourism, education, medical, etc.

In turn, the Upper Midwest Economic Study chose to focus on processes of population concentration in the largest urban places, and the emergence of great urban regions comprising one or more major cities and a "mortar" of surrounding non-farm townships. Borchert and Adams noted the obsolete trade center pattern that exists today. Only complete shopping centers or those of higher level appeared to have long-term prospects for growth, because of the dramatic technological changes in the retail and service industries, improvements in transportation, and the general thinning-out of rural populations. They pointed to the need for new institutions to coordinate provision of facilities in an obsolete governmental network incapable of handling the modern forms of urbanization.

Synthesis: Growth Regions and the Lagging Periphery

By setting the rich insights of the detailed local studies within the systematic framework of national analyses of regional economic structure and change, a picture of the Upper Great Lakes Region emerged with persuasive clarity. The synthesis that was derived is presented in figure 2–46 and it showed that the region consisted of a series of "layers." The southernmost tier comprised the overlapping areas of influence and labor markets of an axis of growing metropolitan and wholesale-retail level centers stretching from eastern Michigan to Minneapolis and St. Cloud in Minnesota, linked by the Interstate Highway System. The northern and western areas of this axis, to Duluth-Superior and Fargo-Moorhead, extended to centers and related regions that are substantially more sluggish, however. In the northern reaches were found peripheries that were weakly linked into the urban fields, but displaying incipient growth in the last decade. Finally, the northern tier of nine Development Districts was almost totally occupied by lagging areas outside the reach of growth impulses spreading from the southern axis.

[a]For comparison, average wage-rates in Detroit are $3.47 per hour, 25 percent more than the $2.79 of Duluth-Superior. Similarly, rates in N.E. Minnesota are 25 percent less than in the Twin Cities—see figure 2–44.

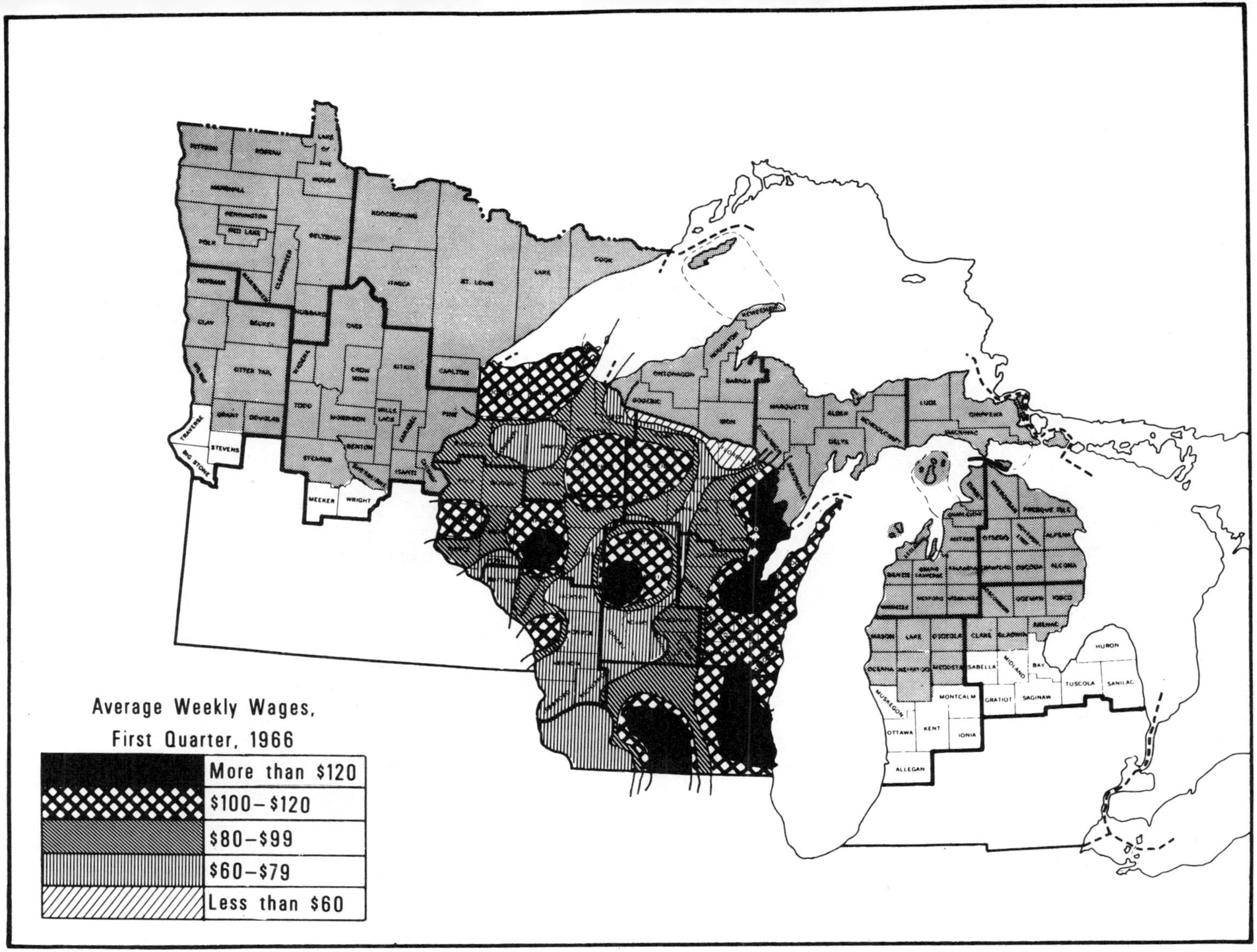

Figure 2–44. Spatial Variations of Wage Rates in Wisconsin.

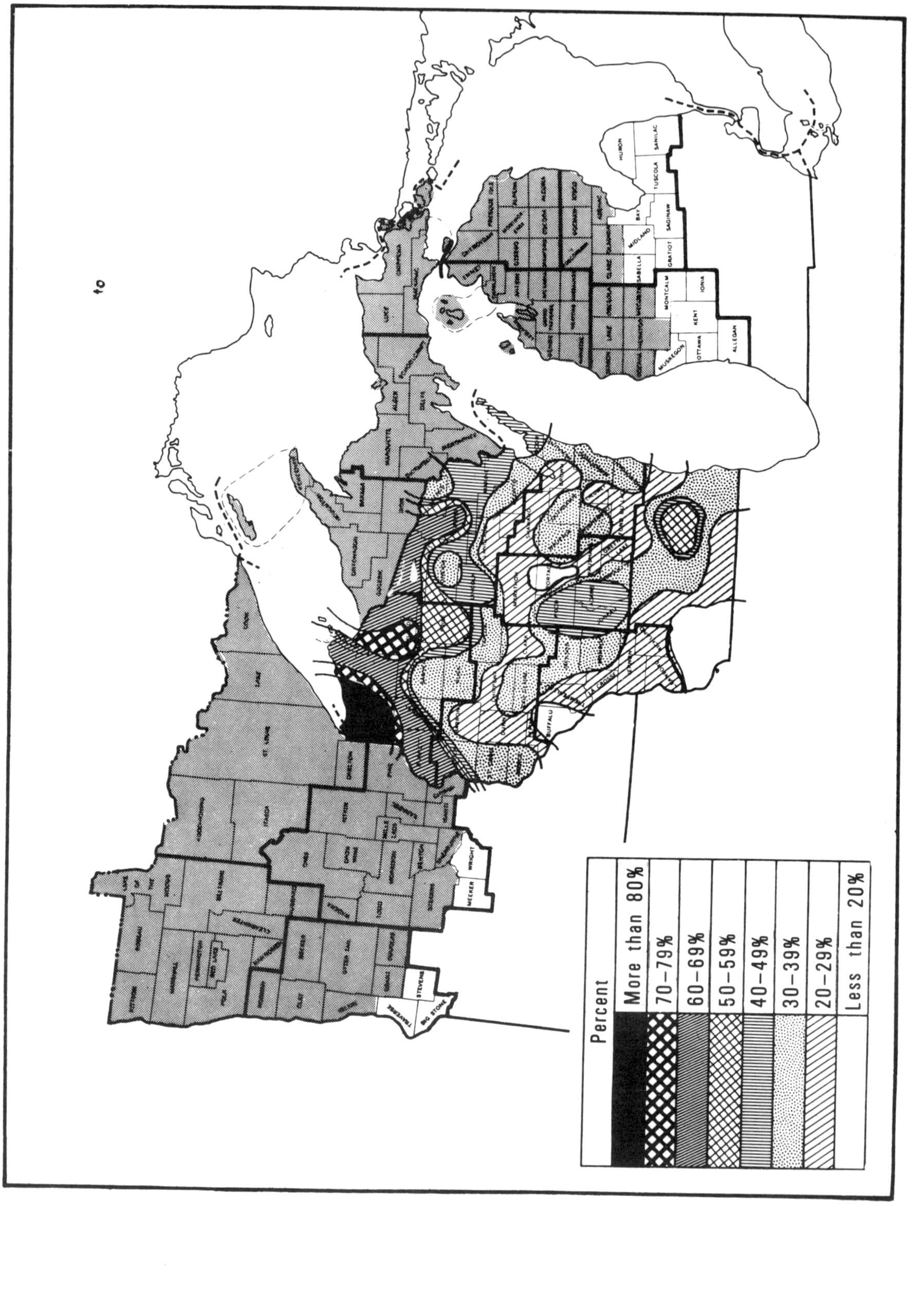

Figure 2-45. Ratio of Income of Farm Residents from Non-Agricultural Sources to Farm Products Sold.

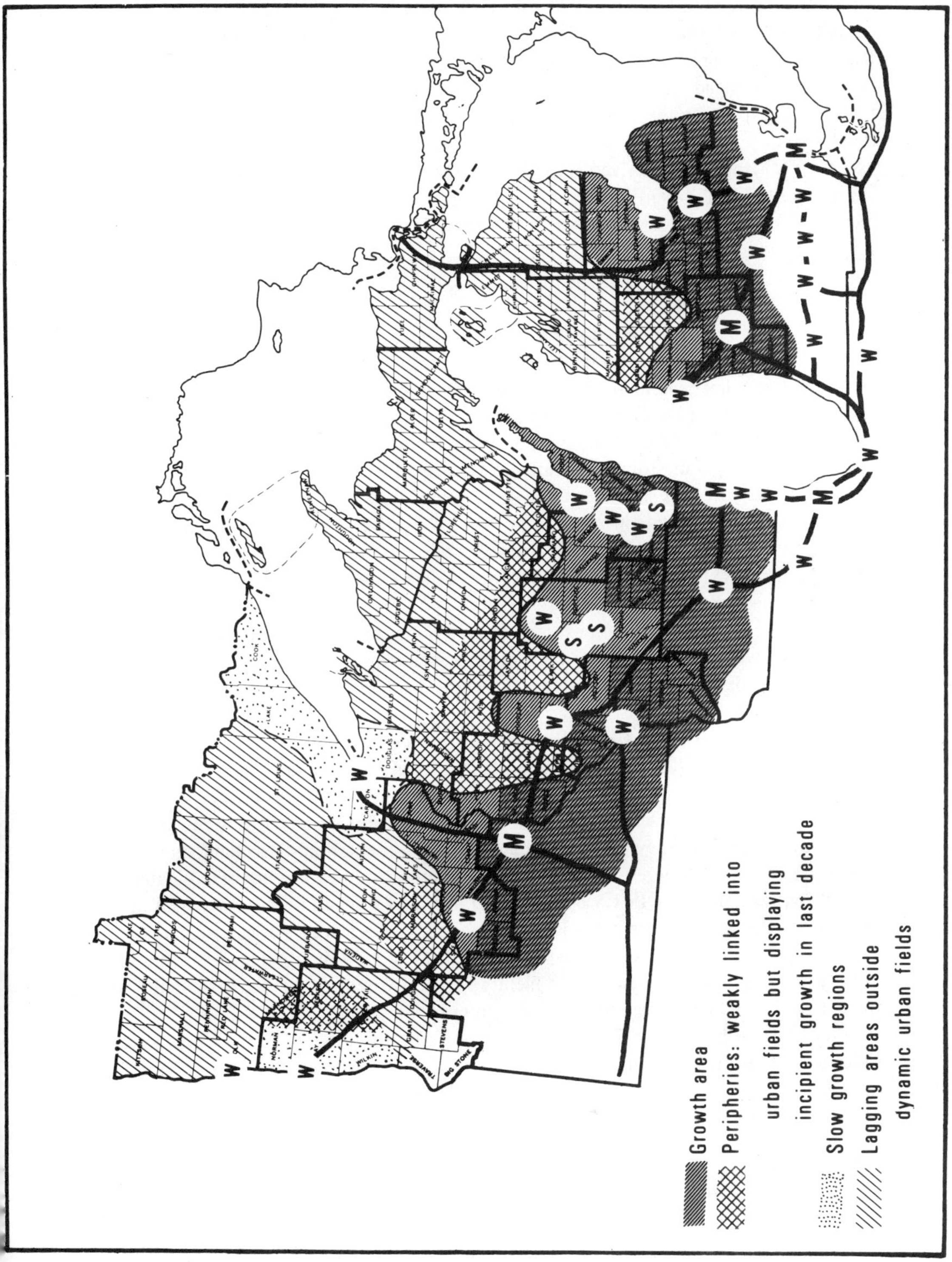

Figure 2–46. Synthesis of Regional Growth Characteristics.

There was much supplementary evidence related to this synthesis. Sources of the differential growth performance of the region's Standard Metropolitan Statistical Areas between 1929 and 1966 are provided in tables 2-4 and 2-5. Of particular interest is the relative dependence of the two slowest growth wholesale-retail level centers, Duluth-Superior and Fargo-Moorhead, on mining and agriculture-related sources of income, the weak manufacturing expansion in these cities 1959-1966, and the consequent lag in their wholesale-retail sectors.

Figure 2-47, derived from the report of the National Advisory Commission on Rural Poverty (1967), confirms the low economic status of rural residents of the lagging areas shown in figure 2-46. Only where the ratio of income derived from non-farm sources to that obtained by farming is high are rural levels of welfare above the nation's median. Compare figure 2-47 with figure 2-45.

The Proposed Growth and Service Centers

All the basic elements of a proposed system of growth and service centers for the Upper Great Lakes Region flowed from this regional systhesis:

1. A southern tier of Development Districts was identified that was already well-integrated into the manufacturing-related growth of the nation's industrial heartland by way of the region's principal metropolitan and wholesale-retail level centers. These cities were shown to be the region's *primary growth centers*, in that they had demonstrated continuing ability to attract private investment, to provide significant expansion of employment opportunities, and to generate income-levels at or above the national average. Figure 2-48 maps these centers, and they are listed in table 2-6.
2. Three other centers of wholesale-retail level, by their size and infrastructure, were also designated as primary growth centers: Duluth-Superior, Fargo-Moorhead, and Grand Forks. However, their recent growth performance indicated that they needed supplementary stimuli if they were to be able to generate significant spillover effects into their labor markets.

Insofar as the first group of centers is concerned, their continued growth and viability was thought to be a direct function of national growth and change. Their continuing growth, was thought to be likely to foster the incipient improvements now evident along the northern edges of their labor markets. One goal of regional policy for the region was thus stated to be to see that they remain linked closely into the nation's heartland, and that these links be strengthened wherever possible. Thus, proposals to provide expressway extensions from Milwaukee along the Fox Valley to Green Bay and from Juneau County to Wausau (and probably to Rhinelander, see below) were recommended as subjects of careful analysis.

The evidence also pointed to the focusing of growth impulses in the Juneau County area, and public investment in facilitative infrastructure was recommended to fashion these growth potentials into a new growth center in that area.

Duluth-Superior, Fargo-Moorhead and to a lesser extent Grand Forks were seen to have many of the essentials of primary growth centers, but they had lagged because of their reliance upon slow-growth sectors of the economy. For them, the problem was seen to be one of finding new externally-related sources of growth. They had many of the factors favoring new industry: Infrastructure, space, water, and the like. Their problem was seen to be one of trading off their abundant supplies of semi-skilled low-cost labor for their relative inaccessibility and the climatic unattractiveness of northern locations. Growth, for them, was seen ultimately to stem from the derived demand for their labor supply; public programs designed to increase their rate of industrial growth were called for.

Table 2-4. Incomes of Standard Metropolitan Statistical Areas, 1929-1966

		U.S.	Bay City	Detroit	Grand Rapids	Mus-kegon	Green Bay	Madison	Mil-waukee	Duluth-Superior	Minne-apolis-St. Paul	Fargo-Moorhead
Personal Income (millions)	1929	80,803	39	2,230	237	59	47	91	849	161	823	43
	1966	580,483	286	15,013	1,610	481	386	808	4,825	715	5,971	309
Ave. Ann. Growth Rate	1929-1940	-0.9	-0.2	-0.4	-1.8	-0.7	0.1	0.1	-1.8	-1.5	-0.8	0.2
	1940-1950	11.2	12.3	11.0	12.6	13.9	11.7	11.7	11.1	10.3	11.1	13.2
	1950-1959	6.0	5.3	5.0	5.7	5.3	6.5	7.2	6.2	4.2	6.7	4.4
	1959-1966	8.5	5.7	6.8	6.4	6.1	6.1	6.8	5.1	4.5	6.4	4.9
Dollars per Capita	1929	705	570	1,027	812	702	665	804	1,013	640	930	597
	1966	2,963	2,890	3,695	3,185	3,023	2,720	3,044	3,591	2,665	3,621	2,797
Percentage of Nat. Ave.	1929	100	81	146	115	100	94	114	144	91	132	85
	1966	100	98	125	107	102	92	103	121	90	122	94

Table 2-5. Source, Type, and Growth Rate of Standard Metropolitan Statistical Area Incomes, 1959-1966

		U.S.	*Bay City*	*Detroit*	*Grand Rapids*	*Mus-kegon*	*Green Bay*	*Madison*	*Mil-waukee*	*Duluth-Superior*	*Minne-apolis-St. Paul*	*Fargo-Moorhead*
Type of Payment (millions)	Wages and salaries	391,066	180	11,007	1,123	335	260	558	3,419	493	4,363	180
	Other labor income	20,792	11.4	693	71	34.2	15.4	27.8	213	23.1	237	7.5
	Proprietor's income	59,277	34.9	1,023	146	36.1	41.7	82.8	342	49.1	398	52.6
	Property income	83,258	46.7	1,885	215	68.1	54.3	119.5	724	101.8	800	56.4
	Transfer payments	43,917	20.5	838	99	30.1	25.9	49.8	280	70.5	372	22.2
Earnings by Source (millions)	Farm	18,812	11.6	13.0	26	4.4	13.6	31.6	25.4	0.6	21.2	29.1
	Government	75,679	19.8	1,247	102	30.0	21.4	175.6	325	98.6	577	38.6
	Federal civilian	20,107	2.8	217	16	3.2	2.8	17.1	58	12.9	132	7.6
	Military	12,763	0.9	52	3.8	1.3	1.2	12.7	19.1	13.1	28.3	1.8
	State & Local	42,809	16.1	978	82	25.5	17.4	145.8	248.4	71.6	416	29.2
	Private nonfarm	376,644	194.9	11,464	1,212	361.6	282.6	455.6	3,623	466	4,396	172.4
	Manufacturing	141,483	95.7	5,971	598	232.8	115.8	121.0	1,770	82.2	1,515	16.1
	Mining	5,097	0.4	8.4	1.4	1.0	0.1	1.3	6.1	78.8	6.0	0.3
	Construction	26,668	14.5	720	92	17.4	22.3	60.4	275	47.6	347	18.5
	Transportation, etc.	33,068	14.1	701	83	20.2	31.1	35.8	252	62.1	446	23.5
	Wholesale, retail	78,966	39.7	1,954	229	47.0	63.2	131.3	647	98.8	1,028	59.9
	Finance, etc.	29,305	4.5	502	45	8.0	9.1	37.6	197	17.7	318	15.6
	Services	64,622	25.6	1,592	160	24.9	40.0	85.3	472	78.3	727	38.2
Average Annual Growth Rates, 1959–66	Government	7.9	8.2	8.2	8.3	8.2	5.9	6.9	5.6	6.8	7.6	8.0
	Federal civilian	6.9	8.1	7.3	7.1	6.9	4.7	2.6	3.7	3.4	7.1	6.5
	Military	5.7	1.4	1.2	2.0	1.1	2.2	-3.6	0.5	3.4	4.0	4.9
	State & Local	9.2	8.7	9.0	9.0	8.8	6.4	9.0	6.5	8.4	8.1	8.7
	Farm	4.2	14.5	3.4	6.3	5.6	7.9	2.3	4.5	-18.1	1.2	9.6
	Manufacturing	5.9	4.6	7.2	6.5	5.8	7.0	7.2	4.6	2.9	7.6	0.9
	Wholesale & Retail	5.0	4.6	5.4	6.9	4.2	5.2	7.1	4.5	1.5	5.8	3.8
	Services	7.1	7.2	7.3	6.4	6.7	8.0	7.5	6.5	6.5	8.9	7.3

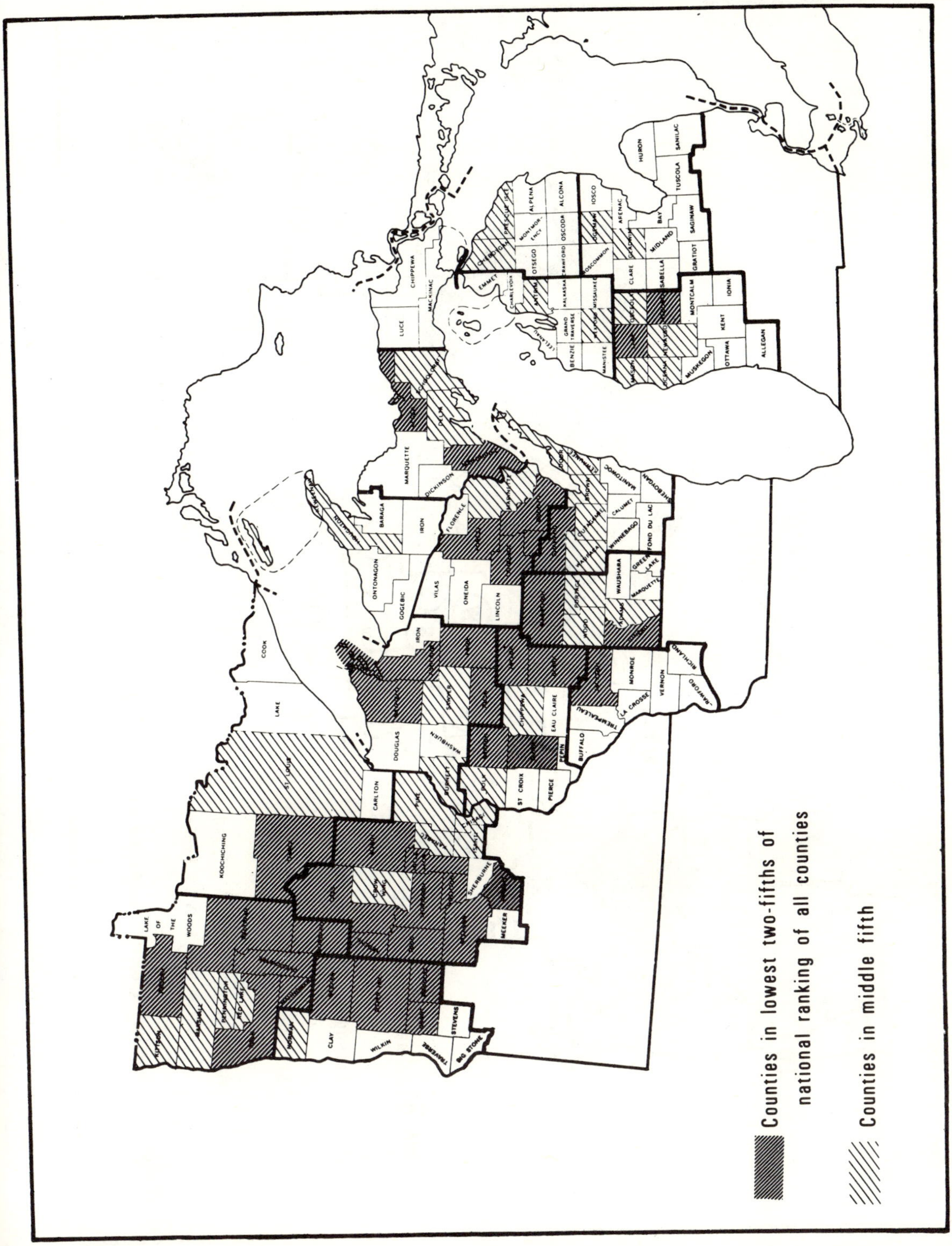

Figure 2–47. Economic Status of the Rural Population in 1960.

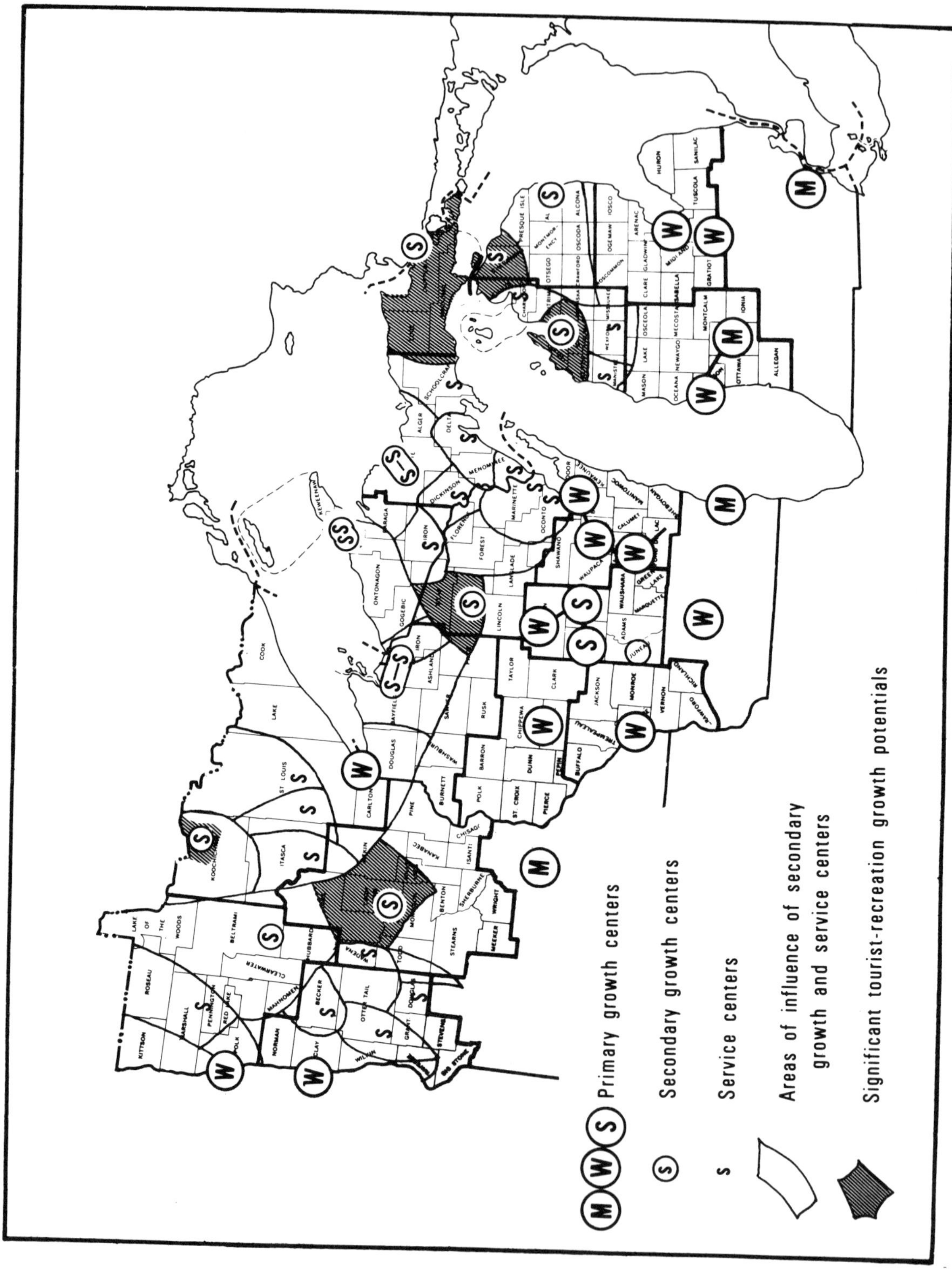

Figure 2–48. The Proposed Growth Centers and their Areas of Influence.

Table 2-6. Proposed Growth and Service Centers

Primary Growth Centers	
Metropolitan Centers:	Detroit Grand Rapids-Muskegon Minneapolis-St. Paul Milwaukee
Wholesale-retail Centers:	Bay City-Saginaw Fox Valley (Green Bay, Appleton Oshkosh, Fond du Lac) Wausau to Juneau County La Crosse Eau Claire-Chippewa Falls St. Cloud
Primary Growth Centers Requiring Supplementary Stimuli	
Wholesale-retail Centers:	Duluth-Superior Fargo-Moorhead
Secondary Growth Centers: Possible Development District Centers with Supplementary Growth Potentials	
Complete Shopping Centers:	Alpena Traverse City** Sault Ste. Marie* Marquette-Ishpeming Hancock-Houghton-Calumet* Rhinelander Ashland-Ironwood* Brainerd** Bemidji (supplements Grand Forks) International Falls*
Service Centers	
Complete Shopping Centers:	Cadillac Manistee Cheboygan Petoska Manistique Escanaba Menominee Marinette Oconto Iron Mt. Iron River Virginia Hibbing Grand Rapids Wadena Alexandria Fergus Falls Detroit Lakes Thief River Falls

*Tourist-recreation development potentials
**Year-round tourist-recreation development potentials

A dilemma in such a recommendation was noted, however. The kinds of industry likely to be attracted are those seeking a low-wage, semi-skilled labor force. But these industries support a level of living below that of the nation. The initial attraction might be that of assurance of adequate infrastructure; or a combination of industry grants, loans and loan guarantees; from liberalized investment tax credits, accelerated depreciation schedules, better carry forward and carry backward provisions, etc. But most of these were seen to be to no avail for an industry seeking low wages, if the wage-differential is not maintained. Since it is in the best interests of the region to maintain wage-rates as high as possible, it is therefore thought to be appropriate to consider using the public treasury for wage subsidies in the form of deductions on wages and salaries for those firms willing to locate in a designated primary growth center, thereby contributing to the general welfare.

Even if new growth were brought to the three lagging wholesale-retail centers, it was shown that most of the northern tier of the Upper Great Lakes region would remain untouched by growth impulses, except in so far as people migrate to the primary growth centers or outside the region, however. Therefore:

3. A network of 30 complete shopping centers was proposed for development to reach—or adequate services to be provided—to the population of the upper tier of lagging areas. See figure 2-48 and table 2-6.

Many of these centers did not have significant growth potential, but they did perform an essential "layer" of functions for a permanent population as part of the region's urban hierarchy. It is from them that permanent residents should be able to obtain requisite educational, health and related services, and in them it should be possible to prepare elements of the local population for successful migration to the other higher order growth areas within the region or beyond it.

It was at this point that the designation of Development Districts, combined with existing differentials in economic power among these thirty centers, was seen to converge with the "filtering" concept of growth center strategy and possibilities for inducing regional growth by exploiting new resources. Activities in the public sector were seen to have the potentiality for creating a *new level* in the urban hierarchy, because:

4. Ten complete shopping centers showed potentialities for becoming secondary growth poles, at the centers of Development Districts.

Further, it was argued that:

5. The balance of the complete shopping centers in the region should be designated as service centers, subsidiary to and linked with the specialized facilities of their Development District Centers, because of the spatial coverage needed for adequate service provision that they provide.

The larger population base, availability of semi-skilled labor, adequate transportation, vocational training and educational facilities, existing industrial base, public services and, more generally, aggregate "economic power" (table 2-4) in cities such as Ashland, Marquette, and Alpena suggested that some of the region's complete shopping centers have the potentialities for new industrial expansion, under essentially the same terms as primary growth centers like Duluth-Superior.

To this, it was felt, could be added opportunities for opening up new all-year-round tourist-recreation activities in the Traverse City, Rhinelander and Brainerd areas. The ingredients in these three cases were the provision of adequate local infrastructure and facilities for tourism, together with superior access, so that each could become drawn tightly into the weekend-vacationing range of the great metropolitan complexes of Detroit-Grand Rapids, Chicago-Milwaukee, and Minneapolis-St. Paul to the south. Thus, further expressway extensions were indicated. Only in this way, was it felt, could the latent potentialities of the resources be converted into externally-derived growth impulses of substantial size. As in Appalachia, then, the growth center proposals were inextricably bound up with an access policy.

Industrialization and tourist-resource related development, it was felt, would only be realized in a new hierarchical level of Development District Centers by effective district-wide leadership. Hence the third critical ingredient was seen to be the focusing of the institutional development implicit in definition of Development Districts in the secondary growth centers. Within the Development Districts, the remaining complete shopping centers then assumed a dominantly service role.

The philosophy involved in the above proposals was thus one of facilitating downward-filtering of industrial development by creating a new stratum of growth centers, exercising leadership within the Development Districts. The public sector is involved, by (1) ensuring that public facilities are adequate; (2) providing incentives and subsidies to industries to move; and (3) stimulating local leadership. Wherever possible, too, downward-filtering was combined conceptually with increased *integration* into the expanding urban fields of the primary growth centers to the south, by improving accessibility and by opening up new resources consistent with the rising real incomes of the residents of these areas and the widening of the space of urban living to include regular use of year-round recreation facilities. Finally, it was recognized that the continuing peripheral position and unfavorable climate of much of the region would, in the foreseeable future, continue to depress the rate of growth. But the residents can still expect a high and rising per capita income by facing up to the need for continuing outmigration. Where development cannot be brought to the people, some people can be prepared to move to development elsewhere by providing good schools, vocational training, and health care in a network of viable service centers that simultaneously ensure that those residents who remain will continue to enjoy a high-quality life.

Chapter Three

The Nation's Growth Centers in the 1960s

Both affirmative guidelines for public intervention and a basic framework for nationwide analysis of growth centers were provided by the Appalachian experience and by the Upper Great Lakes investigations. It is to the realization of the opportunities created by this framework that we turn in this chapter.

THE U.S. URBAN HIERARCHY

The first step was to define the U.S. urban hierarchy on a consistent nationwide basis. Following the example set in the Upper Great Lakes investigations, the sequence of procedures was this: All urban places in the United States with populations exceeding 10,000 in both 1960 and 1970 were subjected to a 97-variable multiple factor analysis, the first factor of which indexed the relative "economic power" or "hierarchical status" of each center. This analysis is described in the *City Classification Handbook* (Berry, 1972).

On the basis of these index values and, for smaller places, population size, all of the nation's urban areas with populations exceeding 1,500 in 1960, were stratified into a hierarchy with the following levels:

metropolis
major wholesale-retail center
complete shopping goods center
partial shopping goods center
complete convenience goods center

The hierarchical breaks were determined on the basis of the consistency checks made earlier in the Upper Great Lakes Region, reported in Chapter 2, and earlier studies of regional hierarchies elsewhere in the United States (Berry, 1967a). Other studies of urban hierarchies completed elsewhere in the nation during the decade of the 1960s also were examined for consistency of the results. Figures 3-1 and 3-2 show the 75 centers of metropolitan status in this hierarchy, together with the extent and configuration of their daily urban systems, as indicated by their daily commuting areas in 1960. Note that these metropolitan-status centers are not metropolitan areas in the sense of the census's Standard Metropolitan Statistical Areas, although they all appear within the current SMSA list. Many SMSAs have a lesser hierarchical status in our scheme.

For purposes of presentation and ease of use at a regional level, the hierarchy materials were organized separately for each of the 171 OBE Economic Areas (Daily Urban

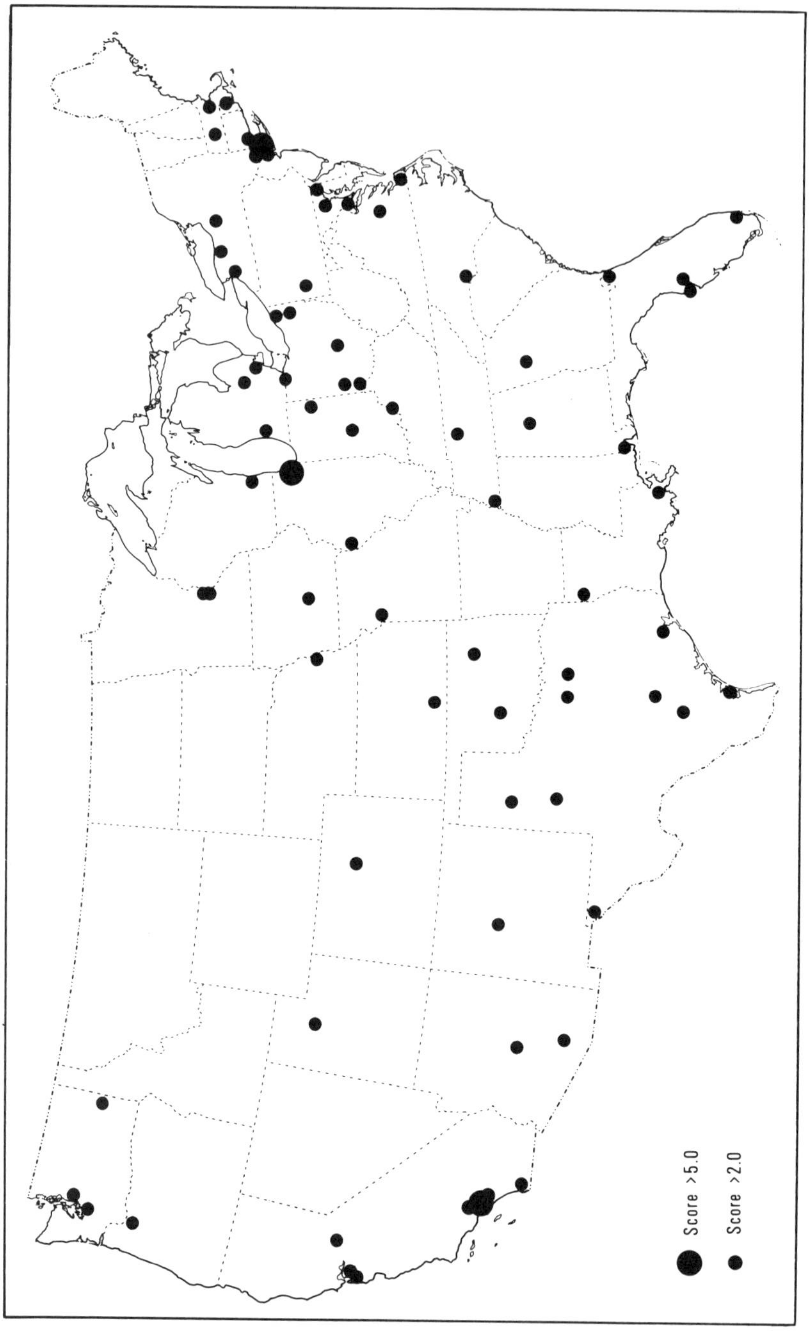

Figure 3–1. Centers of Metropolitan Status in the U.S. Urban Hierarchy.

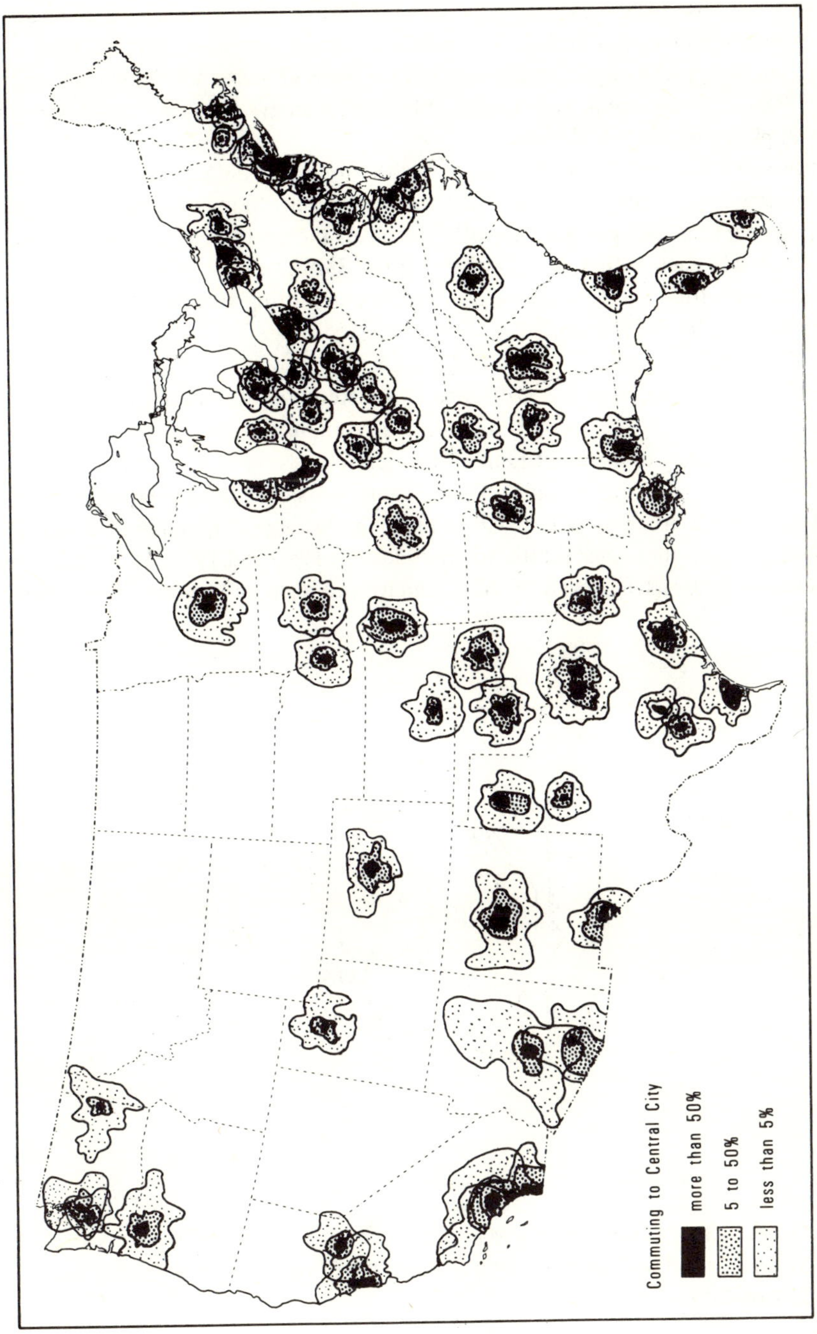

Figure 3-2. The Metropolitan-Status Daily Urban Systems of the U.S. in 1960, as indexed by the Commuting Fields of Central Cities in that Year.

Systems) in the conterminous United States that were discussed and analyzed in Chapter 1. Within each OBE area, several other geographical distinctions were made:

1. If the OBE area had within it an SMSA, as defined by the Office of Management and Budget in 1972, that SMSA was treated as a single "urban place," because SMSAs are treated as functional entities in all U.S. regional policy. In the tables, data are thus presented for the central city of the SMSA and for the SMSA as a whole, with no additional internal differentiation, even though our original analysis did distinguish separate legal urban places within the SMSAs.
2. If the OBE had a dominant economic focus not defined as an SMSA, the county containing the city in question was treated as a functional unit, to maintain some consistency with (1). No detail is thus provided for other than for the central city and its county.
3. Centers located in each OBE area outside its central SMSA or county were separated into those lying within and those lying outside the commuting area of the central city giving its name to the OBE area.

Thus, figure 3-3 shows the Memphis OBE area and differentiates between the part lying within and the part lying beyond the Memphis commuting area. Figure 3-4 shows the location of the centers of different rank in the hierarchy. Note that the hierarchical detail is not provided within the Memphis SMSA. Table 3-1 shows the presentation format of the basic data on the urban hierarchy within the Memphis region. Population data for the urban places, within their legal limits, are provided for 1960 and 1970, as is percentage population change 1960-1970. Levels of the hierarchy and regional location of the centers are specified.[a]

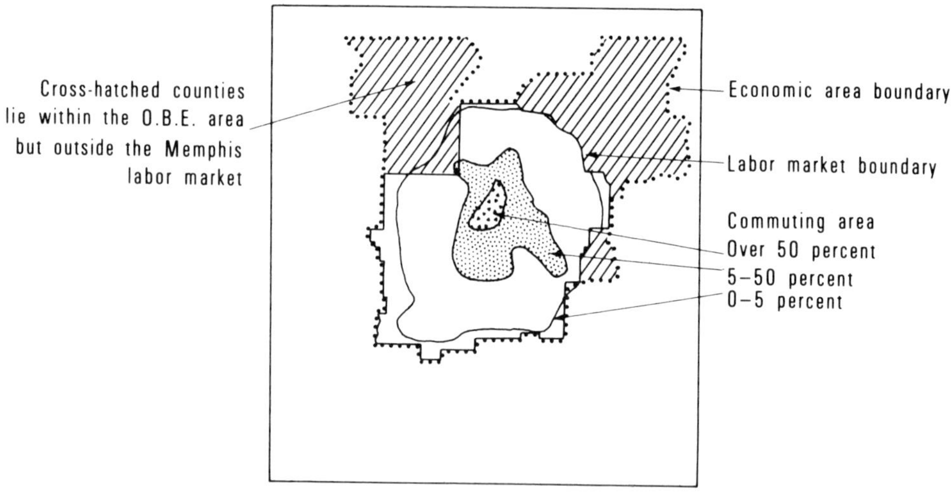

Figure 3-3. A Distinction is Made Within Each OBE Area Between Counties Lying *Within* the Counties Lying *Beyond* the Commuting Area of the Central City.

[a]Volume II contains the complete set of 171 hierarchy tables for every OBE region in the conterminous United States. These tables are identical in format to table 3-1.

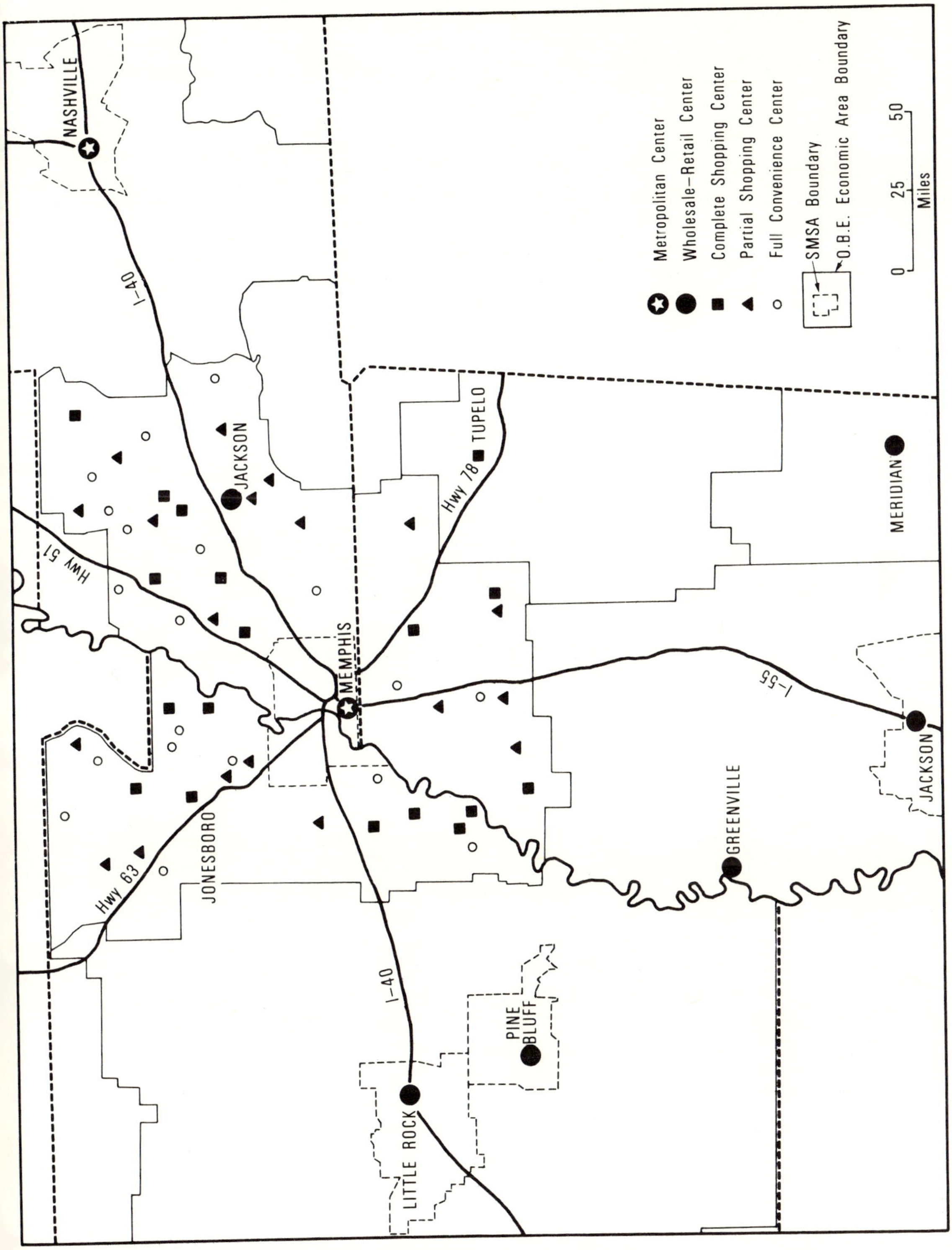

Figure 3–4. The Urban Hierarchy in the Memphis Region. The Highways that are noted are used as Traverses for Plotting Socio-Economic Gradients.

GRADIENTS OF URBAN INFLUENCE AND CHANGE

How do surrounding areas relate to the centers occupying different echelons of the urban hierarchy? Do varying degrees of spatial interdependency have measurable results in terms of the characteristics of the outlying areas and the types and intensities of change unfolding within them? These were the questions that were answered in the second step of the investigation.

Some indication of the path taken in this second step will already be sensed from the discussion in Chapter 2 of gradients of welfare in the Upper Great Lakes Region. Corollary evidence was produced during the 1960s by the U.S. Department of Agriculture, whose research workers found that if the nation's counties were classified from "metropolitan" to "sparsely-settled rural" on the basis of degree of urbanization and population densities, as in figure 3–5, then per capita incomes declined and the poverty population and the proportion of the aged increased along this gradient. See figures 3–6–3–8 (Bluestone, 1970).

Return for a moment to figure 3–4. Certain highways are emphasized as "traverses" along which various "distance-gradients" (i.e., changing values of selected variables along the routes) can be plotted. A distance-gradient can be likened to a time-series graph in which, for example, the Dow-Jones average is plotted from day to day. However, instead of the series being plotted with respect to variations in time, gradients record the variations in selected indices with respect to space. In figure 3–4, the traverses follow major highway routes. Consider the route extending northwards from Jackson, Mississippi to Memphis along 155, and thence towards Paducah, Tennessee along Highway 51. Figure 3–9 shows the way in which the newspaper market penetration and daily commuting drop off with increasing distance from the city centers along this route, thus indexing variations in the interdependency of outlying areas with these cities. Figure 3–10 shows how the rates of population change of blacks and whites, and their migration rates, changed along the same traverse between 1960 and 1970. The rhythms reported in Chapter 2 are to be seen once again. Midway between Memphis and Jackson, a smaller urban center is seen to be partially successful in offsetting the decline that otherwise characterizes the peripheral areas. Figures 3–11 and 3–12, and 3–13 and 3–14 show, respectively, similar gradients between Little Rock and Nashville and between Jonesboro and Tupelo.

In every case the "topography" of migration patterns and population changes among both blacks and whites rises and falls in rhythm with the gradients of urban influence of the larger metropolises and the lower-order wholesale-retail centers. The complete map showing the "topography" of commuting fields was presented in Chapter 1, and the specific commuting areas of the metropolitan-status centers in figure 3–2. Figure 3–15 provides the companion map of newspaper market penetration by the 75 centers of metropolitan status in the hierarchy, noted in figure 3–1, and figure 3–16 adds in a lighter grey shade the market penetration information on the next echelon in the hierarchy, the wholesale-retail centers, to that of the metropolitan centers mapped in figure 3–15.

Linked in every case with this urban-regional system of spatial interdependencies are parallel socioeconomic gradients. On the socioeconomic traverses, the "peaks" correspond to major urban nodes and the "valleys" to the interurban peripheries; a few of the peaks display both population growth and net immigration.

Returning to the Memphis case, most parts of this region display net outflows of people, however–more rapid for blacks than whites. The height of the peaks corresponds to the level of centers in the hierarchy. Very few of the centers classified in table 3–1 that

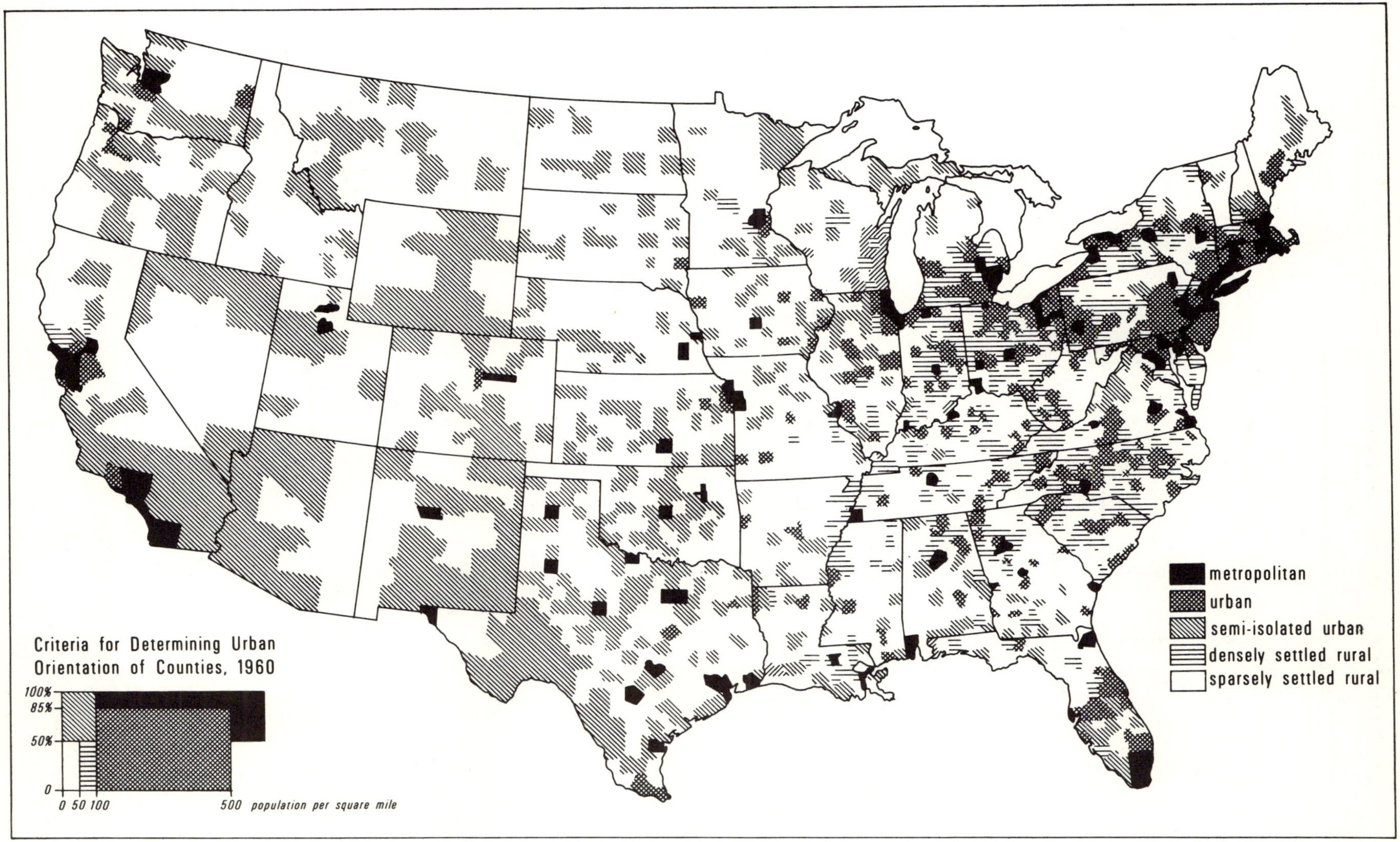

Figure 3–5. Classification of Counties on a Scale of Urbanization and Population Densities in 1960.

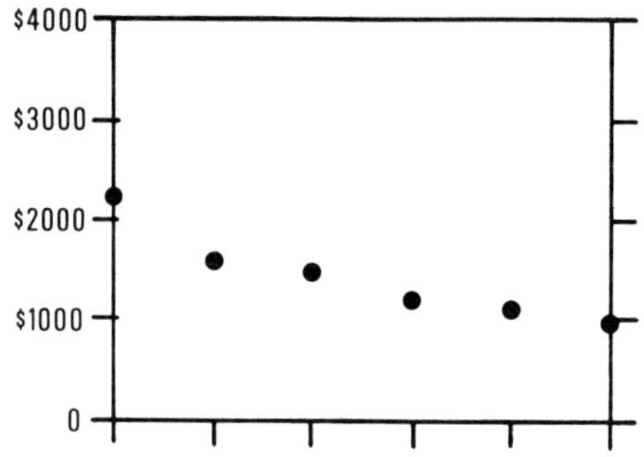

Figure 3-6. Variation of Per Capita Incomes along the Scale of Urban Orientation in 1960.

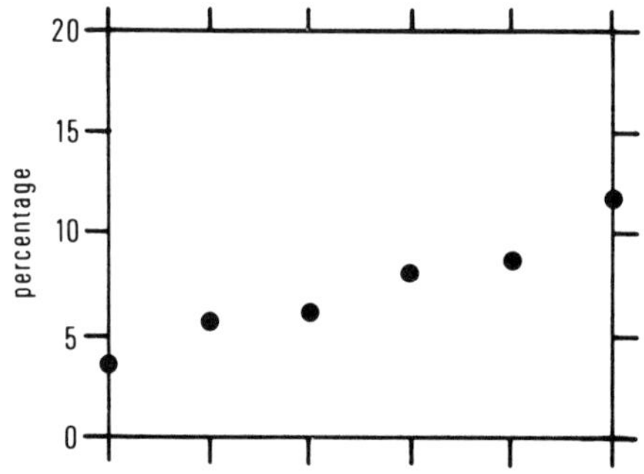

Figure 3-7. Percentage of Families with Incomes Less Than $3,000 in 1960 Related to Urban Orientations.

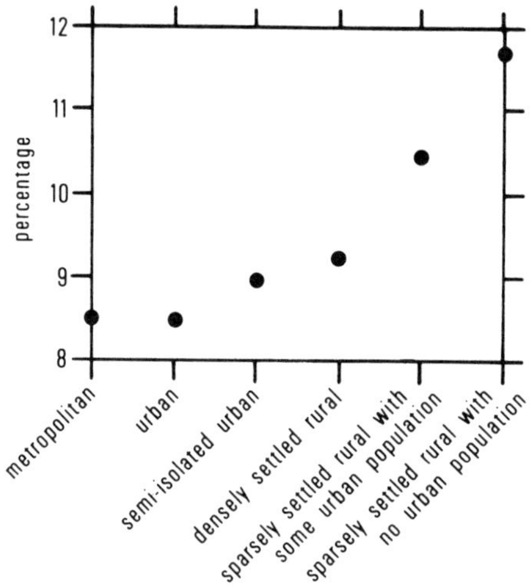

Figure 3-8. Concentration of the Elderly in Areas with Differing Urban Orientations in 1960.

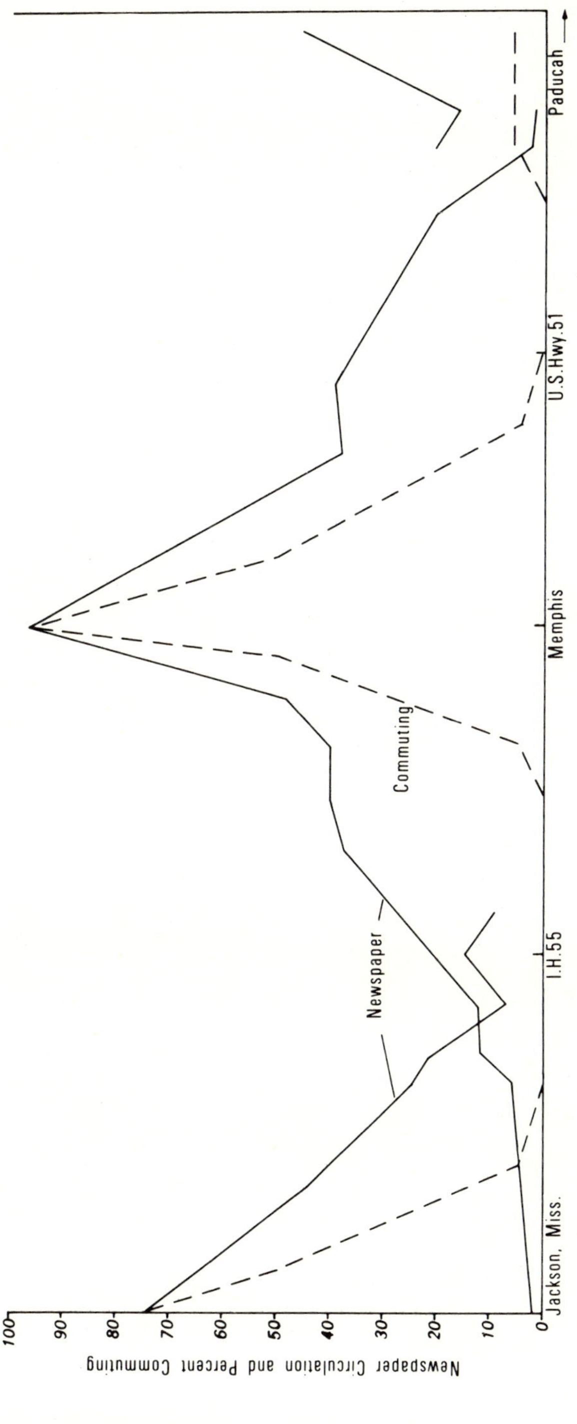

Figure 3–9. Variations in Newspaper Market Penetration and Daily Commuting Along the Traverse between Jackson and Paducah.

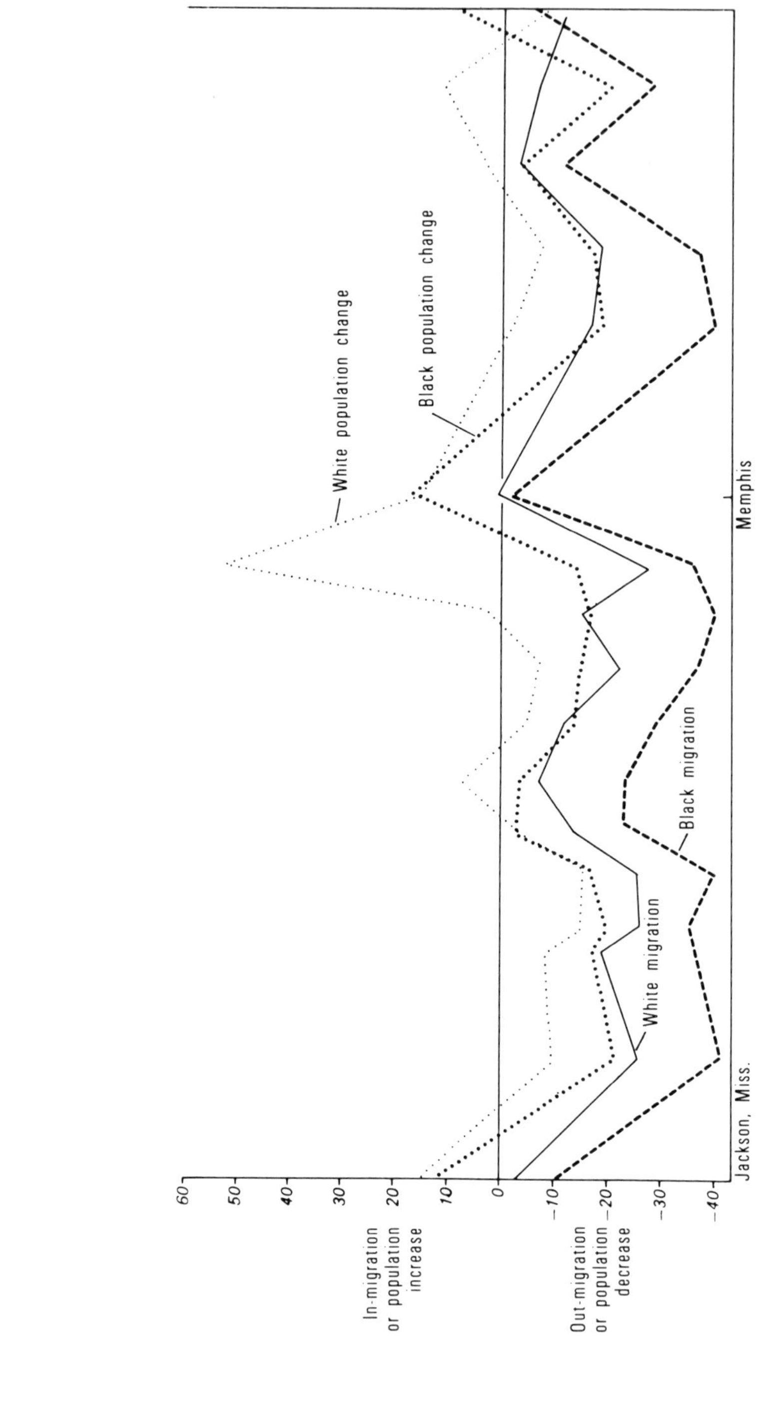

Figure 3-10. Population Change and Migration, 1960-1970, Along the Same Traverse as in Figure 3-9.

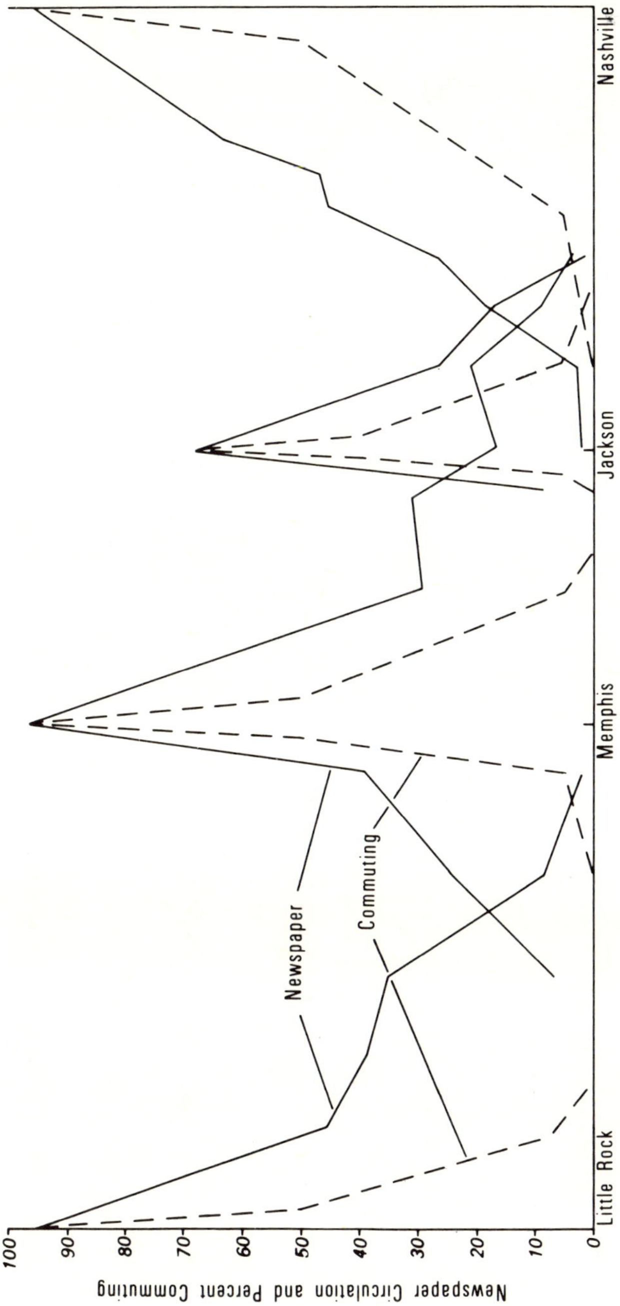

Figure 3-11. Spatial Interdependencies Along a Traverse Between Little Rock and Nashville.

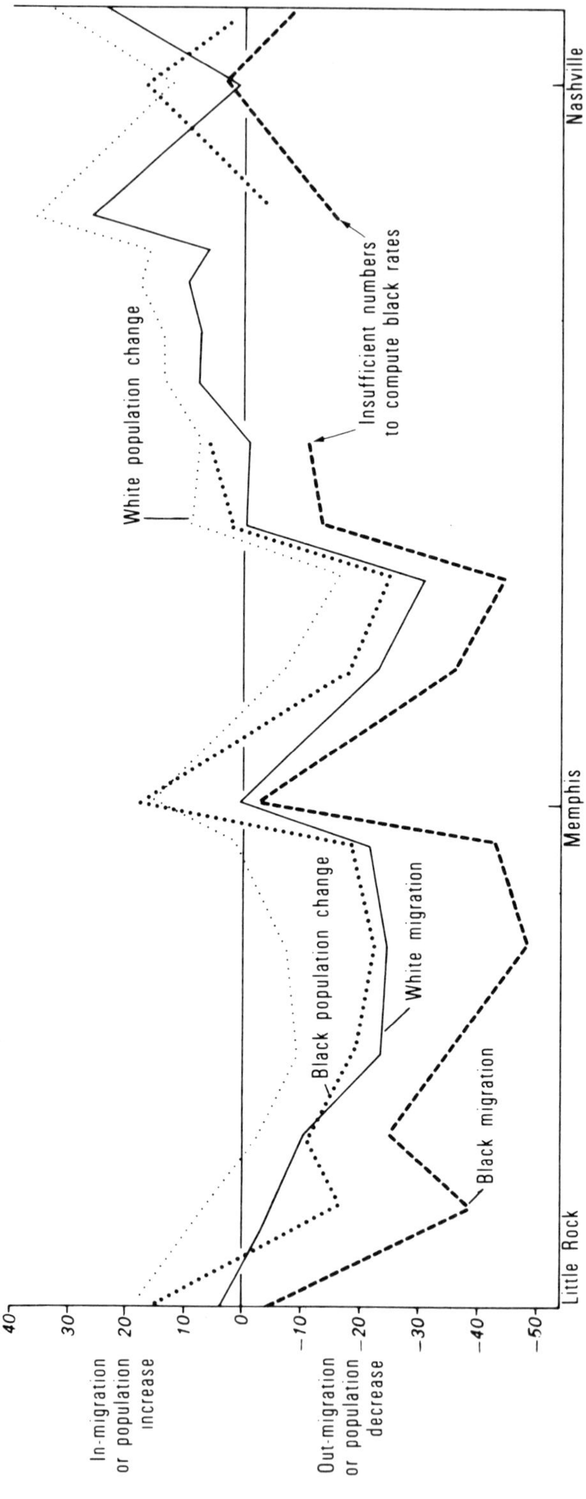

Figure 3-12. Gradients of Change Along the Little Rock-Nashville Traverse.

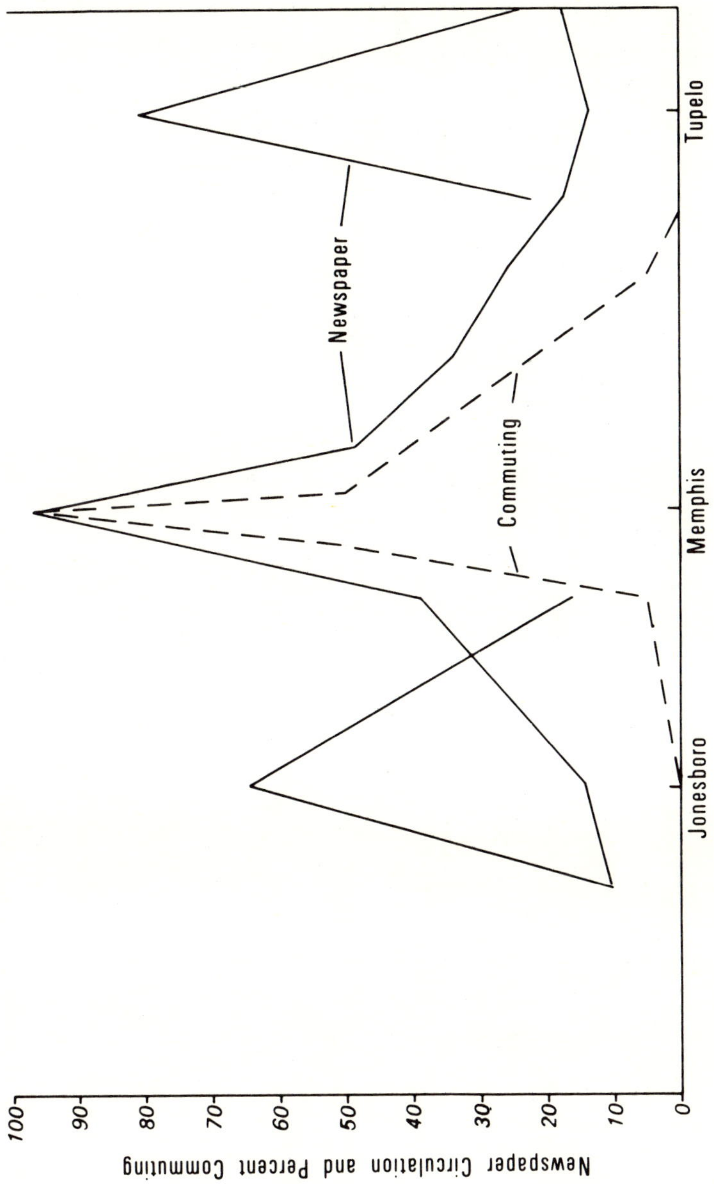

Figure 3-13. Spatial Interdependencies, Jonesboro to Tupelo.

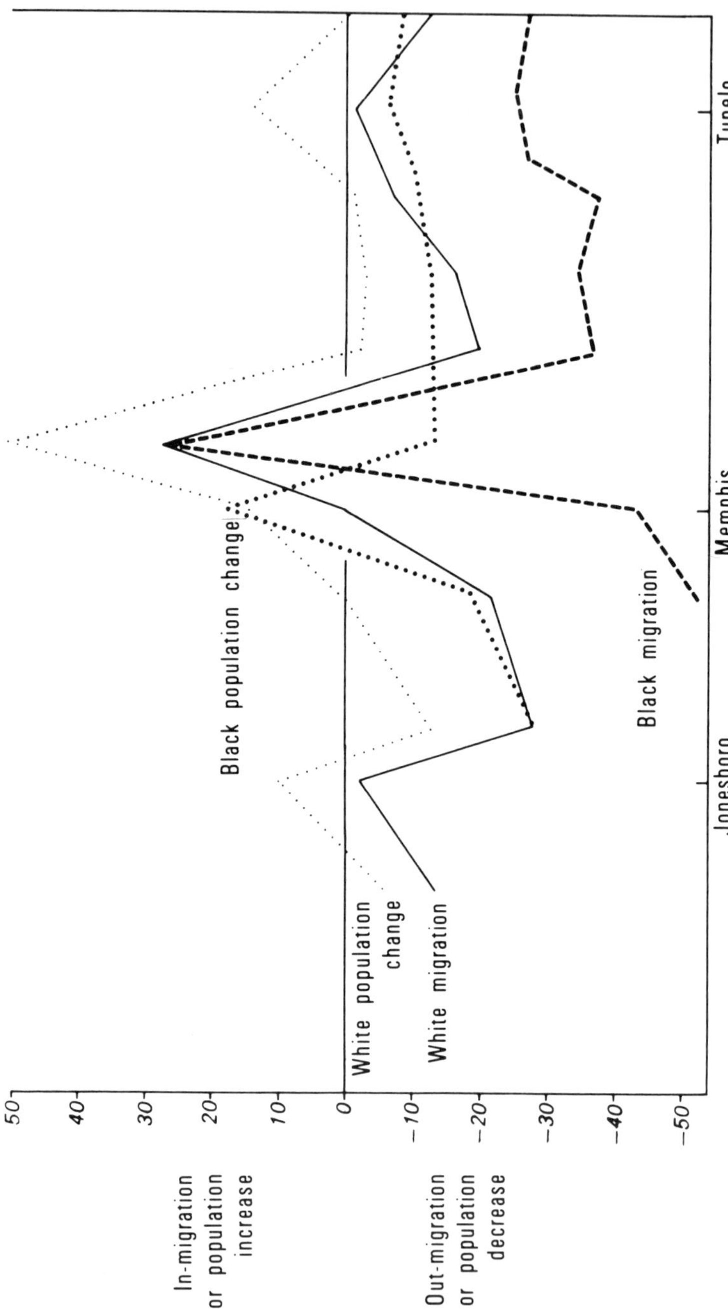

Figure 3-14. Changes in the 1960s, Jonesboro to Tupelo.

Figure 3–15. Newspaper Market Penetration by the Nation's Metropolitan-Level Centers.

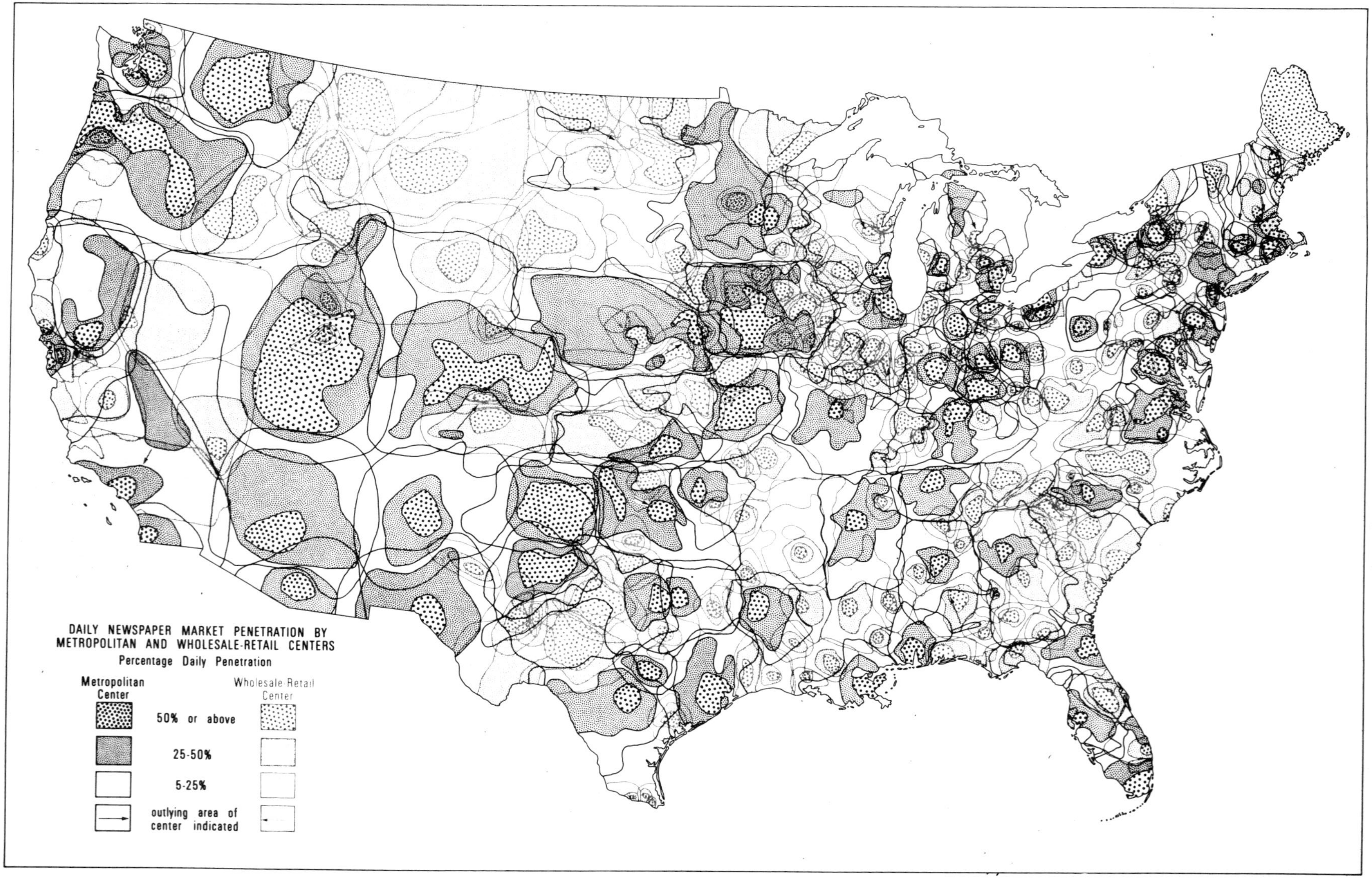

Figure 3–16. Newspaper Market Penetration by Centers Occupying the Top Two Levels of the Urban Hierarchy.

Table 3-1. Urban Hierarchy of the Memphis, Tenn. (Miss.-Ark.) Economic Area (OBE 046)

(a) Within Memphis Labor Market

Level	*City*	*County*	*Population 1960*	*Population 1970*	*Percentage Change*
Metropolis	Memphis (City)		497,524	623,530	25.3
	Shelby County		627,019	722,014	15.2
	Memphis SMSA		674,583	770,120	14.2
Wholesale-retail					
Complete shopping	Blytheville	Mississippi	20,797	24,752	19.0
	Clarksdale	Coahoma	21,105	21,673	2.7
	Helena	Phillips	11,500	10,415	-9.4
	Forrest City	St. Francis	10,544	12,521	18.8
	West Helena	Phillips	8,385	11,007	31.3
	Osceola	Mississippi	6,189	7,204	16.4
	Holly Springs	Marshall	5,621	5,728	1.9
	Brownsville	Haywood	5,424	6,901	27.2
	Covington	Tipton	5,298	5,771	8.9
	Oxford	Lafayette	5,283	13,846	162.1
	Marianna	Lee	5,134	6,196	20.7
Partial shopping	Wynne	Cross	4,922	6,696	36.0
	Trumann	Poinsett	4,511	5,938	31.6
	Ripley	Lauderdale	3,782	4,637	22.6
	University	Lafayette	3,594		
	Bolivar	Hardeman	3,338	6,578	97.1
	Batesville	Panola	3,284	3,796	15.6
	Senatobia	Tate	3,259	4,247	30.3
	Marked Tree	Poinsett	3,216	3,208	-0.2
	Marks	Quitman	2,572	2,609	1.4
Full Convenience	Sardis	Panola	2,098	2,391	14.0
	Hughes	St. Francis	1,960	1,872	-4.5
	Hernando	DeSoto	1,898	2,499	31.7
	Halls	Lauderdale	1,890	2,281	20.7
	Somerville	Fayette	1,820	1,779	-2.3
	Manila	Mississippi	1,753	1,961	11.9
	Lepanto	Poinsett	1,585	1,846	16.5
	Leachville	Mississippi	1,507	1,582	5.0

(b) Beyond Memphis Labor Market

Level	*City*	*County*	*Population 1960*	*Population 1970*	*Percentage Change*
Wholesale-retail	Jackson	Madison	34,376	39,262	14.2
Complete shopping	Jonesboro	Craighead	21,418	27,050	26.3
	Dyersburg	Dyer	12,499	13,942	11.5
Complete shopping	Paragould	Greene	9,947	10,639	7.0
	Paris	Henry	9,325	9,803	5.1
	Humboldt	Gibson	8,482	10,000	17.9
	Milan	Gibson	5,208	7,115	36.6

(continued)

Table 3-1. (continued)

	(b) Beyond Memphis Labor Market				
			Population		
Level	*City*	*County*	*1960*	*1970*	*Percentage Change*
Partial shopping	Martin	Weakley	4,750	7,738	62.9
	Trenton	Gibson	4,225	4,181	-1.1
	Lexington	Henderson	3,943	4,986	26.5
	McKenzie	Carroll, Weakley	3,780	4,813	27.3
	Pocahontas	Randolph	3,665	4,544	24.0
	Walnut Ridge	Lawrence	3,547	3,800	7.1
	Bemis	Madison	3,127		
	Piggott	Clay	2,776	3,087	11.2
	Henderson	Chester	2,691	3,512	30.5
	Ripley	Tippah	2,668	3,482	30.5
Full convenience	Corning	Clay	2,192	2,705	23.4
	Huntingdon	Carroll	2,119	3,525	66.4
	Dyer	Gibson	1,909	2,430	27.3
	Hoxie	Lawrence	1,886	2,265	20.1
	Parsons	Decatur	1,859	2,119	14.0
	Greenfield	Weakley	1,779	2,051	15.3
	Rector	Clay	1,757	1,990	13.3
	Newbern	Dyer	1,695	2,081	22.8
	Marvell	Phillips	1,690	1,980	17.2
	Alamo	Crockett	1,665	2,385	43.2
	Dresden	Weakley	1,510	1,933	28.0

are located on the highways selected as traverses show any capability of developing any "spread effect" (i.e., gradient of influence) around them with respect to either *static* measures such as incomes (i.e., *as centers of spatial organization*) or *dynamic* indicators such as changes in incomes (i.e., *as growth centers*). The traverses also pick up other details. Within the spatially-extending labor markets of the metropolises, internal polarizing shifts are seen to be taking place. For example, inverse black-white patterns of change discussed in Chapter 1 are quite clear within the Nashville labor market in figure 3-12 and also are represented in the southward and westward thrusts of the Memphian white population indicated in figures 3-12 and 3-14.

Note other features, too: the westward pattern of white immigration and population increase in the outer extremes of the Nashville labor market, towards Jackson, in the only zone with too few blacks for the census to report data for blacks, and the absence of any real gradient of influence around Jackson itself (fig. 3-10); the subsidiary peaks of Jonesboro and Tupelo, growing in population and almost holding net migration among whites to zero, and the conformity of gradients of change around these places to the configuration of their newspaper circulation territories (figs. 3-13 and 3-14); and the suggestion that there are a few lower-order outlying poles of *relative* importance in generating local spread effects, such as Grenada and Dyersburg, the lesser "peaks" in figure 3-10.

These results were substantially the same as were found in analyses of 1960 census data (Berry, 1967b), so a systematic process of plotting gradients nationwide was completed using data from the 1970 census. Figure 3-17 shows the complete nationwide set of

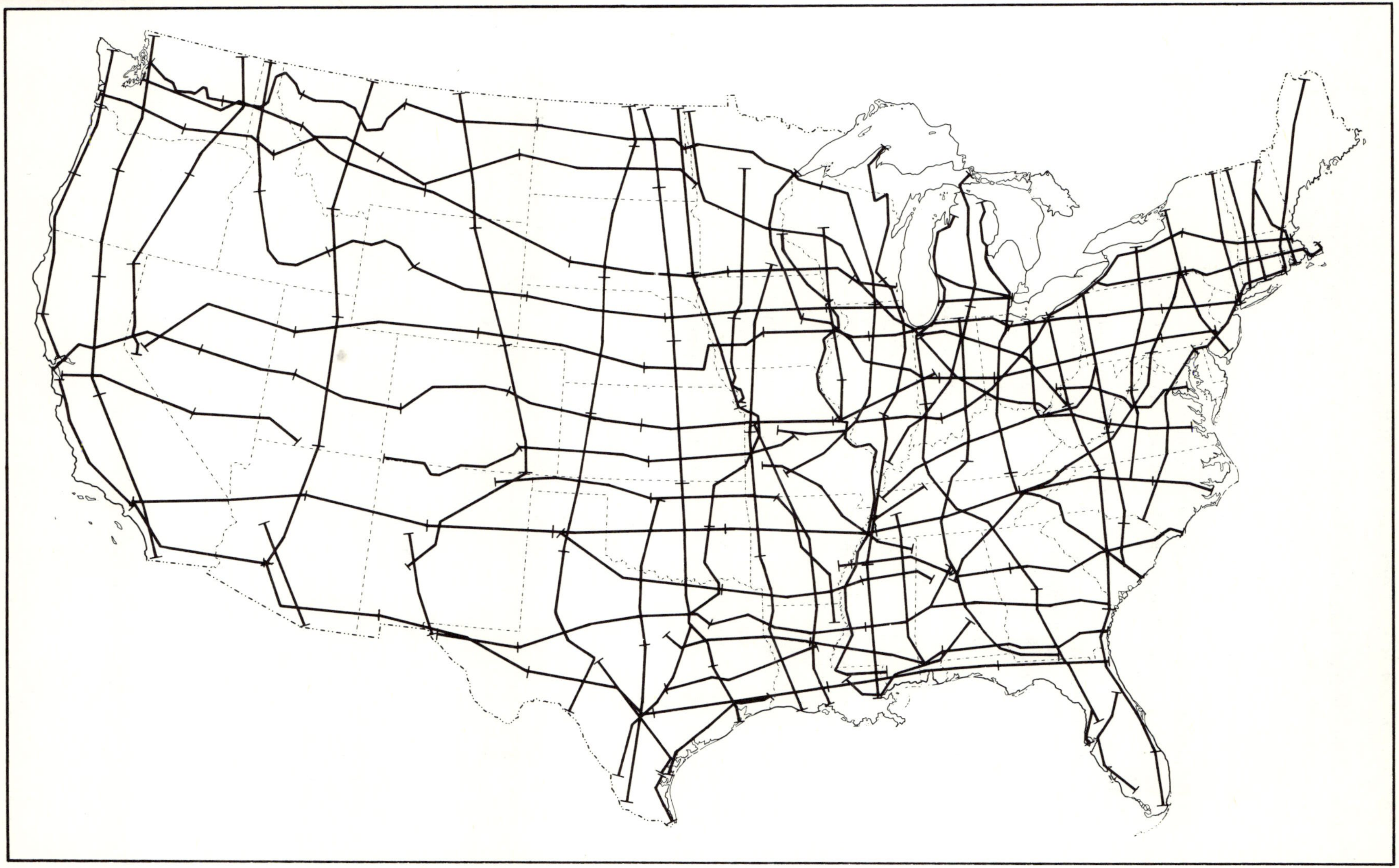

Figure 3-17. Socioeconomic Transect Network.

traverses for which graphs are available and figure 3-18 provides one example. Each traverse is approximately 400 miles long.[b] For each traverse the gradient information is recorded in four parts:

1. Newspaper market penetration and daily commuting are used to index the ways in which centers relate to surrounding areas via gradients of urban influence.
2. Population change and immigration rates are reported by race between 1960 and 1970, to show the extent to which population redistribution mirrors spatial organization and urban influence.
3. Median income levels in 1960 and 1970 are graphed, again by race, to show the extent to which spread effects with respect to these gradients shape levels of welfare.
4. The joint effects of population change and urban influence in leading to changes in income levels and in the proportion of the population beneath the poverty line are likewise graphed.

Figures 3-19 and 3-20 show, respectively, the generalized nationwide patterns of changes in median family income and of the percentage of families beneath the poverty line between 1960 and 1970 that are graphed in more detail along the traverses.

GROWTH CENTERS, BOTH CONTINUING AND EMERGENT

Taken together, the information on the urban hierarchy of the United States in the 1960s, patterns of spatial interaction of outlying areas with centers of each rank in the hierarchy, and the gradients of urban influence and patterns of change, enabled both the continuing and newly-emergent growth centers of the nation to be identified.

A continuing growth center, termed a *continuing focus for regional growth* or a *center of spatial organization*, was identified by exploring the topography of the commuting, newspaper circulation, income, population density and related maps and gradients for "peaks", downward from which gradients of urban influence flowed into the "valleys" in the interurban peripheries. Two kinds of peaks were identfied by this screening process, the "major" and the "minor"; a minor peak appears as a lesser "hill" part of the way down the slope of a major peak's "mountain." Not all urban centers listed in the hierarchy tables in Volume II will be found to have been classified as continuing foci for regional growth for the following reason. When the level of welfare in an urban place is simply consistent with its position in the urban field of a larger place, and it generates no peak around itself—i.e., it reveals no separately identifiable spread effect—this was taken as indicative of the fact that the center performs a continuing service role within the fabric of the larger urban-regional system, but does not have the independent generative capacity necessary to exert a definable spread effect on surrounding areas, with the resultant emergence of another peak-and-gradient feature in the regional topography.

Newly emergent growth centers were identified by a similar screening process applied to maps and gradients of *changes* in the 1960s—changes in the rate of population growth or the immigration rate, growth in income levels or declines in the poverty populations, etc. First, all peaks in the pattern of change were identified. Second, those peaks that had already been classified as continuing foci for regional growth were eliminated from

[b]The set of graphs is presented in Volume II.

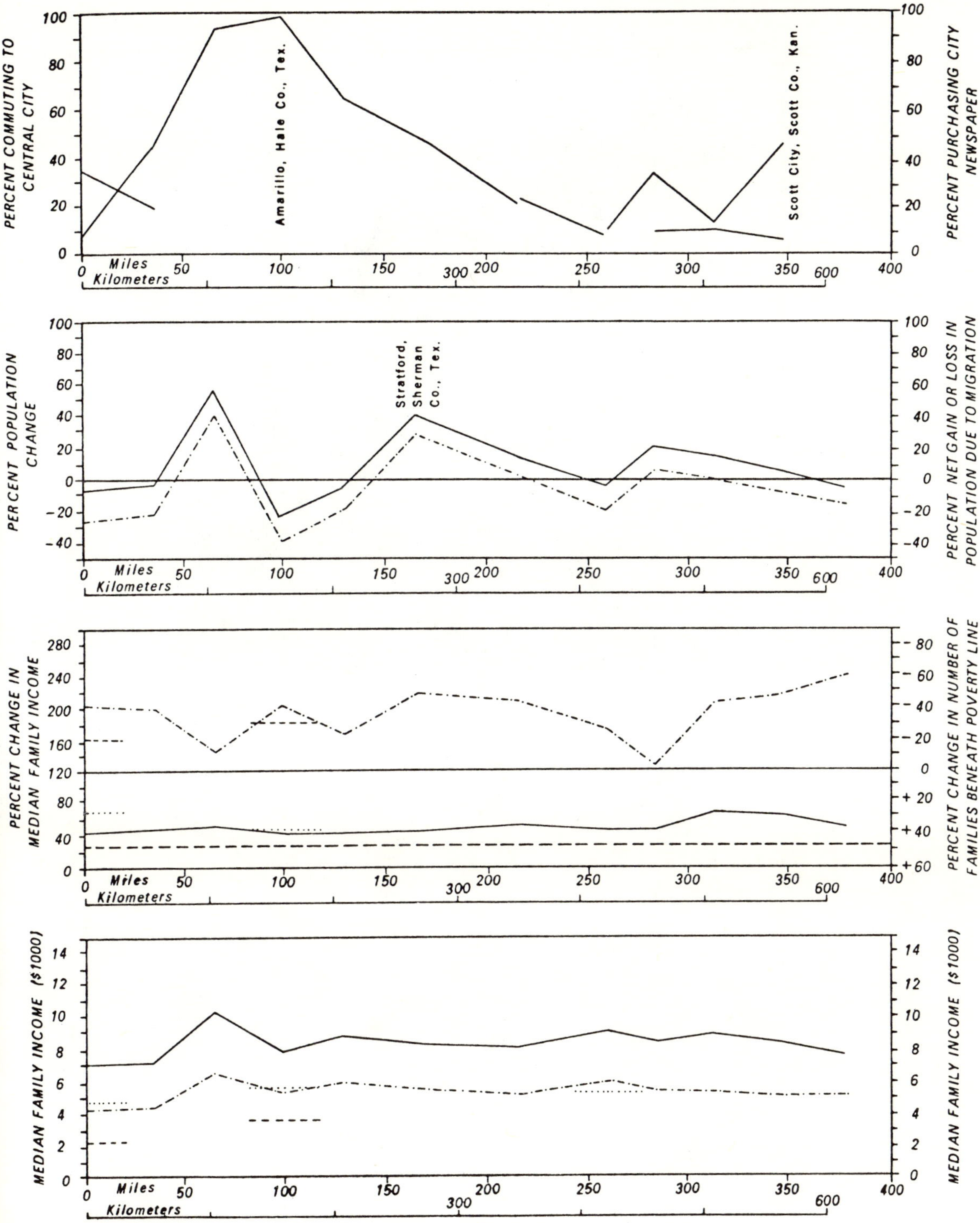

Figure 3-18. A Sample of the Set of Gradients Presented in Volume II.

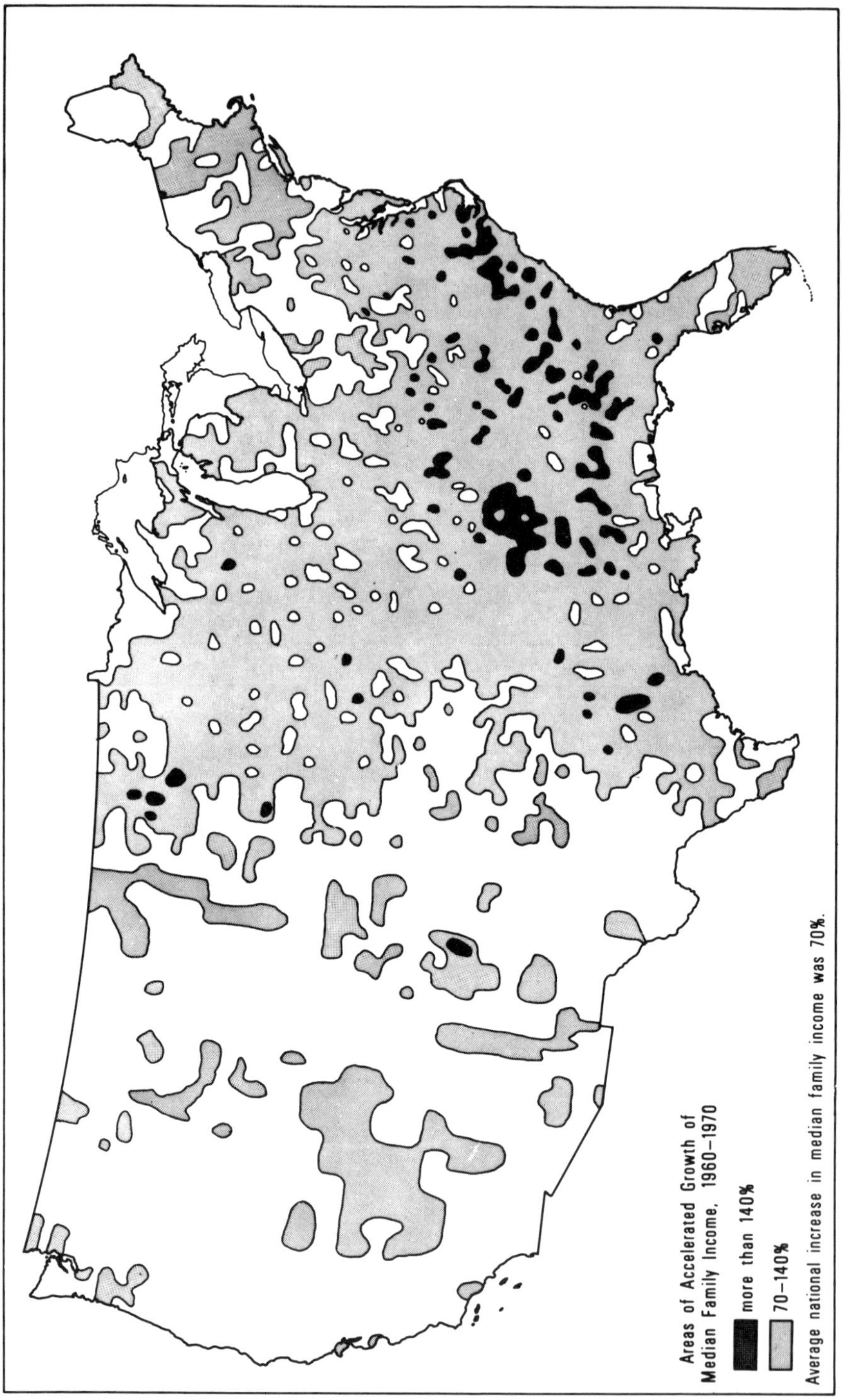

Figure 3-19. Changes in Median Family Income, 1960-1970.

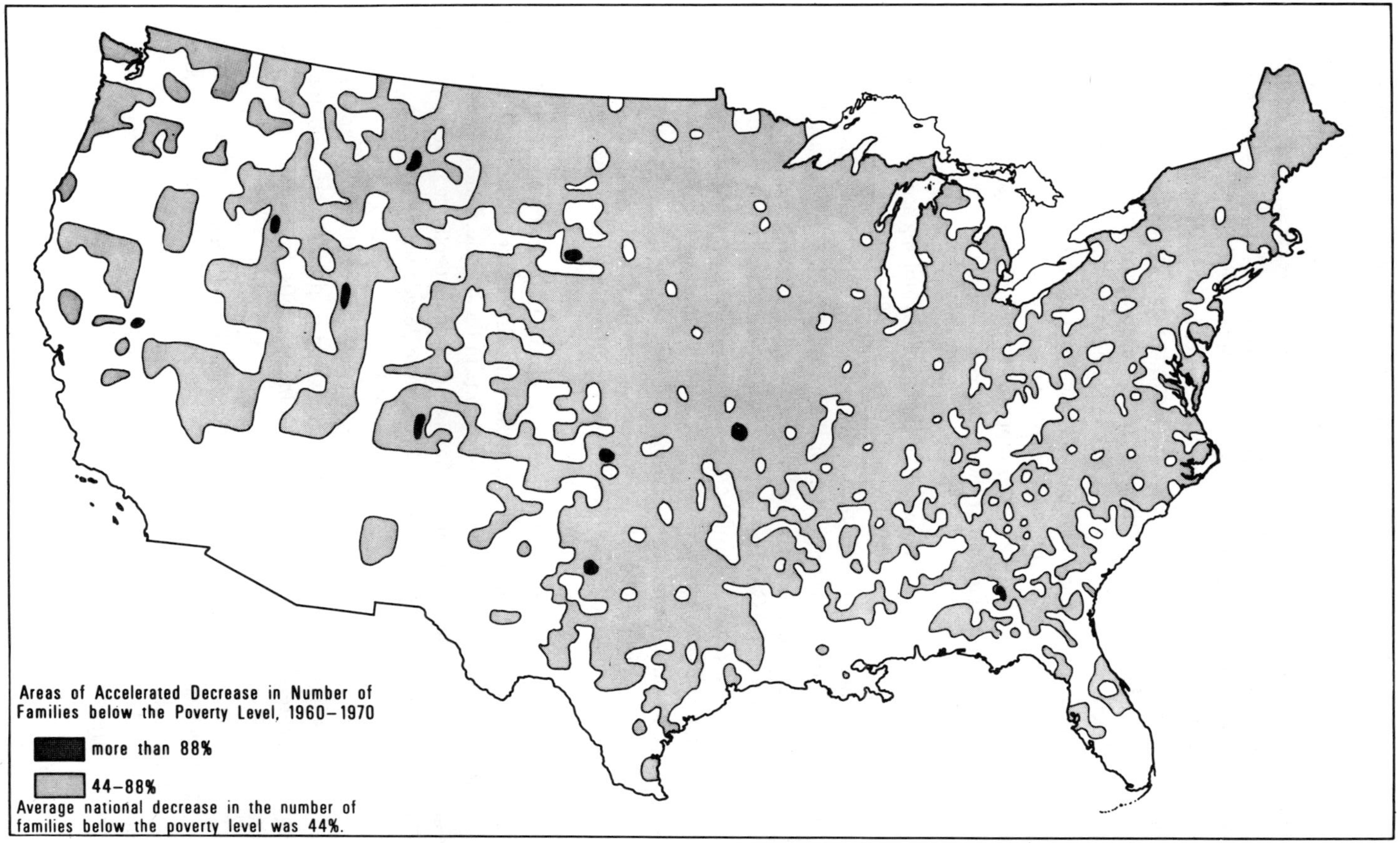

Figure 3-20. Changes in the Percentage of Families Beneath the Poverty Line, 1960–1970.

the list. The resultant set comprised the emergent growth centers, characterized by one or more type of accelerated positive change during the 1960s.

The results of the classificatory process were first tabulated for each of the 171 OBE regions in the conterminous United States. See, for example, tables 3-2 and 3-3, which refer to the Salina, Kansas region (OBE 109). Table 3-2 presents the urban hierarchy of the region. Table 3-3 shows how the results of the growth center analysis are tabulated.

First, in Section A of table 3-3, the continuing foci for regional growth are identified—in this case the Wichita SMSA, which is outside OBE 109. Colby, Concordia, Hays, and Great Bend are all lesser peaks on the Wichita gradient. No other center within OBE 109, including Salina, shows any ability to develop a separate urban field peaking above that declining away from Wichita. Rather, they dance to the rhythms of welfare and growth emanating from Wichita. Indeed, only beyond the Salina labor market are subsidiary peaks to be seen, developed around the outlying small towns of Colby, Concordia, Hays, and Great Bend. That Colby appears is indicative of a greater centrality or locally-influential generative capability than the classification as a partial shopping center might suggest. That Russell and Abilene do not appear indicates that these complete shopping centers perform only a service role in the regional economy.

Section B of table 3-3 shows all of the places exhibiting accelerated growth during the 1960s, together with the nature of this growth. The peaks were identified after the maps and gradients had been smoothed by using county averages, because city statistics may be biased by such things as annexation or the location of new growth just beyond the city limits. Among the growth centers are McPherson and Lindsberg within the Salina labor market, and Hays, Ellis, Goodland and Norton outside that labor market. McPherson and Lindsberg showed rapid growth of median income and decline of their poverty populations; they were the only two towns within the Salina commuting area to show greater growth during the decade that might have been predicted on the basis of gradients flowing from Wichita. Goodland evidenced rapid population growth and immigration. In addition, several outlying counties without centers of at least partial shopping status revealed some signs of economic improvement.

Section C of table 3-3 is reserved for centers with mixed records, declining in some respects and growing in others. For example, Lincoln Center and Council Grove both were successful in offsetting certain effects of decline in the decade: Lincoln Center declined in population, yet experienced growing median incomes and a declining poverty population. Council Grove declined in population, yet ended up the decade with a smaller poverty population.

The final part of the summary table, Section D, identifies whether or not the region contains any designated EDA growth or redevelopment centers, and whether or not such designated centers actually displayed growth in the 1960s. In the case of the Salina region there was none.

The complete set of tables identifying the centers of spatial organization and the various types of new growth centers is to be found in Volume II. This collection records both the spatial structure of regional development in the 1960s, and the nation's growth centers in the decade. Comparison of the tables in Volume II also enables local service centers to be distinguished from both the continuing and newly-emergent centers of growth.

THE NATIONAL PATTERNS

Several maps were prepared from the materials listed in Volume II. Figure 3-21 shows the continuing foci for regional growth—i.e., the nation's principal continuing growth centers—

Table 3-2. Urban Hierarchy of Salina, Kans. Economic Area (OBE 109)

Level	City	County	Population 1960	Population 1970	Percentage Change
	(a) Within Salina Labor Market				
Wholesale-retail	Salina (City)		43,202	37,714	-12.7
	Saline County		54,715	46,592	-14.8
Complete shopping	McPherson	McPherson	9,996	10,851	8.6
	Abilene	Dickinson	6,746	6,661	-1.3
Partial shopping	Herington	Dickinson	3,702	3,165	-14.5
	Lindsborg	McPherson	2,609	2,764	5.9
Full convenience	Ellsworth	Ellsworth	2,361	2,080	-11.9
	Minneapolis	Ottawa	2,024	1,971	-2.6
	Lincoln Center	Lincoln	1,717	1,582	-7.9
	(b) Beyond Salina Labor Market				
Wholesale-retail					
Complete shopping	Great Bend	Barton	16,670	16,133	-3.2
	Hays	Ellis	11,947	15,396	28.9
	Concordia	Cloud	7,022	7,221	2.8
	Russell	Russell	6,113	5,371	-12.1
Partial shopping	Clay Center	Clay	4,613	4,963	7.6
	Lyons	Rice	4,592	4,355	-5.2
	Goodland	Sherman	4,459	5,510	23.6
	Hoisington	Barton	4,248	3,710	-12.7
	Colby	Thomas	4,210	4,658	10.6
	Beloit	Mitchell	3,837	4,121	7.4
	Scott City	Scott	3,555	4,001	12.5
	Norton	Norton	3,345	3,621	8.4
	Phillipsburg	Phillips	3,233	3,241	0.2
	Plainville	Rooks	3,104	2,627	-15.4
	Belleville	Republic	2,940	3,063	4.2
	Wakeeney	Trego	2,808	2,334	-16.9
	Ellinwood	Barton	2,729	2,416	-11.5
	Council Grove	Morris	2,664	2,403	-9.8
Full convenience	Hill City	Graham	2,421	2,071	-14.5
	Smith Center	Smith	2,379	2,389	0.4
	Oberlin	Decatur	2,337	2,291	-2.0
	Sterling	Rice	2,303	2,312	0.4
	Ellis	Ellis	2,218	2,137	-3.7
	Oakley	Logan	2,190	2,327	6.3
	Stockton	Rooks	2,073	1,818	-12.3
	Osborne	Osborne	2,049	1,980	-3.4
	Atwood	Rawlins	1,906	1,658	-13.0
	LaCrosse	Rush	1,767	1,583	-10.4
	Ness City	Ness	1,653	1,756	6.2
	St. Francis	Cheyenne	1,594	1,725	8.2
	Dighton	Lane	1,526	1,540	0.9

Table 3-3. Growth Centers in the Salina, Kans. Economic Area (OBE 109)

A. (i) *Continuing Foci for Regional Growth: Centers for Spatial Organization*

Level	*Center*
M	Wichita SMSA (not in OBE 109)

(ii) *Subsidiary Peaks on the Income Gradient Dipping Away From: Wichita*

(a) Within Major Labor Market

Level	*Center(s)*	*County*

(b) Beyond Major Labor Market

Level	*Center(s)*	*County*
PS	Colby	Thomas
CS	Concordia	Cloud
CS	Hays	Ellis
CS	Great Bend	Barton

B. *Areas of Accelerated Relative Growth in the 1960's*

(i) Within Major Labor Market

Level	*Center(s)*	*County*	*Type of Accelerated Relative Growth*			
			Population	*Migration*	*Income*	*Welfare Decline*
CS	McPherson	McPherson			x	x
PS	Lindsberg	McPherson			x	x

(ii) Beyond Major Labor Market

Level	*Center(s)*	*County*	*Population*	*Migration*	*Income*	*Welfare Decline*
CS,FCC	Hays, Ellis	Ellis	x			
PS	Goodland	Sherman	x	x		
PS	Norton	Norton				x
–	–	Wichita		x		
–	–	Jewell, Wallace			x	x

C. *Areas Partially Successful in Offsetting Decline in the 1960's*

(i) *Combined Population Decline and/or Emigration with Median Family Income Increase and/or Poverty Level Decline*

(a) Within Major Labor Market

Level	*Center(s)*	*County*		*Median Family Income Increase*	*Poverty Level Decline*
FCC	Lincoln Center	Lincoln	Pop'n Decline	x	x

(b) Beyond Major Labor Market

Level	*Center(s)*	*County*			
PS	Council Grove	Morris	Pop'n Decline		x

(ii) *Relatively Less Rapid Decline Than Surrounding Areas*

Types of Less Rapid Decline: *Population* | *Migration*

(a) Within Major Labor Market

Level	*Center(s)*	*County*

(b) Beyond Major Labor Market

Level	*Center(s)*	*County*

D. *Designated EDA Growth Centers Within the Region*

EDA Center	*Level in Hierarchy*	*EDA District*	If actual growth center in the 1960's, category under which EDA center is listed above.

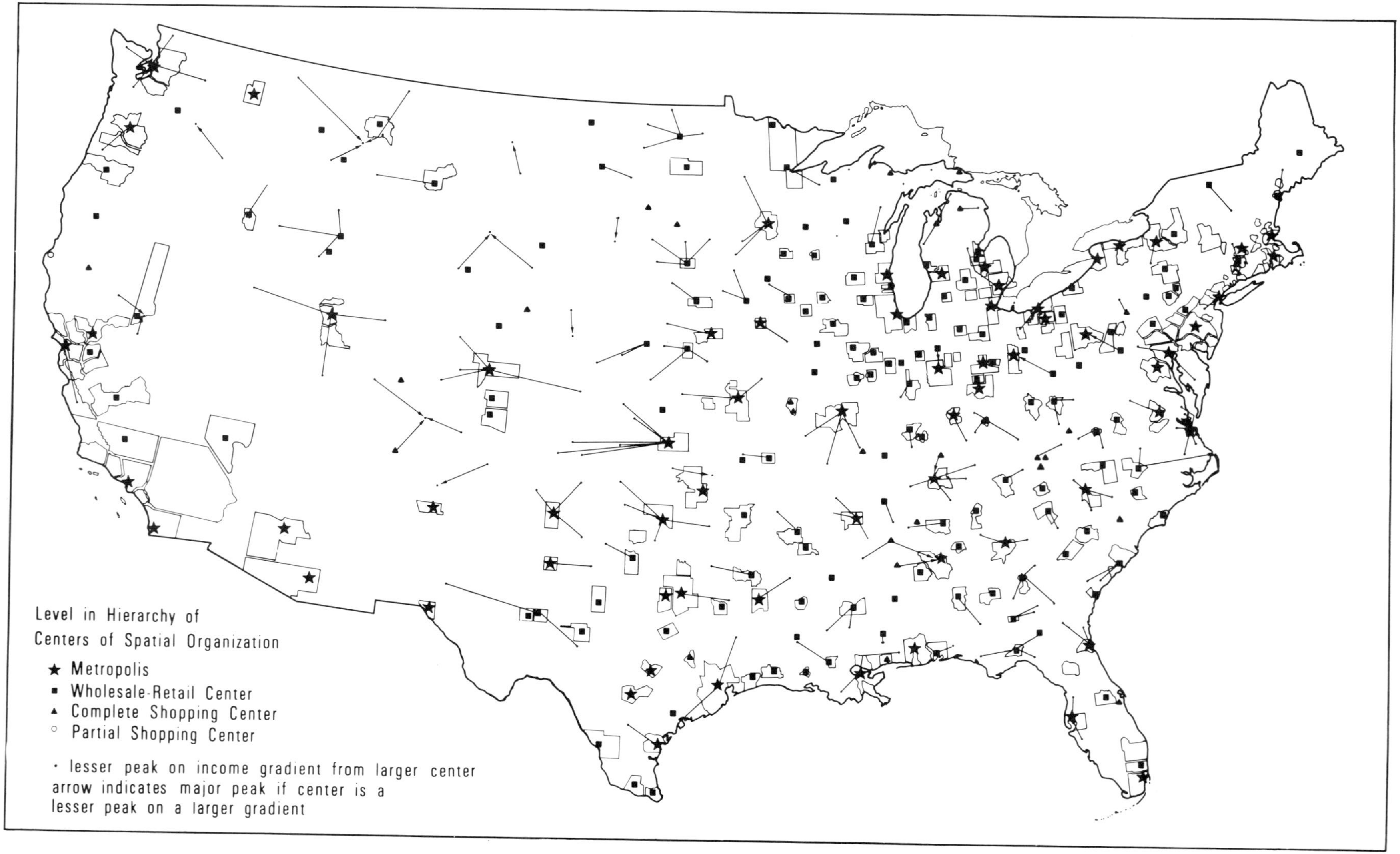

Figure 3–21. Continuing Foci for Regional Growth.

classifying the major peaks by their status in the urban hierarchy and showing, for each of the lesser peaks, the major peaks to which they are related. The outlines of the SMSAs, as of the end of 1970, are also shown, because many of the continuing centers of spatial organization are the SMSAs. This map, then, summarizes the continuing centers responsible for the fabric of regional growth and change in the United States.

Figures 3-22 and 3-34 plot the accelerated growth points of the 1960s for, respectively, population and immigration, and income and welfare. Because the general patterns underlying these maps may not be evident upon first inspection, they have been summarized in figure 3-24 into three types:

a. Those related to the diffusion and decentralization of metropolitan growth beyond existing SMSA boundaries. In this case, the individual urban places are not identified, but instead, because the places are becoming functional parts of the metropolitan complex, the *extra-metropolitan growth area* is shaded.
b. "*Major*" *growth areas*: 34 counties which contain several individual growth centers with multi-criteria peaks in the tables.
c. "*Other*" *non-metropolitan growth centers*: Some 105 centers occurring one one to a county.

Just as figure 3-21 summarizes the continuing foci of regional growth in the United States, figure 3-24 summarizes the new growth directions—predominantly those of metropolitan decentralization, but also involving a variety of the more remote places that grew more rapidly than their environs during the 1960s. It is to preliminary analysis of figures 3-21 and 3-24 that we turn in the next chapter.

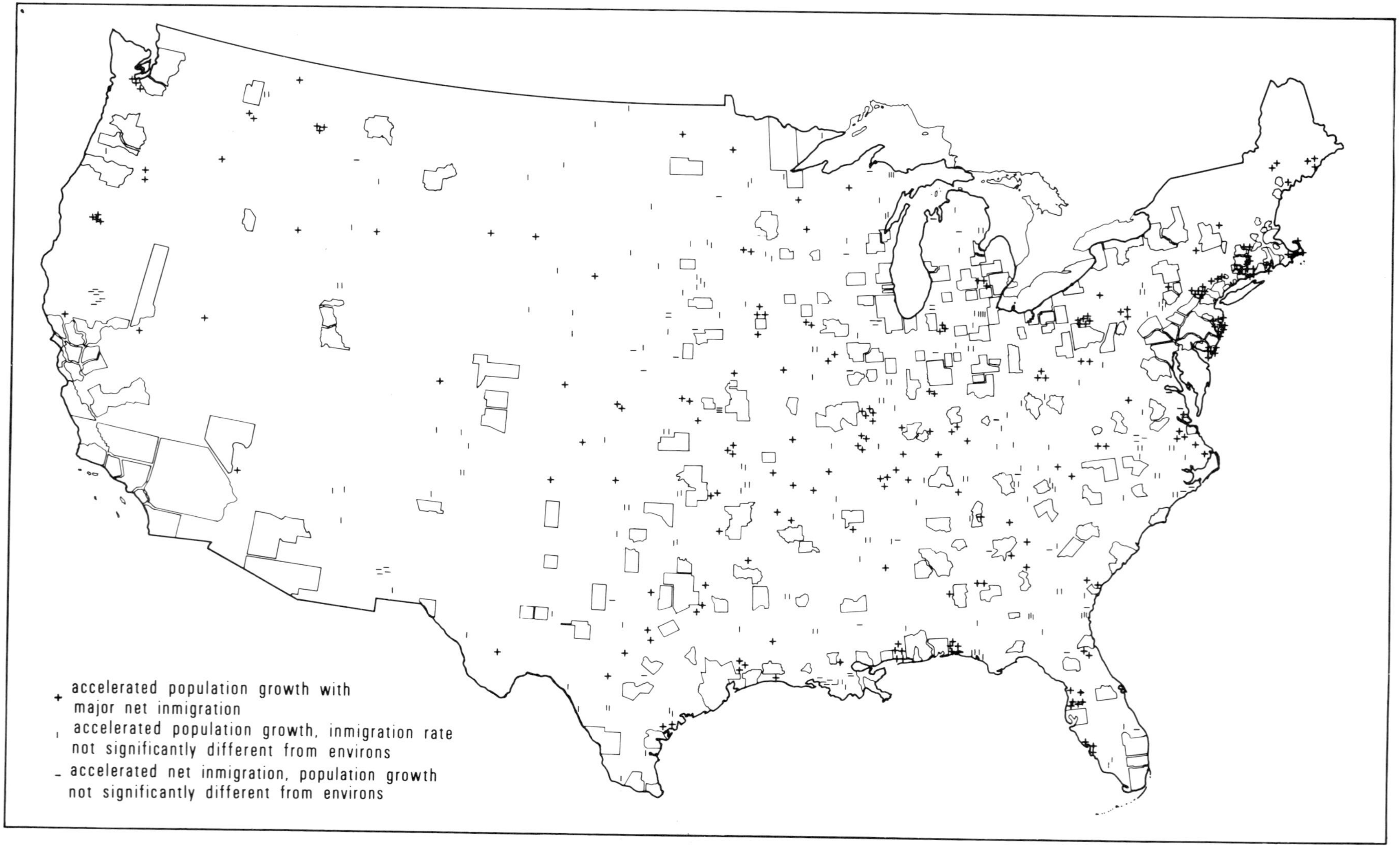

Figure 3–22. Population Growth Points.

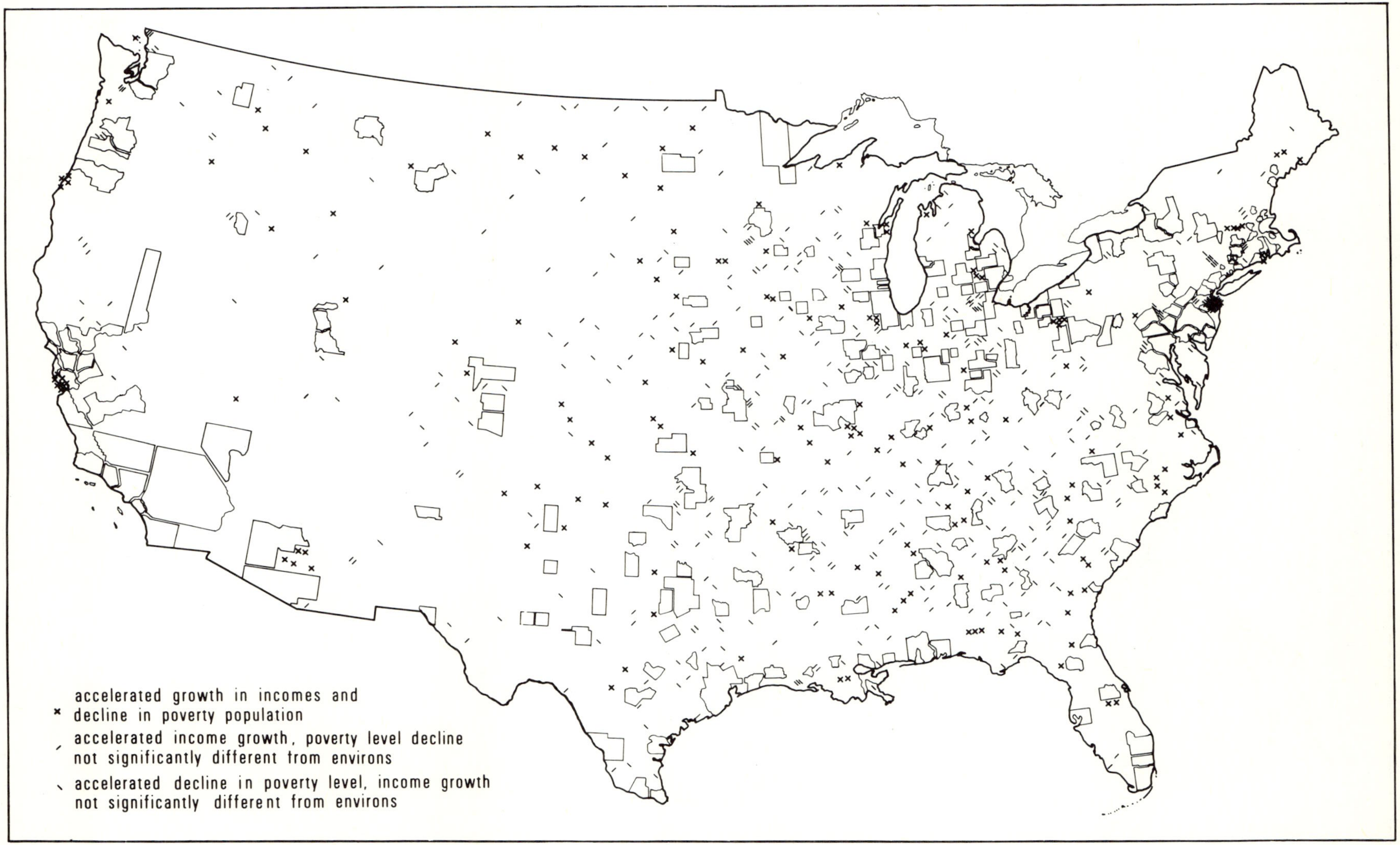

Figure 3–23. Income/Welfare Growth Points.

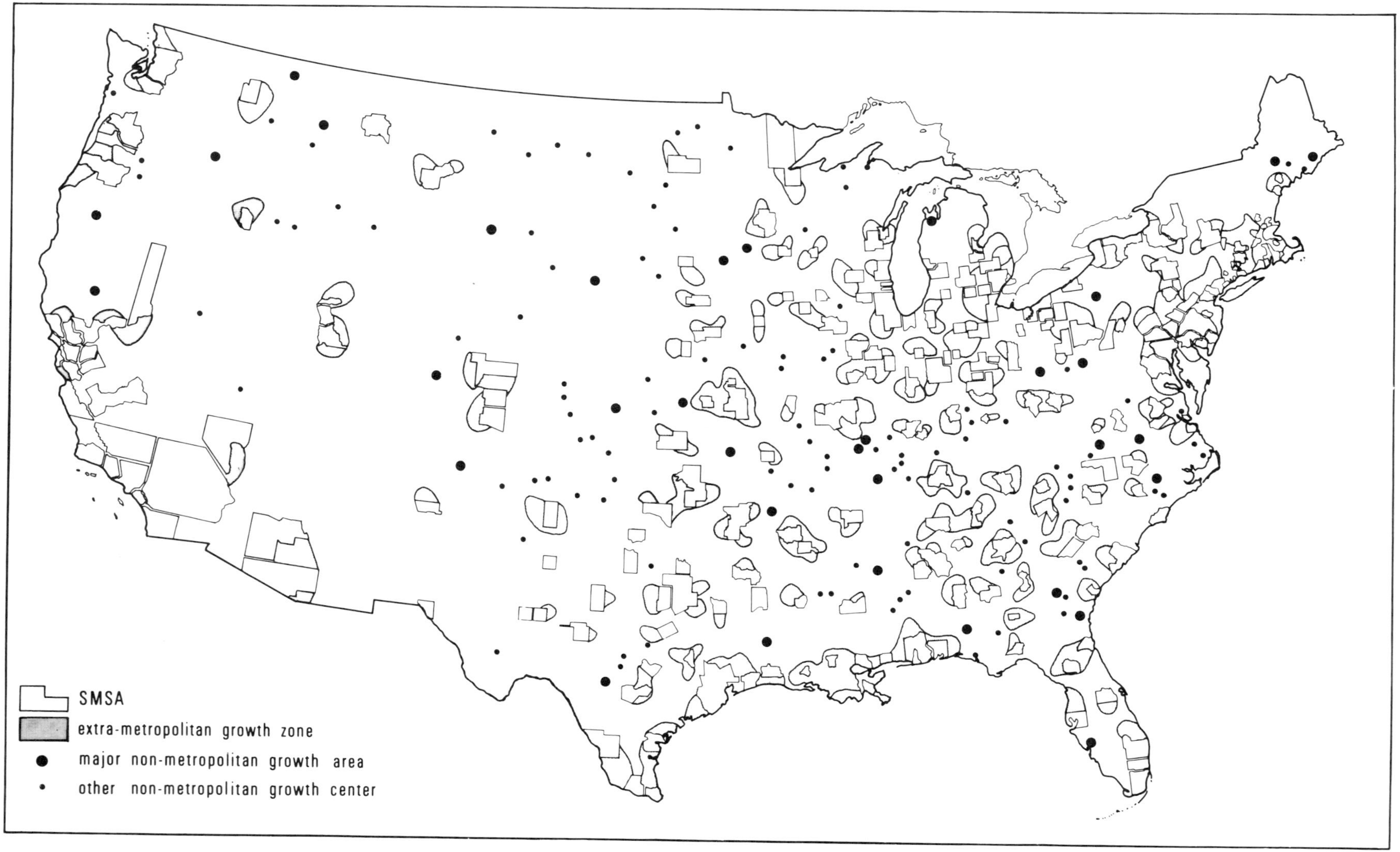

Figure 3–24. Non-Metropolitan Growth Patterns in the 1960's.

Chapter Four

The Patterns Analyzed

Many of the growth characteristics of the continuing centers of spatial organization depicted in figure 3-21 were anticipated in the latter part of Chapter 1. They include: convergence of growth rates on the national average with increasing size; slower rates of growth in regions relying heavily upon primary activities; convergence of growth on the national average with an increasing secondary component to the economic base; and higher-than-average growth where the region displays heavy dependence upon the tertiary and quaternary sectors and/or upon governmental expenditures. What, then, of the new growth centers shown in figure 3-24?

THE UPPER MIDWEST CASE

One organization, the Upper Midwest Council, a nonprofit corporation concerned with growth problems of an area including Montana, North and South Dakota, Minnesota, northwest Wisconsin, and Upper Michigan, has attempted to address this question in its region of concern. They write that in the Upper Midwest, growth areas fall into three general categories: *urban-related, high amenity*, and *special investment areas* (Gustavson, 1973).

Urban-Related Growth

The urban-related growth accounted, the Council found, for the greatest share of population increase, especially around the larger, diversified centers. The Twin Cities metropolitan area is the most obvious of these, influencing an area within a range extending more than 50 miles from the Twin Cities, which has been growing at a rate more than twice the national average. Within the area of most rapid growth, a majority of the employed persons are commuting into the Twin Cities area from the small towns and rural areas. Population increases in this commuting zone are accounted for both by persons moving in and the retention of rural population. Farms have increased in size much more slowly in this area than in other parts of the Upper Midwest, with a very high proportion of the farms having become part time operations as their operators find supplemental nonagricultural income in and near the Twin Cities area. Accompanying the spreading of population growth around the Twin Cities, there has been a spreading of labor intensive manufacturing taking advantage of generally high quality, low cost labor.

These trends were most evident in the Upper Midwest in and around the Twin Cities metropolitan area during the 1960s, but they were also said to exist to a lesser degree in most of the larger urban centers in the Upper Midwest. Spreading areas of influence were to be seen around Eau Claire, La Crosse, Winona, Rochester, Mankato, St. Cloud, Duluth-Superior, Fargo-Moorhead, Grand Forks, Minot, Bismarck, Dickinson, Sioux Falls, Aberdeen, Rapid City, Billings, Bozeman, Helena, Great Falls, Missoula, Kalispell, and to a lesser extent around the smaller growing centers. Each urban area was expanding its scope of influence and affecting growth in nearby small towns and rural areas much the same as the area around the Twin Cities is affected.

Special Investmant Areas

Special and highly specific investments in higher education, military bases, construction, and mining also contributed to the growth of certain urban centers. The highly specialized growth centers, according to the Upper Midwest Council, include Vermillion and Brookings, S.D., and Marshall, Minnesota, each influenced by college growth. Military installations at Kincheloe and K. I. Sawyer Air Force Bases in the Upper Peninsula of Michigan affected growth in the nearby towns of Saulte Ste. Marie and Marquette respectively. Air Force bases at Grand Forks and minot, North Dakota; Ellsworth Air Force Base near Rapid City, South Dakota; and Malmstrom Air Force Base adjoining Great Falls, Montana, each had a substantial population, and an important impact on nearby communities.

High Amenity Areas

The third major factor identified as influencing population growth in the region was the accelerating development of year-around residences in high amenity areas, which include cities, towns, and rural areas with special scenic attributes such as water, trees, and topographic relief. Two general growth areas of this type were most noticeable in the Upper Midwest in the 1960s—the valleys of western Montana and the lake regions of Wisconsin and Minnesota. Amenity-related growth was most noticeable in Montana between Kalispell and Hamilton, including the Flathead Valley, the Missoula area and the Bitterroot Valley; the Gallatin Valley south of Bozeman also experienced some noticeable amenity-related growth. Expansion of the lumber and wood products industry also was an important stimulant to growth in Western Montana. Northern Wisconsin from Vilas and Oneida Counties in the east to Washburn County in the west and between Brainerd and Bemidji in the central Minnesota Lake District were important high amenity growth areas in the eastern part of the Upper Midwest. This phenomenon also was to be seen to a lesser extent in the Detroit Lakes-Fergus Falls-Alexandria-Willmar area in west central Minnesota, in Itasca and northern St. Louis Counties in Minnesota and in the Black Hilis of South Dakota.

METROPOLITAN DECENTRALIZATION, MEGALOPOLITAN EVOLUTION AND HIGH-AMENITY GROWTH: LEADING ELEMENTS IN THE NATIONWIDE PATTERN

The conclusions of the Upper Midwest Council may be generalized throughout the United States, provided that the accelerated filtering of industries into certain peripheral areas is recognized as an additional theme. Metropolitan and major wholesale-retail centers remain the principal centers of spatial organization (fig. 3-21), and their accelerated decentralization beyond the boundaries of the Standard Metropolitan Statistical Areas is bringing substantial segments of the country into their fields of growth (fig. 3-24). Where existing metropolitan centers are close to one another, this is contributing to the replacement of the spatial order composed of the metropolis and its gradients of influence, extending downward into the inter-metropolitan peripheries in the manner discussed in Chapter 2, by a new spatial order, that of the megalopolis, within which the spatial patterns of growing metropolis and declining periphery are reversed.

Consider the situation diagrammed in figure 4-1. The top illustration shows typical income gradients declining with distance from the city center as urban influences are extended over the coutryside. Substantial urban-rural differences in incomes emerge as a consequence of the resulting spread effects. At metropolitan scale, these income differences lead to massive immigration of the peripheral poor into the metropolitan core, where incomes then decline, and countervailing waves of emigration of the rich and middle class to the periphery take place. A deepening and widening "volcanic" formation develops as shown in the second graph. Incomes are at their highest levels in the extending suburbs and exurbs. But where metropolitan areas are close to one another, the outward waves from adjacent metropoli begin to converge, as shown in the third diagram. Initially, peripheral incomes are lower than the crest of the waves, but are higher than in the traditional metropolitan cores. The megalopolis emerges when waves meet in a common zone in which new growth opportunities are concentrated (bottom diagram). Much of what is to be seen in figure 3-24 is indicative of the emergence of "megalopolitan confluence zones" as the most dynamic growth areas in the nation, combining tertiary and quaternary employment growth with high-income residential developments in amenity-rich environments.

Beyond the megalopolitan confluence zones and, in the case of isolated metropolitan areas, beyond their encircling rings of metropolitan expansion, the most widespread type of new growth also is in high-amenity areas–by lakes, rivers, and oceans; where there are winter sports opportunities; and in other scenic or natural areas. Many of the nonmetropolitan communities which have such facilities have had considerable population increases and development. The lake areas in the Ozark-Appalachian region have been growing as have the winter sports areas in New England and the northern and central Rocky Mountains. But in such areas, the per capita income has not increased at the same pace as population because much of recreational employment is seasonal and low paid.

Related to recreational developments are the burgeoning retirement communities, again emphasizing particular amenity resources. Many of the original developments of this type were in the desert Southwest; however, this phenomenon has now spread to many other parts of the United States. Florida for two decades has received large numbers of such retirees, and more recently a very significant number of such communities has begun to develop in the Missouri and Arkansas Ozarks and, to a lesser extent, in the mountainous areas of Southern Appalachia and the southern Rockies.

Filtering of Manufacturing Industries

Beyond the emerging megalopolis, decentralizing metropolis, and high-amenity concentrations, many of the other cases of accelerated growth in the 1960s involve state colleges, military bases, the spillovers from construction projects, and mining. Indeed, of the 34 major nonmetropolitan growth areas identified in figure 3-24, one-third involve major college expansions and four are military-related. Interstate location appears to be of some significance, especially in regions where past highway investment has lagged (Bohm and Patterson, 1972). However, the force of greatest significance–and one that differentiates the rest of the nation from the conclusions of the Upper Midwest Council reported in the previous pages–is the filtering of manufacturing industries into small towns and rural areas in the intermetropolitan periphery. The patterns are shown in figures 4-2 and 4-3. These maps record manufacturing employment increments in, first, nonmetropolitan counties which had

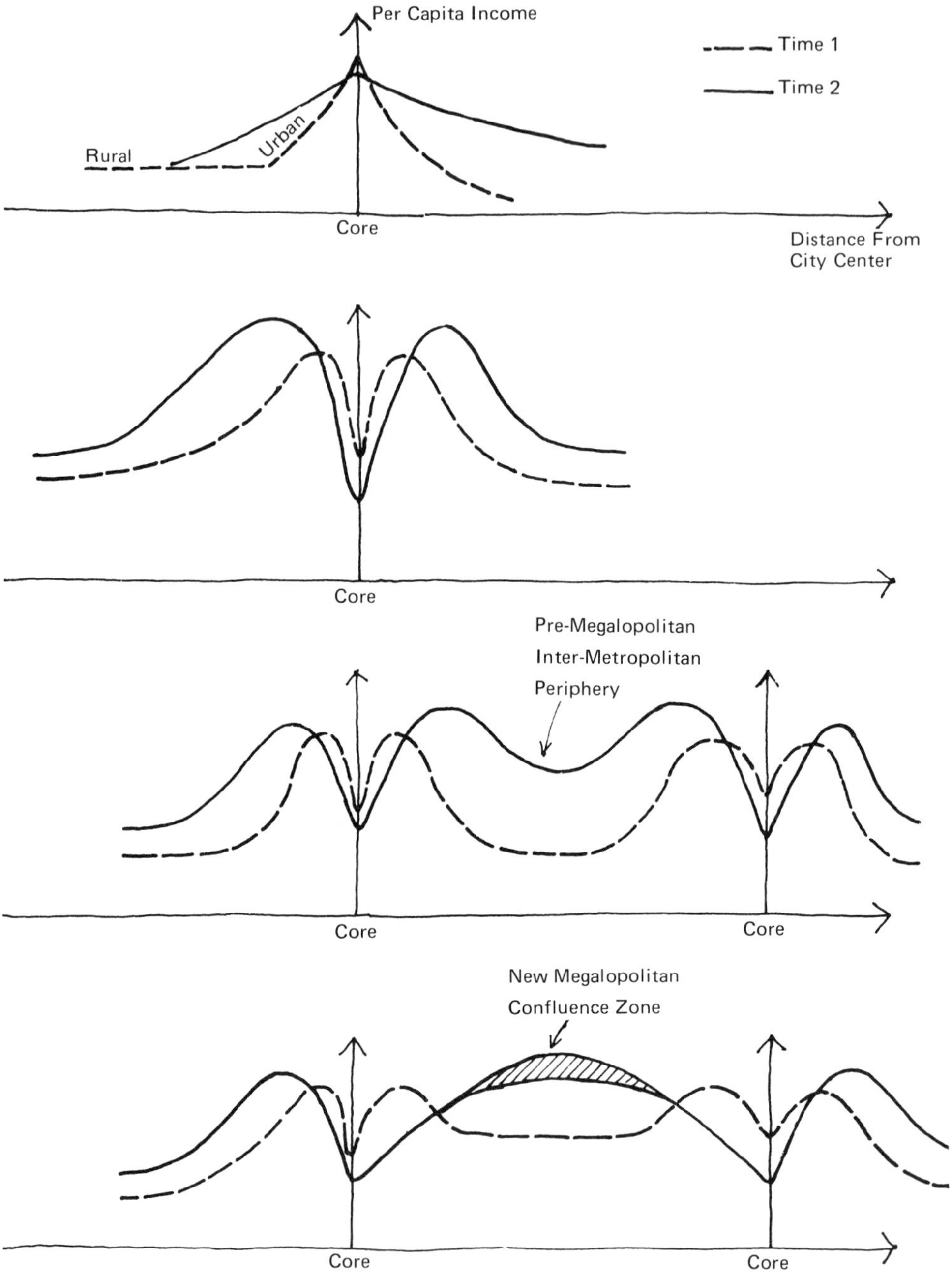

Figure 4-1. Changing Income Gradients as the Metropolitan Order is Replaced by that of the Megalopolis.

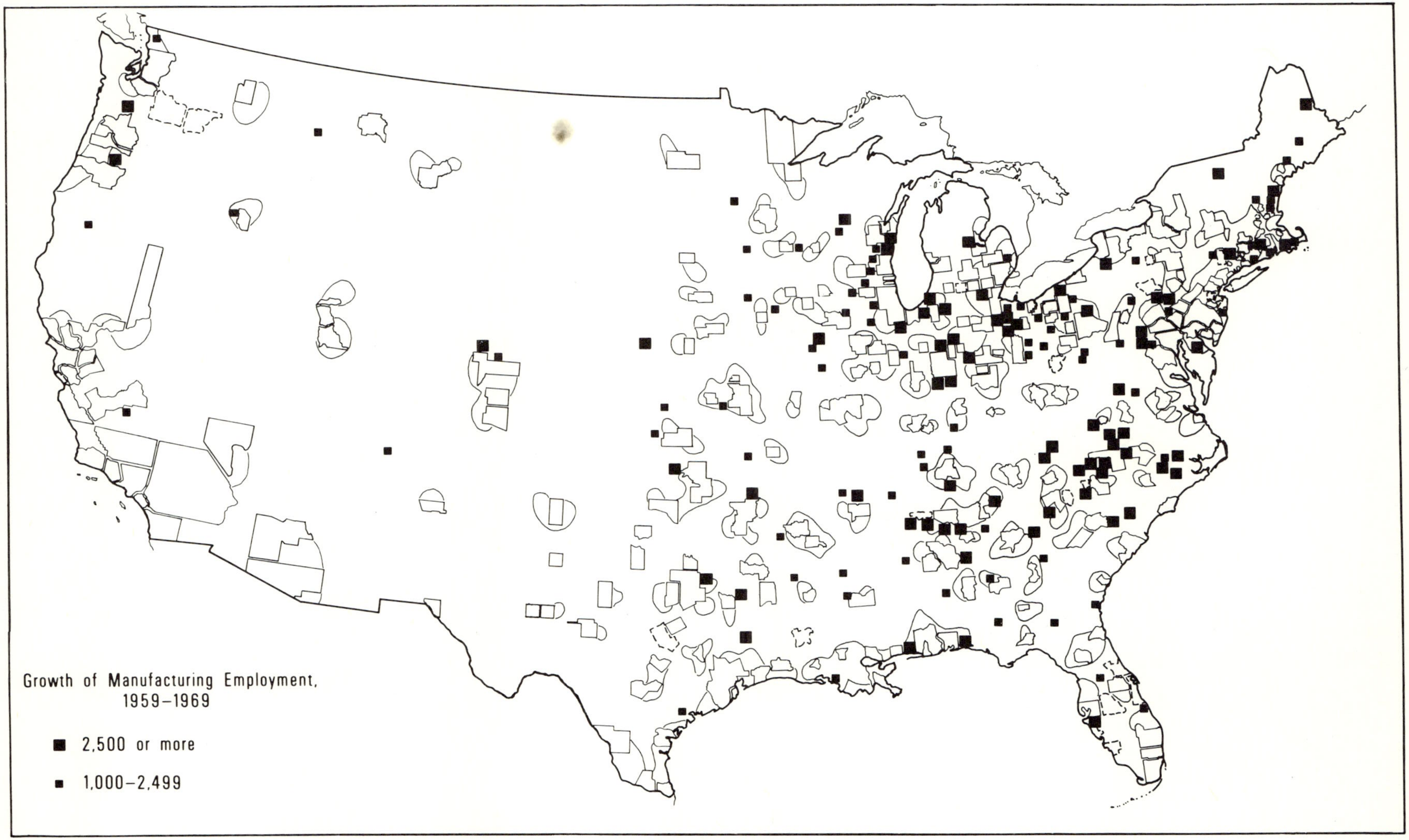

Figure 4–2. Filtering of Manufacturing Employment into the Inter-Metropolitan Periphery: (a) Employment Expansion in More Urbanized Counties.

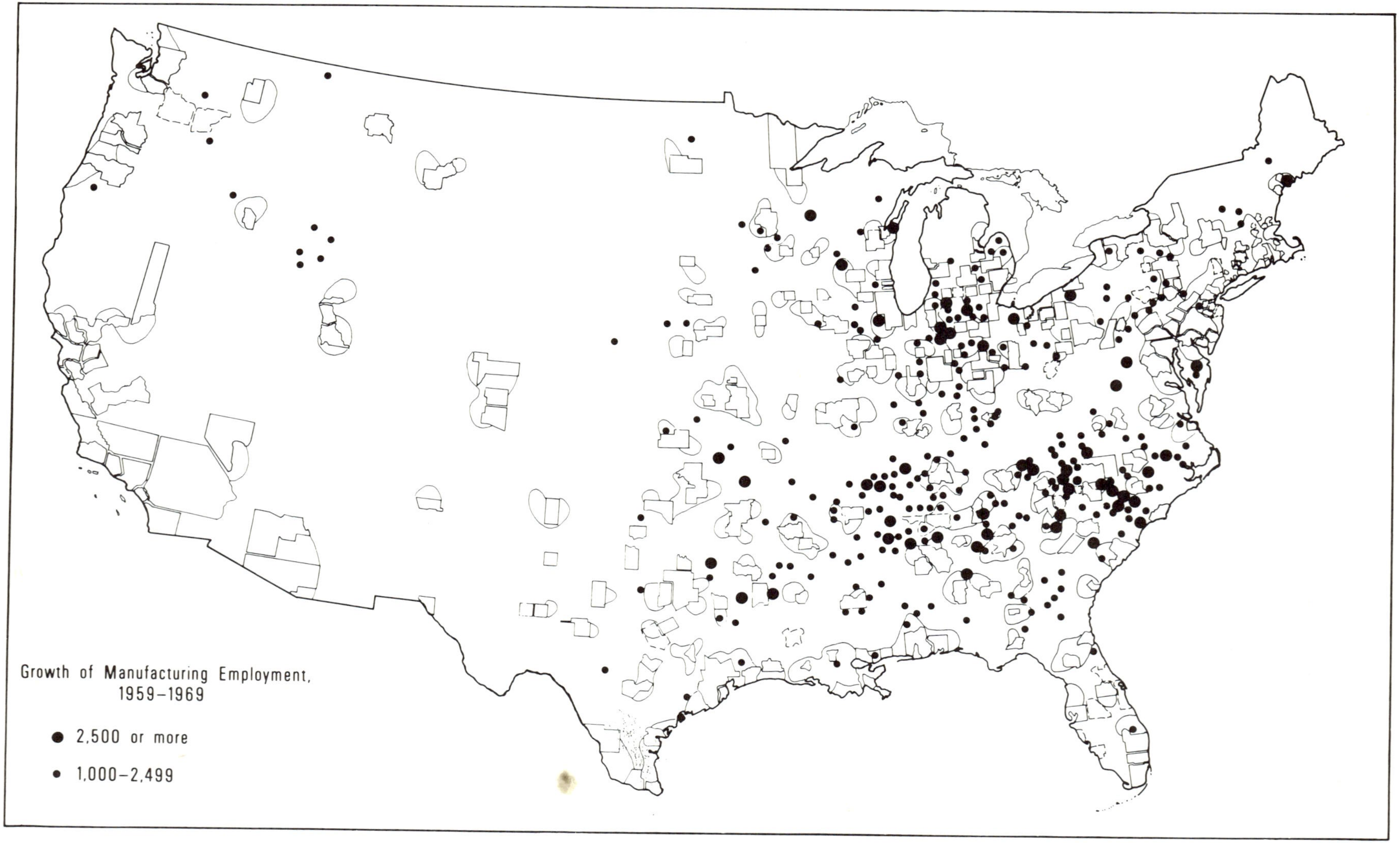

Figure 4–3. Filtering of Manufacturing Employment into the Inter-Metropolitan Periphery: (b) Employment Expansion in More Rural Counties.

more than 25,000 urban population in 1970, and second, in nonmetropolitan counties with less than 25,000 urban population in 1970. As the maps reveal, the filtering process was highly selective in spatial terms. Filtering was directed into smaller towns within and just beyond the metropolitan growth zones; and into more rural settings in, first of all, the megalopolitan confluence zones, and second, the Carolinas, Georgia, the mid-South, and Arkansas. The pattern in the latter areas is even more highly selective. The greater the rural white population, especially in more wooded areas, the greater the increase of new manufacturing employment; the greater the minority population concentrations, the greater the tendency to be by-passed by decentralizing or filtering industries. Among the principal types of manufacturing shifts are the relocation of large numbers of soft goods (primarily clothing), small electrical and electronic assembly, furniture, and other industries which utilize comparatively large numbers of low paid, unskilled employees into the Ozark-Appalachian area. These employ large numbers of previously unemployed white women and underemployed white farmers. In the Midwest, meatpacking and newer kinds of food-processing and frozen-meal preparation plants have moved from the metropolitan areas to small towns which are closer to the sources of supply. Other cases will occur to the reader. The story is a familiar one, and one that has been reported many times.

SYNTHESIS: THE REGIONAL GEOGRAPHY OF GROWTH

Figure 4–4 draws together what may be concluded from the analysis so far. Growing metropolitan areas remain the principal centers of spatial organization and have produced the most concentrated forms of growth outside the SMSAs, as their influences have extended into surrounding rural territory. Where metropolitan growth influences converge in megalopolitan confluence zones, the most dynamic growth patterns in the nation are to be found. Small towns in intervening areas in the northeast are growing rapidly as manufacturing centers. A new manufacturing belt is emerging across the mid-South, as industry decentralizes and filters from the central cities of the old manufacturing belt. Zones of superior environmental amenity are growing quite rapidly, attracting the non-job oriented population, accommodating an increasing demand for second homes, and providing new settings for the quaternary industries and their employees and for a range of new growth areas. And even beyond these settings, growth is taking place—in college towns and state capitols, where new construction and mining are to be found, where military expenditures have mushroomed, and in smaller regional centers endowed with new national accessibility by the interstate highway system.

What areas are left out of this new and wide-spread growth? They are predominantly those populated by minorities—rural blacks and Chicanos, reservation Indians, and far-backwater hillbillies—together with the ghetto areas of the central cities to which they are migrating and from which enterprise is decentralizing, for no area is left untouched by the dynamics of contemporary America. Indeed, the peripheral areas with the greatest growth in real incomes in the 1960–1970 decade were those from which the migration to the cities had been the greatest. Where, then, do these complex dynamics leave the question of the formulation of a national growth center policy and community development strategy? That is the question to which we turn in the final chapter. What do the dynamics imply for the value of the USDA, EDA, and ARC growth center schemes? The answer to this question will be found in the Appendix to this volume.

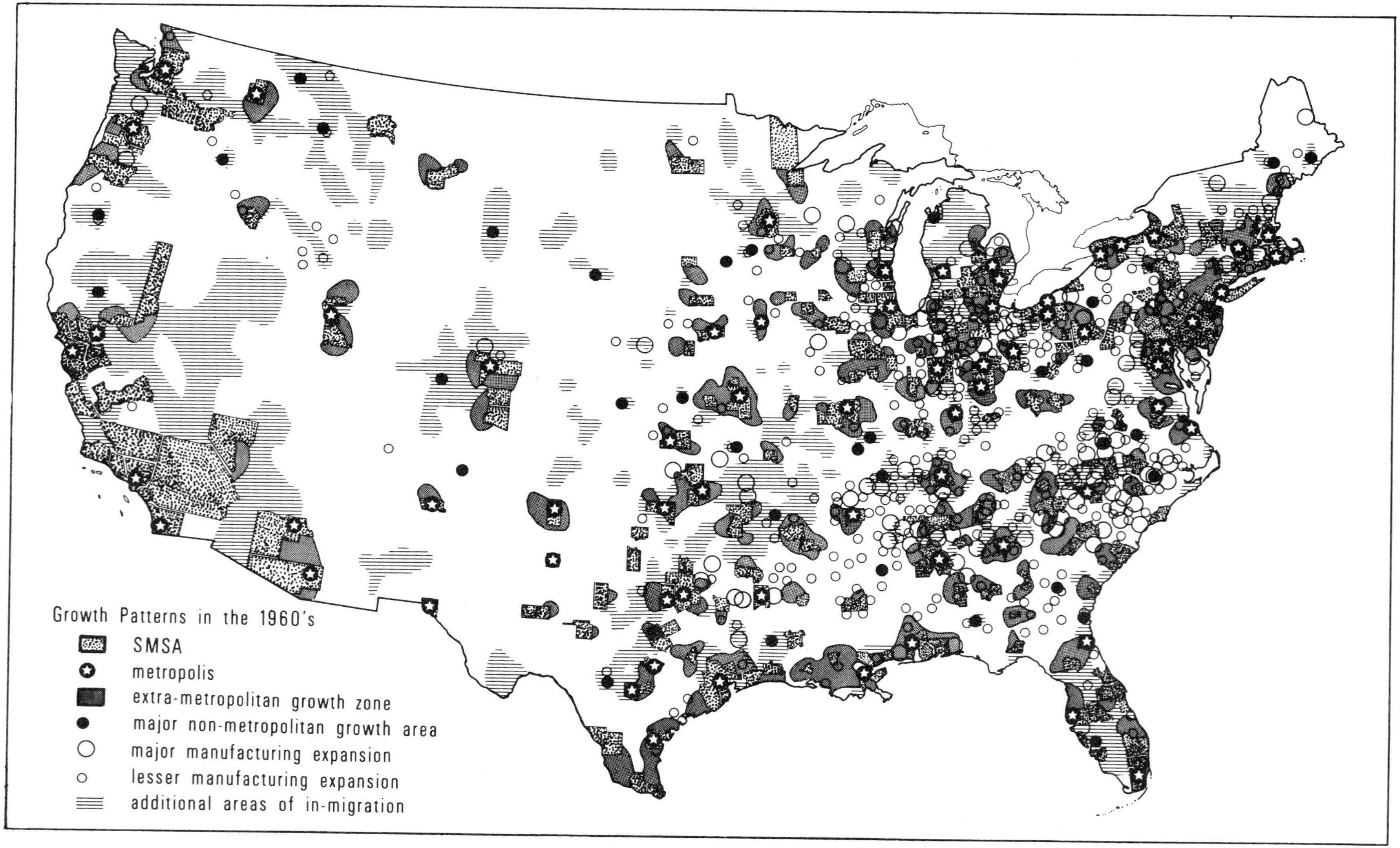

Figure 4–4. Synthesis of Growth Patterns in the 1960's.

Chapter Five

Review and an Agenda

There are various ways in which one can look at the problem of urban-regional growth. From the perspective of national productivity, such growth should enhance the nation's efficiency and international competitiveness. From the perspective of environmental quality, growth is a threat—something to be slowed to avoid possible ecological catastrophe. From an antipoverty perspective, growth is to be redirected by the use of public resources to stimulate flows of private resources in ways that will achieve greater equity by eliminating pockets of poverty. It is the latter perspective that has provided much of the impetus for growth center strategies. It may be demonstrated, however, that the objectives of such strategies may be achieved without sacrificing national efficiency and growth.

Of course, ultimately all growth can be traced back to individual location decisions by people and by business establishments. From a market viewpoint, the entrepreneur should select the most profitable location for his enterprise, and the citizen a place to live that maximizes his satisfactions. From the welfare viewpoint, the problem for society becomes one of diverting individually-optimal locational choices toward sites that generate a greater social good, if it is determined that this social good is unlikely to arise out of the collective decisions of profit-maximizing businessmen and satisfaction-maximizing citizens.

The reasons why such welfare and equity considerations may be necessary are several: negative externalities remaining unaccounted within individual cost-benefit schemes may thwart the opportunities of some to fully exercise free market choices; some, either through inability, inaccessibility, age or infirmity may simply be left out of the market scheme; yet others—blacks, Chicanos, Indians—continue to be afflicted by multiplex barriers of discrimination from full and productive participation in the mainstream of growth that has so benefited majority America.

This being admitted, a variety of basic issues remain (Cumberland, 1971): How should one intervene in the market process to produce greater welfare? Are people or places to be aided? Should programs be designed primarily to alleviate poverty, or to spur regional growth? Should the adjustment process involve relocating jobs to the poverty population or relocating people to where the jobs are located? Should aid go to the most distressed regions first, or to those with the greatest potentialities for growth? Should assistance be widely dispersed or concentrated?

The answers that appear to be indicated in this study are, first of all, that any sound national program of economic development must emphasize the location of jobs and people in the most advantageous places; without efficient national growth, lagging areas and poverty populations cannot be helped. Efforts to develop economically or culturally-poor areas may not produce long-term advantages for either the nation or for more than a small proportion of the inhabitants of a region. On the other hand, regions in decline but possessing useful social overhead facilities and good location may be candidates for significant public action if this will at least stabilize the situation.

Beyond this, what is increasingly clear is that a combination of migration and filtering-enhancement, both supported by growth-center policies, can and do work. On the one hand, provision of adequate social and educational infrastructure that systematically improves the quality of human resources makes it more feasible for workers to migrate to growing employment complexes, materially improving both their own welfare and the welfare of those remaining in the region left behind—indeed, the greatest relative growth in incomes in the decade 1960–1970 was in the areas with the highest emigration rates, and several recent studies have shown the considerable lifetime income gains to those who migrate. Enhancement of the quality and, via migration, the productivity of human resources is important not only from a welfare standpoint. As the national birth rate slows, it will become increasingly important to use an increasingly scarce human resource as wisely as possible.

On the other hand, growth centers serve as filtering enhancement devices when keyed to an accessibility policy that brings peripheries effectively within the orbit of metropolitan America, and to an infrastructure policy designed to increase the hierarchical status of the chosen growth centers. Recall the basic spatial filtering and diffusion sequence, moving down the urban hierarchy from large centers to small, and outward from accessible areas towards inaccessible areas. An accessibility policy reduces diffusion times, and a growth center infrastructure policy reduces filtering times. That the combination of the two appears to effect substantial changes in both industrial and residential choices is already clear from the Appalachian experience or from any reading of the earlier history of the railroads or the consequences of the Interstate Highway System in the last decade. When filtering and diffusion work well, they do result in rapid integration of the nation's economic space, as illustrated by figures 5-1 to 5-5. The national community development agenda should and must include a consistent nationwide approach aimed at ensuring that such national integration is promoted, by ensuring that all citizens are provided with the essential preconditions for making free choices about where to live and work, and by closing the gaps of inaccessibility and inadequate scale and quality of services, so that the range of locational choice is widened. All national opinion surveys taken in the past decade point to the yearning among Americans for alternatives to megalopolis. A growth center policy can increase the range of such alternatives and contribute to the quality of the nation's human resources without sacrificing the nation's efficiency and growth.

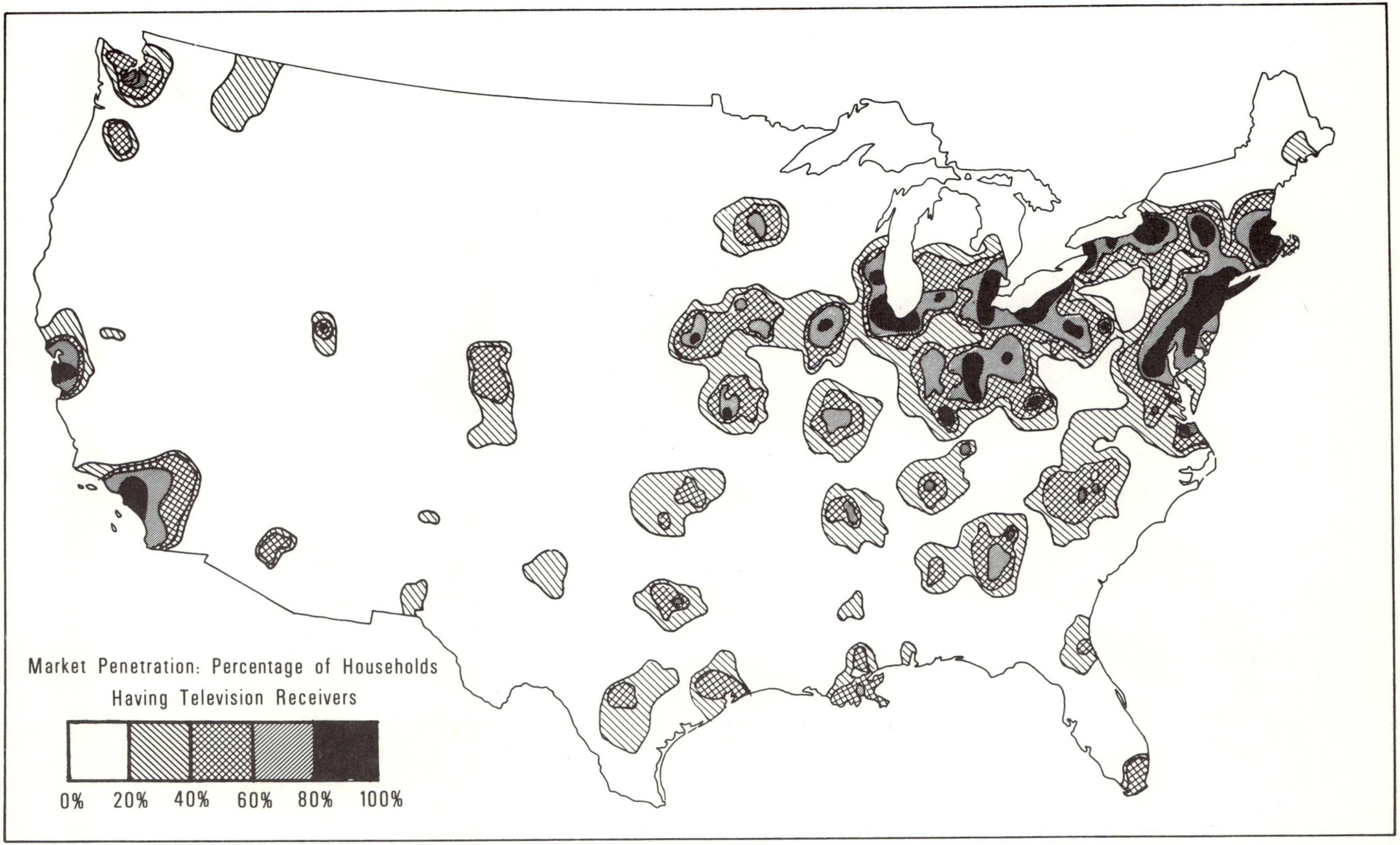

Figure 5-1. Market Penetration by Television in 1953.

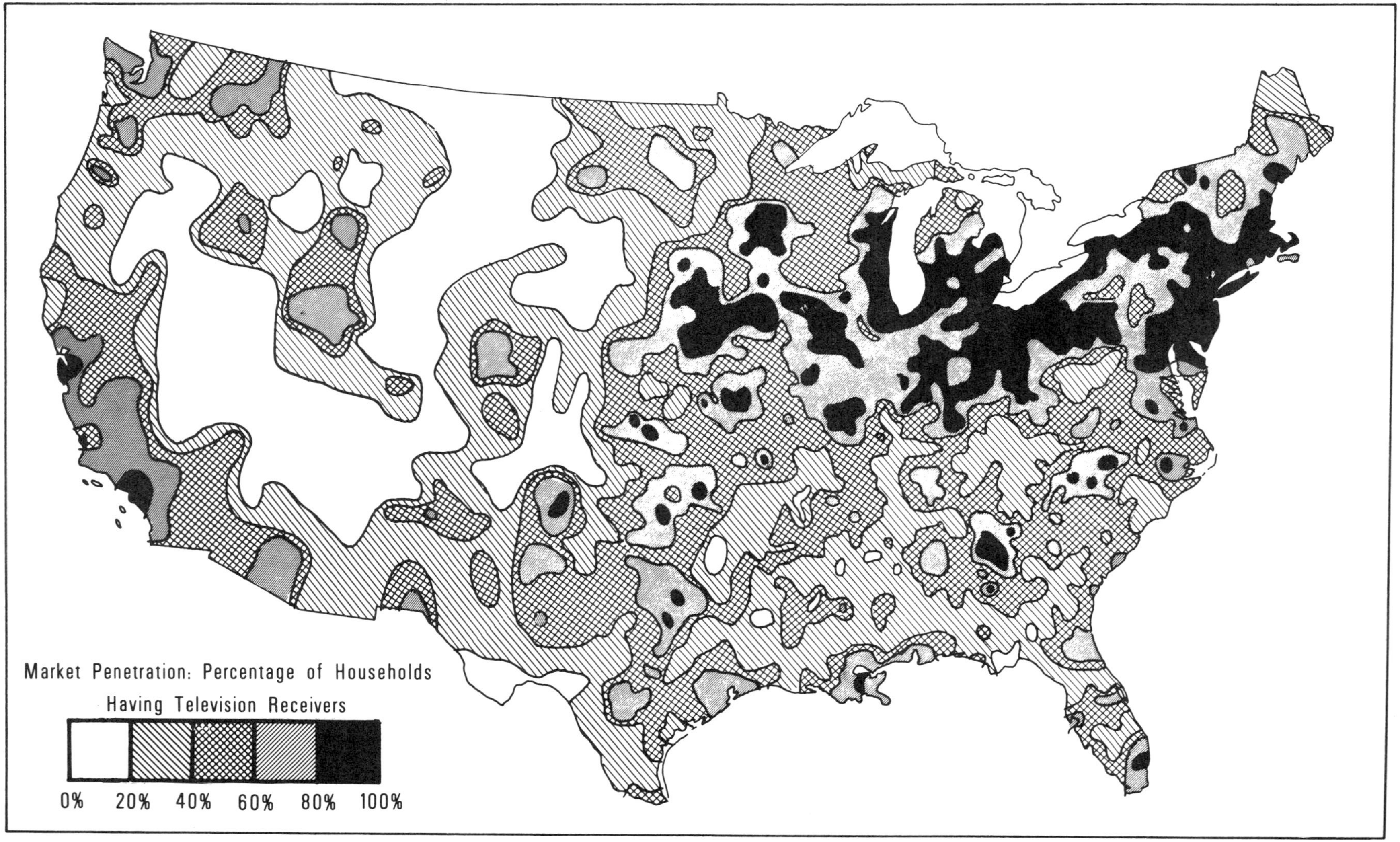

Figure 5–2. Market Penetration by Television in 1956.

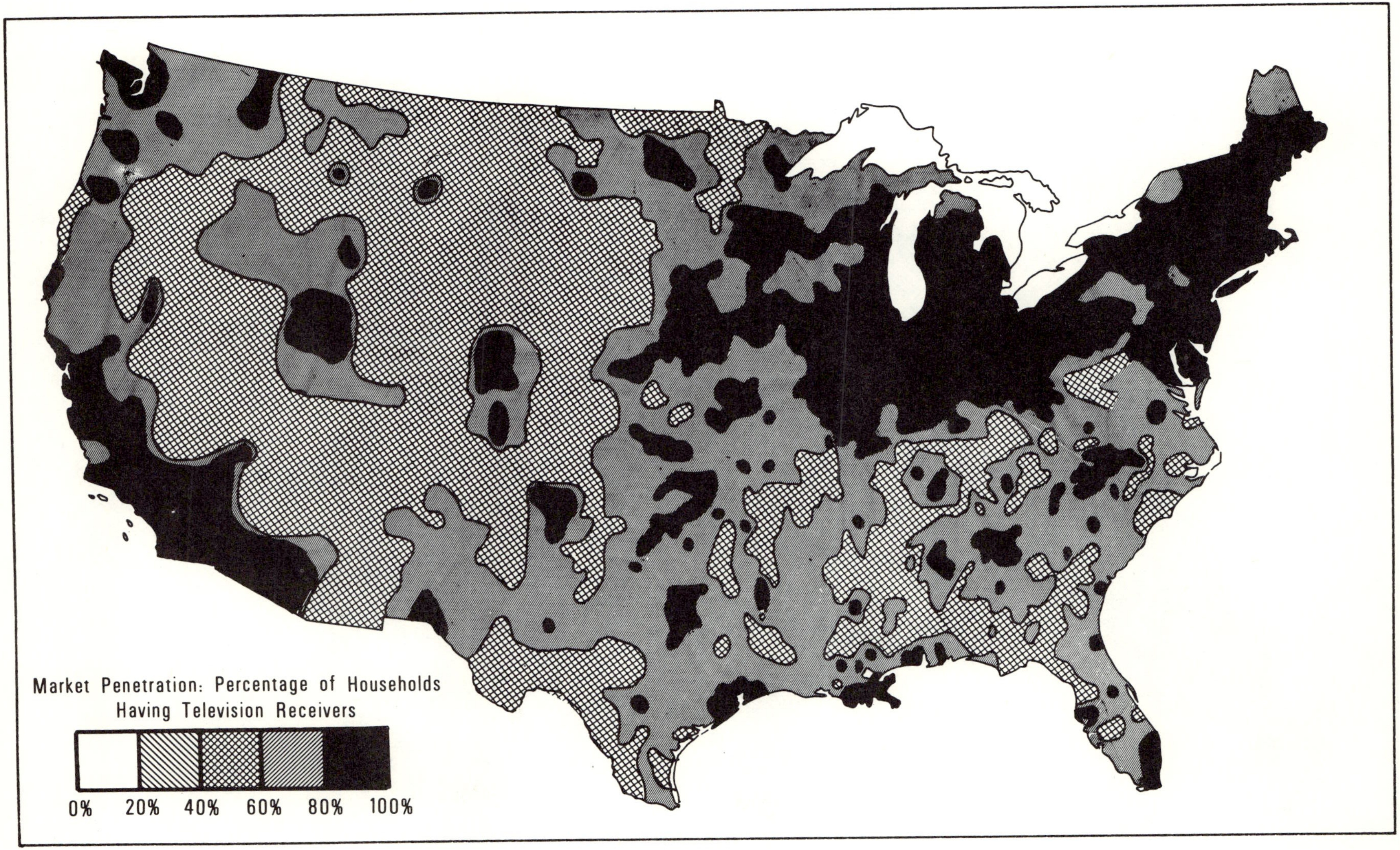

Figure 5–3. Market Penetration by Television in 1959.

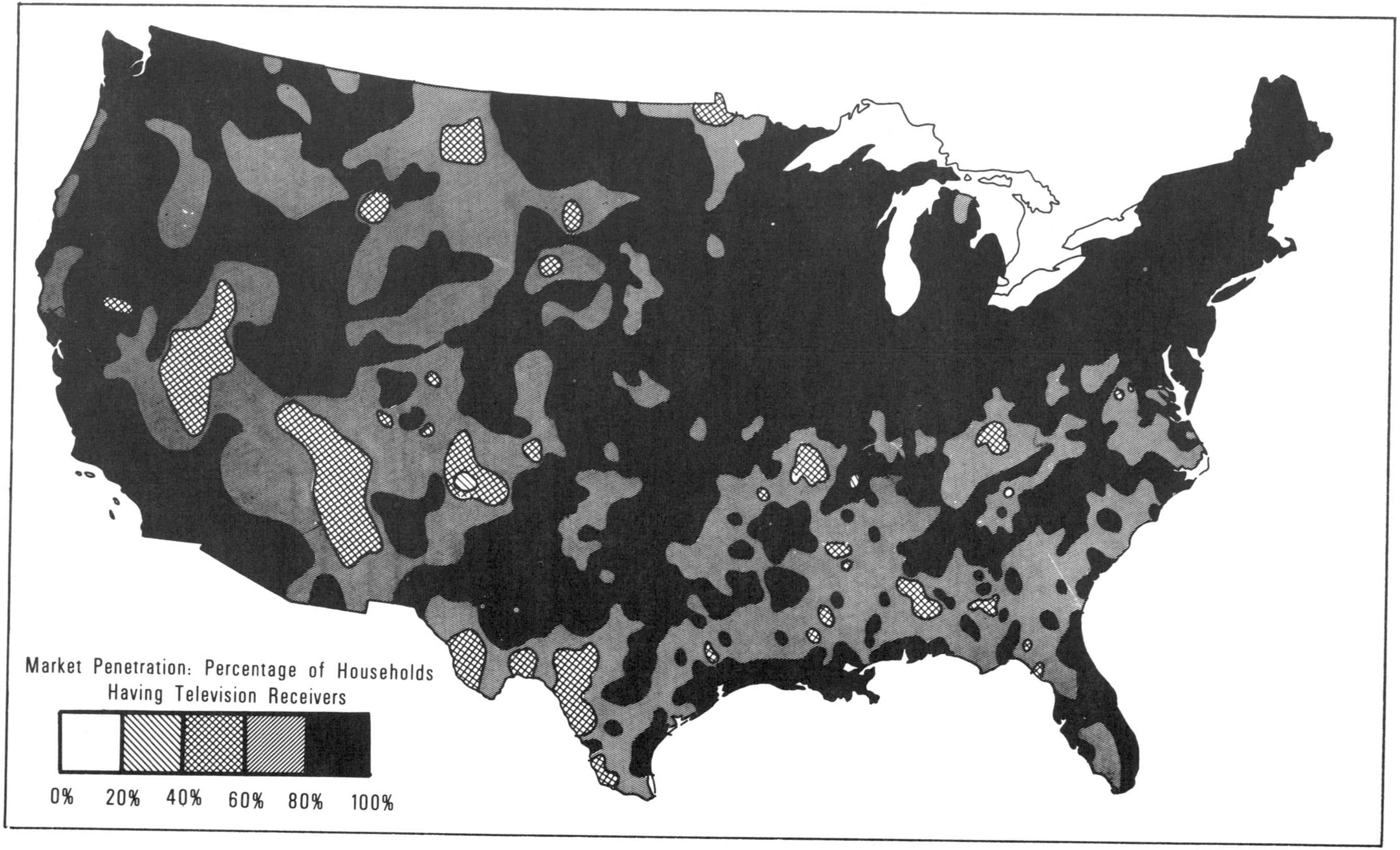

Figure 5–4. Market Penetration by Television in 1962.

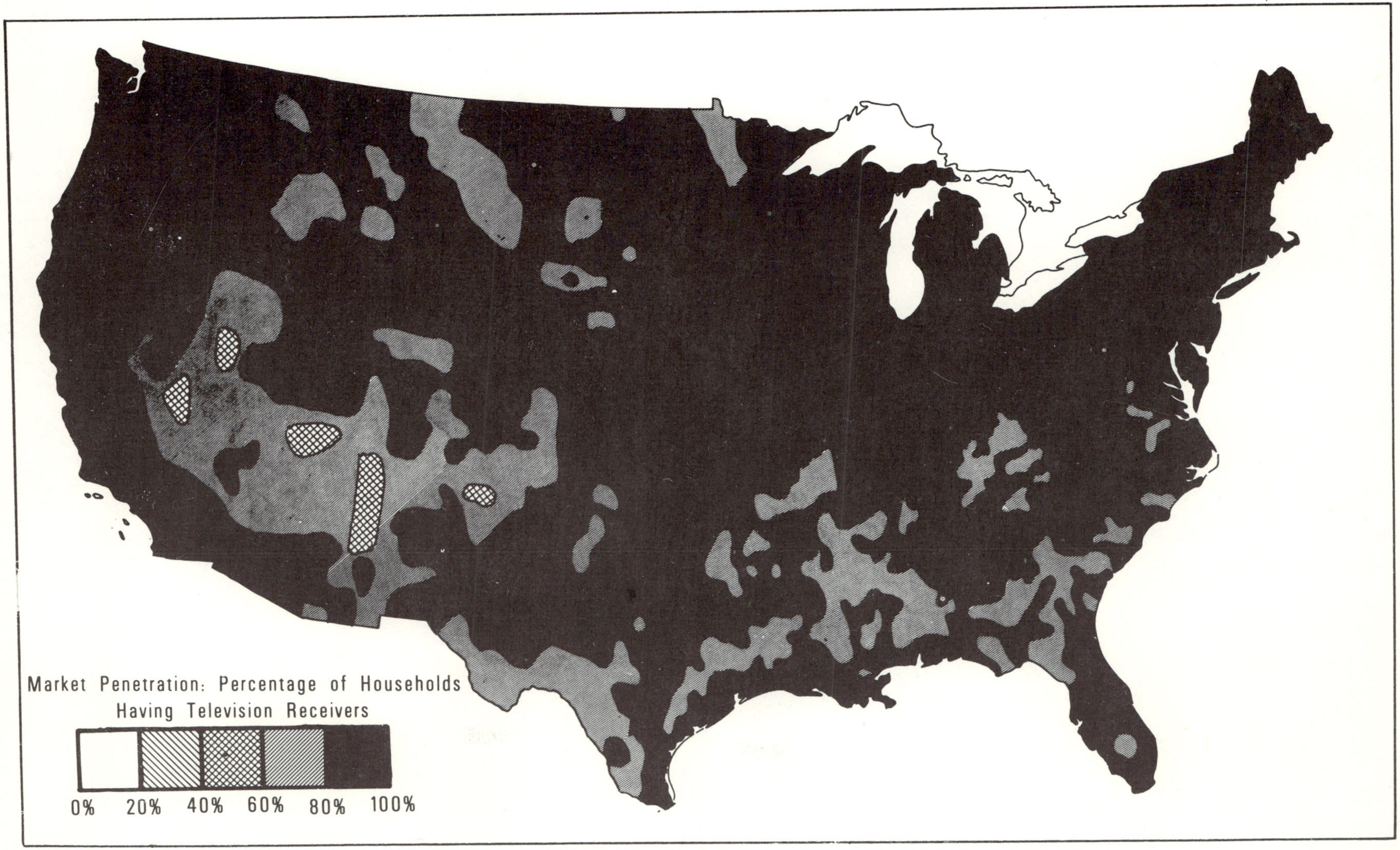

Figure 5-5. Market Penetration by Television in 1965.

Appendix

Growth Center Schemes Evaluated

Richard Lamb and Quentin Gillard

The conclusions presented so far enable a variety of growth center schemes, proposed or designated, to be evaluated from the perspective of a consistent nationwide set of materials on urban-regional growth. Of particular concern are the U.S. Department of Agriculture's presentations to the Congress, the selection of centers to receive concentrations of investment in the Appalachian program, and the Economic Development Administration's growth center designations.

THE USDA PROPOSALS

Calvin L. Beale of the Economic Research Service, U.S. Department of Agriculture (USDA), made a series of presentations before House and Senate committees in 1969 and 1971 concerning growth center strategies that might reverse current migration flows and the perceived progressive increase of metropolitan concentration of the nation's population. He argued that during the 1960s about 200 nonmetropolitan towns of 10,000 to 50,000 population grew by 15 percent or more, i.e., at a rate well above the national average, implying net immigration; and that these smaller urban places (10,000 to 50,000 population) can play a sizable role in serving as rural growth centers for nonmetropolitan territory. Beale acknowledged that if such a role is to be assigned to these small urban centers, the towns must remain sufficiently viable in the future to provide growing numbers of jobs and services for the surrounding rural population, as distinguished from "mere population" dependent on a metropolitan center, and that to adequately serve as growth centers, the jobs that are created must be of sufficient quality to maintain and raise in most cases, present rural family incomes. Further, employment should be stable over the long run and not be subject to the whims of closing or relocating a single major enterprise, the stability of which is largely unpredictable.

USDA listed their proposed set of growth centers in two sources:

1. A map depicting nonmetropolitan counties which contained towns of 10,000 to 50,000 population in 1970 that grew by 15 percent or in the 1960–1970 decade. One hundred and ninety-eight rural centers located within these counties may be identified for analysis from this report (USDA, 1971a).
2. A list prepared later and submitted to the Commission on Population Growth and the American Future for futher analysis. Ninety-four rural centers were

identified on this list, including several from the previously mentioned source, but adding some new ones. All towns on this list were reported to be at least 75 miles from a metropolitan center, a criterion utilized by USDA to identify rural regions which could be served by outlying places which lay beyond the commuting field of a metropolis (USDA, 1971b).

If these urban centers are examined in terms of: (a) population growth, 1960–1970, (b) relative location, and (c) reasons for vitality or apparent vitality it will be found the conclusions belie USDA's recommendations. USDA's method of identifying potential growth centers is totally inadequate.

For example, while all the centers exhibited population growth greater than the national average as determined by the number of inhabitants listed in the 1960 and 1970 Censuses of Population, a sizable portion of such recorded increase was due to annexation. When population change within the 1960 census area is noted (i.e., discounting the effects of annexation), the actual growth of many of the listed towns is questionable (tables A-1 and A-2). Although such figures do not give a totally accurate picture of the true population change in or near the centers in question, neither do growth figures that include annexed population. The basic problem with using the annexed population represents new growth in the 1960–1970 decade, and how much was already there in 1960 in the areas annexed in the following decade.

What may be made of this? As a first approximation we may see that when considering population increase in broad terms, decline, or growth of less than 5 percent in the 1960 census area is perhaps indicative of lack of vitality. By the same token, real population growth of at least 15 percent in the same area (not fictitious growth due to annexation of a preexisting population) might be considered to be indicative of vitality in the sense of accelerated expansion. Population increases somewhere between these extremes is then taken to be indicative of questionable vitality. In these terms, the following can be concluded:

–29 percent of the listed towns did not display vitality

–41 percent of the towns are questionable

–30 percent of the towns did display vitality

How about employment change in the towns? Two types of data are currently

Table A-1. Population Growth in 1960 Census Area, Discounting Effects of Annexation (Number of Towns)

	Towns on list submitted to Population Commission		*Towns cited in* The Economic & Social Condition of Rural America in the 1970's, *but deleted from later list.*			
	More than 75 miles from metropolitan area		*More than 75 miles from metropolitan area*		*Less than 75 miles from metropolitan area*	
	Pop. 10,000–25,000	*Pop. 25,000–50,000*	*Pop. 10,000–25,000*	*Pop. 25,000–50,000*	*Pop. 10,000–25,000*	*Pop. 25,000–50,000*
Decrease	13	5	–	–	10	5
Increase 0–4.9%	6	3	6	1	8	5
5–9.9%	20	3	6	–	13	3
10–14.9%	13	9	2	1	10	13
15%+	17	4	6	1	27	9
Total Number	69	25	14	3	68	35

Table A-2. Population Growth in 1960 Census Area, Discounting Effects of Annexation (Percentage of Towns)

Population Change 1960–1970 in 1960 Census Area	*Towns on list submitted to Population Commission*		*Towns cited in* The Economic & Social Condition of Rural America in 1970's, *but deleted from later list.*		*Total*	
	Number	*Percentage*	*Number*	*Percentage*	*Number*	*Percentage*
Decrease	18	19%	15	13%	33	15%
Increase 0–4.9%	9	10%	20	17%	29	14%
5–9.9%	24	26%	16	13%	40	19%
10–14.9%	22	23%	16	13%	40	22%
15%+	21	22%	43	36%	64	30%
Total Number	94	100%	120	100%	214	100%

Table A-3. Change in Number of Manufacturing Employees, Counties, 1963–1967

	Counties on list submitted to Population Council	*Counties cited in* The Economic & Social Condition of Rural America in the 1970's *but deleted from later list*	*Total*
Number of Counties			
Declined (Negative change)	11	10	21
Modest Gain (1 to 999 employees)	60	62	122
Sizable Gain (1,000 or more employees)	15	44	59
Percentage of Counties			
Declined (Negative change)	13%	9%	10%
Modest Gain (1 to 999 employees)	70%	53%	60%
Sizable Gain (1000 or more employees)	17%	38%	30%

available for use as measures of industrial growth: (1) Change in the number of manufacturing employees as determined from the 1963 and 1967 Censuses of Manufacturing, and (2) changes in employment patterns by industrial sectors as obtained from *Growth Patterns of Employment by County, 1950–1960* (U.S. Department of Commerce, 1965).

Table A-3 illustrates changes in manufacturing employment from 1963 to 1967. Modest gains (1 to 999 employees) were most characteristic of the centers. Larger gains (1,000 or more employees) occurred in only 17 percent of the places in the list submitted to the Population Commission, while a higher percentage, 38 percent, showed such gains among the centers deleted from the previously prepared list (i.e., those *within* 75 miles of a metropolis, and the part of its labor market). Also about 10 percent of the cities and towns showed declines in manufacturing employees.

Although these figures indicate that the smaller places did not show any lack of vitality in terms of manufacturing growth, neither did they show many very dramatic increases. However, it is reasonable to expect some degree of continuity between trends which took place in the decade 1950–1960 and the decade 1960–1970. There are available for the 1950–1960 period, data showing changes within industrial sectors of each county in the United States, and attributing such changes to either: (a) national employment growth, (b) the specific growth rates of the industries located in the counties, or (c) employment growth particular to a specific county discounting changes attributable to the above two factors. Briefly, this type of analysis yields two significant figures after discounting the effects of national employment growth:

1. Employment change attributed to *Industrial Mix.* If the change is positive, the implication is that the county is characterized by growth industries. If the change in industrial mix is negative, the county is characterized by lagging industries showing relative national declines in number of employees, and further relative declines in such industries might be anticipated.
2. Employment change attributed to *Regional Share.* A positive change implies that the county in question fared better than average in retaining or increasing employment in its particular industrial sectors, whether or not these sectors were growing or lagging as indicated by industrial mix. A negative change indicates the opposite. Such changes can be interpreted as competitive regional shifts.

Table A-4 illustrates employment changes during the 1950–1960 decade in the selected counties, noting positive or negative changes in both industrial mix and regional shares. These results show that *most of the counties on the USDA list possessed relatively slow growing or declining industries.* A majority of the counties, however, showed a positive change attributed to regional shares indicating their better than average success in retaining employees in industrial sectors which displayed relative national decline. Their industrial growth, then, is largely based upon the downward filtering of "second hand" industries.

How did relative location affect growth? Of the total 214 urban centers contained in the two USDA lists, 111 are at least 75 miles from a metropolitan area, a criterion deemed necessary by USDA to support the assertion that the smaller urban places can serve as rural growth centers independent of influences directly attributable to nearness to a large metropolitan center. The 94 centers identified on the list submitted to the Population Commission plus an additional 17 centers cited on the previous list lay beyond the 75 mile limit.

To support the notion that these outlying urban places are capable of sustained growth, the location of several of them on the Interstate Highway System was mentioned as a positive factor by Beale. The actual number of such places located on interstate highways is shown on table A-5, which indicates that about 37 percent of the centers located more than 75 miles from the nearest metropolitan area have such favorable locations, while the percentage of centers located on interstate highways within the 75 miles criterion is greater, about 54 percent. Only about one-third of the smaller places (10,000 to 25,000 population) appearing on USDA's list submitted to the Population Commission have such favorable locations.

A variety of source materials can be utilized to identify reasons for growth of the centers on the USDA list during the 1960–1970 decade. The results of this analysis are summarized in tables A-6 and A-7.

About 16 percent of all centers almost certainly did not display significant population growth at all. Rather, their apparent "growth" was attributable to annexation.

A large percentage of centers displayed population growth by virtue of substantial increases in university or college enrollment. Thus, net in-migration in these cases was made up in large part of college students, or temporary short-term residents, rather than persons

Table A-4. Change in Industrial Composition, Counties, 1950-1960

Number of Counties

		Change in Regional Share 1950-1960					Change in Regional Share 1950-1960		
		+	-				+	-	
Change in Industrial Mix 1950-60	+	7	4	11	Change in Industrial Mix 1950-60	+	18	7	25
	-	45	36	81		-	60	22	82
		52	40				78	29	

Percentage of Counties

		Change in Regional Share 1950-1960					Change in Regional Share 1950-1960		
		+	-				+	-	
Change in Industrial Mix 1950-60	+	8%	4%	12%	Change in Industrial Mix 1950-60	+	17%	6%	23%
	-	49%	39%	88%		-	56%	21%	77%
		57%	43%				73%	27%	

Table A-5. Number of Towns Located on the Interstate Highway System

	Towns on list submitted to the Population Commission		*Towns cited in* The Economic & Social Condition of Rural America in the 1970's, *but deleted from later list.*			
	More than 75 miles from Metropolitan Area		*More than 75 miles from Metropolitan Area*		*Less than 75 miles from Metropolitan Area*	
	Pop. 10,000–25,000	*Pop. 25,000–50,000*	*Pop. 10,000–25,000*	*Pop. 25,000–50,000*	*Pop. 10,000–25,000*	*Pop. 25,000–50,000*
Number of towns located on Interstate Highway System	22	13	3	3	36	20
Total number of towns in category	69	25	14	3	68	35
Percent of towns located on Interstate Highway System	32%	52%	21%	100%	53%	57%

employed full time in the labor force. About 40 percent of the centers cited on the list submitted to the Population Commission were of this type. A variety of military installations and their neighboring towns also experienced rapid growth. In addition, missile proving grounds and National Aeronautical and Space Administration facilities such as those at Cape Kennedy fostered growth. Of the centers on the lists under analysis, about 11 percent displayed growth clearly attributable to such influences, located for the most part in the south and west.

About 8 percent of the towns within 75 miles of a metropolitan center contained a significant commuting population in 1960, i.e., from 5 to 50 percent of the resident population commuting to a nearby metropolis. Such places cannot be considered independent "self-sustaining" rural growth centers because they are being integrated with the metropolitan complex. As was seen in figure 3–24, many more centers experienced such growth in the 1960–1970 decade.

About 5 percent of the centers contained a high percentage (20% or more) of elderly persons in 1970. Such high percentages are indicative of retirement communities. Immigration to these communities in large part consisted of non-job oriented persons, not employed full time in the labor force, and the population increases are consequently not indicative of potential for sustained employment growth of the type thought necessary by USDA, except insofar as the elderly bring in transfer payments supporting the service sector.

Another source of apparent growth was expansion of an institutionalized population. Five centers were state capitols, growing due to increases in governmental employees. Next, about 10 percent of the centers exhibited significant increases in the number of manufacturing employees employed within their municipal boundaries. An additional 10 percent of the respective counties containing the towns displayed similar increases, but outside the city limits. Many of these places are located in the south, although all regions contain some centers of this type.

Table A-6. Reasons for Vitality or Apparent Vitality

	Towns on List submitted to the Population Commission		*Towns listed in* The Economic and Social Condition of Rural America in the 1970's, *but deleted from later list.*			
	More than 75 miles from a Metropolitan Area		*More than 75 miles from a Metropolitan Area*		*Less than 75 miles from a Metropolitan Area*	
Number of Towns with Growth attributed to:	*Pop. 10,000–25,000*	*Pop. 25,000–50,000*	*Pop. 10,000–25,000*	*Pop. 25,000–50,000*	*Pop. 10,000–25,000*	*Pop. 25,000–50,000*
Annexation[1]	10	6	3	1	12	2
Significant Increases in University or College Enrollment[2]	28	10	4	1	22	18
Military or Government installations[3]	5	3	1	–	8	6
Commuting to a Metropolitan Area[4]	–	–	–	–	10	–
High Percentage of Elderly[6]	4	1	1	–	2	3
State Capitol	–	2	–	–	2	1
Manufacturing Growth[7] (in town or city)	4	3	2	–	6	6
Manufacturing Growth[7] (in county)	9	2	–	–	10	1
Unexplained by Available Data	15	6	3	1	8	3
Total Number of Towns in Category[8]	69	25	14	3	68	35

1. Defined as towns in which population growth in the 1960 census area did not exceed 5 percent *and* which are located in counties that did not exceed the national rate of growth at 13 percent.

2. Defined as an increase of at least 1,000 in enrollment between the fall of 1960 and the fall of 1968. Most increases, however, were significantly greater than this figure.

3. Includes army bases, marine bases, air force bases, missile proving grounds, National Aeronautical and Space Administration installations, etc.

4. Five to fifty percent of the labor force commuting to a metropolitan center in 1960.

5. More than 20 percent of the 1970 population aged 65 or older. Indicative of planned unit developments, or housing for the elderly.

6. Significant numbers of institutionalized persons in 1970 other than university, college or military.

7. Increase of at least 500 employees between 1963 and 1967 as determined from U.S. Census of Manufacturing.

8. Figures do not add to column totals due to multiple factors involved in some cases.

The results indicate that affirmative growth center proposals should be developed with real care. Although at least 200 nonmetropolitan towns of sizes 10,000–50,000 gained population in the 1960–1970 decade at a rate exceeding the national average, according to numbers of inhabitants recorded in the 1970 census, significant portions of such increases were due to annexation. In only about 38 percent of the centers did population increase exceed the national average when considering changes only in the 1960 census area. It can be

Table A-7. Reasons for Vitality or Apparent Vitality (Percentage of Towns)

Percentage of Towns with Growth Attributed to:	*Towns on List Submitted to the Population Commission*	*Towns cited in* The Economic & Social Condition of Rural America in the 1970's, *but deleted from later list.*	*Total*
Annexation	17.0%	15.0%	15.9%
Significant increases in University or College Enrollment	40.4%	37.5%	38.8%
Military or Government installation	8.5%	10.8%	10.7%
Commuting to a Metropolitan Area	–	8.3%	4.7%
High Percentage of Elderly	5.3%	5.0%	5.1%
State Capitol	2.1%	2.5%	1.4%
Manufacturing Growth (in town or city)	7.4%	11.7%	9.8%
Manufacturing Growth (in county)	11.7%	9.2%	10.3%
Unexplained by Available data	22.3%	12.5%	16.8%

estimated that no more than 84 percent of the towns exhibited true population growth after discounting the effects of annexation.

In about 56 percent of the towns, in-migration consisted of large portions of either: (1) university or college students, (2) military personnel, (3) an elderly population, or (4) other institutionalized population, implying that population increase in such cases is not commensurate with growth of the labor force.

If we were to take the Beale proposals seriously, the result would be that, of the total of 214 small urban places he cited in support of his proposals, most must be eliminated as likely "natural" growth centers when applying his criteria that only centers at least 75 miles from a metropolitan center should be considered; that a population increase of at least 13 percent in the 1960 census area and a corresponding 13 percent increase in the county where the town is located is needed (to insure true population growth discounting the effects of annexation); that centers in which the change in college or university enrollment exceeds one-half of the total recorded population increase in the 1960 census area are excluded; that centers in which the elderly population in 1970 exceeds 20 percent of the total 1970 population are excluded; and that centers which owe their growth to a neighboring military or government installation are excluded. Using the above criteria, only seven small urban centers remain as real "growth centers". These are: Enterprize, Alabama; Spenard, Alaska; Rogers City, Arkansas; Atascadero, California; Tifton, Georgia; Tupelo, Mississippi; Bismark, North Dakota. Two are located on the Interstate Highway System.

With modification of the criteria to include centers with at least a 5 percent population increase in the 1960 census area of the city, but retaining the 13 percent figure for growth in the county where the city is located, together with all the other criteria listed above, an additional 31 centers can be identified. These are: Dothan, Alabama; Calexico, California; Hanford, California; Redding, California; Ocala, Florida; Lewiston, Idaho; Pocatello, Idaho; Spencer, Iowa; Garden City, Kansas; New Ulm, Minnesota; Willmar,

Minnesota; Jefferson City, Missouri; Grand Island, Nebraska; Lenoir, North Carolina; Bend, Oregon; Coos Bay, Oregon; Grants Pass, Oregon; Medford, Oregon; Humboldt, Tennessee; McMinnville, Tennessee; Tullahoma, Tennessee; Union City, Tennessee; Eagle Pass, Texas; Longview, Texas; Lufkin, Texas; Port Lavaca, Texas; Sulphur Springs, Texas; Victoria, Texas; Kelso, Washington; Longview, Washington; Port Angeles, Washington. Thirteen are located on the Interstate Highway System. Twenty-five are located in either the south or west.

EDA'S DESIGNATED GROWTH CENTERS

In his 1965 message on Area and Regional Economic Development, President Johnson outlined a new regional development program which was to work in the framework of economic development districts, regional action planning commissions, and economic development centers. The latter were defined as "places where resources can be most swiftly and effectively used to create more jobs and higher income for the people of the surrounding area", places which would benefit from the cumulative advantages flowing from size itself, and able to spread these effects to surrounding areas, and stem in-migration from the nation's depressed areas.

The program was enacted in the Public Works and Economic Development Act of 1965. This act resulted in the creation of the Economic Development Administration and linked the growth center strategy to the Economic Development District Program in which counties were urged to pool their resources and talents to achieve common aims. Each district was to contain two or more redevelopment areas and to be of sufficient size and resources to foster development on a multi-county basis. The growth centers: (a) had to be identified and included in an approved district overall economic development program (OEDP) and recommended for such by the states affected; (b) had to be geographically and economically so related to the district that their economic growth might reasonably be expected to contribute significantly to the alleviation of distress in the redevelopment areas of the district, and (c) could not exceed 250,000 population.

In January 1967, shortly before the first growth center was designated, EDA issued an Order on "Qualification and Delineation of Economic Development Centers" which reiterated the legislative requirements, especially that the centers contribute to the alleviation of economic distress. Primary emphasis was placed on directly improving the employment opportunities of unemployed or underemployed residents of redevelopment areas and/or making public services more readily available to residents of such areas. Further, each center should have a sizable local market, a relatively large well-trained labor force, the prospect of developing a diversified economy and (normally) a population of at least 25,000.

By the end of 1971, EDA had designated over 200 economic development or redevelopment centers. The list is provided in table A-8. Data are organized by OBE area to permit comparisons with the materials in Volume II. To relate to the materials in these appendixes, each center is classified according to its hierarchical status, and with respect to its growth category, viz:

A (i) Continuing center of spatial organization

A (ii) Subsidiary peak on a major gradient of urban influence
  (a) within the labor market of the OBE center
  (b) beyond that labor market

Table A-8. Growth Categories of Designated EDA Growth Center in Each OBE Area

OBE Area	Name of Center	Level in Hierarchy	EDA District	If actual growth center in the 1960s category under which EDA center is classified
001	Bangor	WR-CS	Pride, Maine	A (i)
002				
003	Berlin (Redevelopment Center)	CS	New Hampshire - Vermont	–
	St. Johnsbury - Lyndon	CS	New Hampshire - Vermont	C (ii)
	St. Albans (Redevelopment)	CS	New Hampshire - Vermont	–
	Newport	CS	New Hampshire - Vermont	–
004	New Bedford (Redevelopment)	WR	Southeastern, Mass.	–
	Fall River	WR	Southeastern, Mass	–
	Taunton	WR	Southeastern, Mass.	–
005	–			
006	–			
007	Rome - Utica	WR-WR	Mohawk Valley, N.Y.	A (i)
	Watertown (Redevelopment)	WR	Black River - St. Lawrence, N.Y.	C (i), (a)
	Ogdensburg (Redevelopment)	CS	Black River - St. Lawrence, N.Y.	–
	Massena (Redevelopment)	CS	Black River - St. Lawrence, N.Y.	–
008	–			
009	–			
010	–			
011	–			
012	–			
013	–			
014	–			
015	–			
016	Huntingdon	CS	Turnpike, Pa.	C (i), b
	Bedford (Redevelopment)	PS	Turnpike, Pa.	–
017	Dover	CS	Delmarva, Del.	B (ii)
	Salisbury	CS	Delmarva, Del.	A (ii), b
018	–			

019	Martinsburg - Charles Town	CS-PS	Upper Potomac, W. Va.	–
	Moorefield (Redevelopment)	–	Upper Potomac, W. Va.	–
020	–			
021	–			
022	–			
023	Fayetteville	WR	Southeastern, N.C.	A (i)
	Greeneville (Redevelopment)	CS	Mid East, N.C.	C (ii), b
	Goldsboro	CS	Neuce River, N.C.	B (i)
	Washington	CS	Mid East, N.C.	C (i), b
	Williamstown	CS	Mid East, N.C.	–
024	Wilmington	WR	Southeastern, N.C.	A (i)
	Kinston	CS	Neuce River, N.C.	–
	New Bern	CS	Neuce River, N.C.	–
025	–			
026	Laurinburg	CS	Southeastern, N.C.	B (ii)
027	–			
028	Greenwood	CS	Upper Savannah, N.C.	A (ii), a; B (i)
029	Orangeburg (Redevelopment)	CS	Lower Savannah, N.C.	–
030	Florence-Darlington	CS-CS	Pee Dee, S.C.	A (i); C (ii), a
	Conway - Myrtle Beach - North Myrtle Beach	CS-CS	Waccamaw, S.C.	–
031	–			
032	Augusta	WR	Central Savannah River, Ga.	A (i)
	Aiken - North Augusta	CS-CS	Lower Savannah, S.C.	–
	Swainsboro	CS	Central Savannah River, Ga.	–
033	Hinesville	PS	Coastal Area, Ga.	B (i)
034	Brunswick	CS	Coastal Area, Ga.	B (i)
	Waycross	CS	Slash Pine, Ga.	A (ii), (a)
035	–			
036	–			
037	–			

(continued)

Table A-8. (continued)

OBE Area	Name of Center	Level in Hierarchy	EDA District	If actual growth center in the 1960s category under which EDA center is classified
038	Panama City	WR	Northwest, Fla.	A (ii), (b); B (ii)
	Marianna	CS	Northwest, Fla.	–
039	–			
040	Montgomery	WR	South Central, Ala.	A (i)
	Dothan	WR	Southeast, Ala.	–
	Troy (Redevelopment)	CS	South Central, Ala.	B (i)
	Greenville (Redevelopment)	CS	South Central, Ala.	–
041	Albany	WR	Southwest, Ga.	A (i)
	Valdosta	WR	Coastal Plain, Ga.	A (i), A (ii), (b); B (ii)
	Tifton	CS	Coastal Plain, Ga.	A (ii), (a); B (i); C (ii), (a)
	Bainbridge	CS	Southwest, Ga.	–
042	Dublin - East Dublin	CS	Heart of Georgia, Ga.	–
	Milledgeville	CS	Oconee, Ga.	A (ii), (a)
043	Columbus	WR	Lower Chattahoochee Valley, Ga.	A (i)
	La Grange	CS	Chattahoochee - Flint, Ga.	–
	Americus	CS	Middle Flint, Ga.	A (ii), (a)
044	Athens	CS	Northeast, Ga.	B (i)
	Gainsville	CS	Georgia Mountains, Ga.	–
	Carrollton	CS	Chattahoochee - Flint, Ga.	–
	Toccoa	CS	Georgia Mountains, Ga.	–
045	–			
046	Jonesboro	CS	East Arkansas, Ark.	A (ii), (b); B (ii); C (ii), (b)
	Clarksdale (Redevelopment)	CS	North Delta, Miss.	C (ii), (a)
	Forrest City (Redevelopment)	CS	East Arkansas, Ark.	–
	Batesville (Redevelopment)	PS	North Delta, Miss.	–
047	–			
048	Chattanooga	WR	Southeast, Tenn.	A (i)
	Cleveland - Athens	CS-CS	Southeast, Tenn.	C (i), (a)
049	Bowling Green	CS	Barren River, Ky.	A (i); A (ii), (b); B (ii)
	Clarksville	CS	Mid Cumberland, Tenn.	–

	Murfreesboro (Redevelopment)	CS	Mid Cumberland, Tenn.	–
	Hopkinsville	CS	Pennyrill, Ky.	–
	Cookeville	CS	Upper Cumberland, Tenn.	A (ii), (b); B (ii)
	Glasgow	CS	Barren River, Ky.	–
	McMinnville	CS	Upper Cumberland, Tenn.	B (i)
050	Knoxville	WR	East Tennessee, Tenn.	A (i)
	Oak Ridge	CS	East Tennessee, Tenn.	–
	Morristown	CS	East Tennessee, Tenn.	A (ii), (a); B (i)
	Alcoa - Maryville	CS-CS	East Tennessee, Tenn.	–
	Middlesborough (Redevelopment)	CS	Cumberland Valley, Ky.	–
	Crossville	PS	Upper Cumberland, Tenn.	–
	London - North Corbin	PS	Cumberland Valley, Ky.	B (ii); C (ii), (b)
051	Johnson City	CS	First Tennessee - Virginia, Tenn.	A (i); B (i)
	Kingsport	CS	First Tennessee - Virginia, Tenn.	A (i)
	Bristol	CS	First Tennessee - Virginia, Tenn.	A (i)
	Bluefield - Princeton (Redevelopment)	CS-CS	Southern West Virginia, W. Va.	A (i)
	Bristol (Va.)	CS	First Tennessee - Virginia, Tenn.	–
	Richlands (Redevelopment)	PS	Cumberland Plateau, Va.	–
	Lebanon (Redevelopment)	FCC	Cumberland Plateau, Va.	–
052	Ashland	WR	Fiveco, Ky.	A (i)
	Portsmouth	WR	Ohio Valley, Ohio	–
	Beckley (Redevelopment)	CS	Southern West Virginia, W. Va.	–
	Williamson (Redevelopment)	CS	Southern West Virginia, W. Va.	–
	Prestonburg - Paintsville (Redevelopment)	PS-PS	Big Sandy, Ky.	–
	Pikeville (Redevelopment)	PS	Big Sandy, Ky.	–
053	Somerset	CS	Lake Cumberland, Ky.	–
	Campbellsville	CS	Lake Cumberland, Ky.	A (ii), (b); B (ii)
	Hazard (Redevelopment)	CS	Kentucky River, Ky.	A (ii), (b); C (i), (b)
054	Elizabethtown - Radcliffe - Vine Grove Corridor	CS-PS-FCC	Lincoln Trail, Ky.	–
055	Madisonville	CS	Pennyrill, Ky.	A (ii), (a)
	Harrisburg (Redevelopment)	CS	Southeastern, Ill.	–
056	Terre Haute	WR	West Central, Ind.	A (i)
057	–			
058	–			

(continued)

Table A-8. (continued)

OBE Area	Name of Center	Level in Hierarchy	EDA District	If actual growth center in the 1960s category under which EDA center is classified
059	–			
060	–			
061	–			
062	–			
063	–			
064	Chillocothe	CS	Ohio Valley, Ohio	–
	Athens	CS	Buckeye Hills - Hocking Valley, Ohio	B (i)
	Marietta	CS	Buckeye Hills - Hocking Valley, Ohio	–
065	–			
066	Johnstown	WR	Turnpike, Pa.	A (i)
	Martin's Ferry - Ballaire	CS-CS	Buckeye Hills - Hocking Valley, Ohio	–
	Somerset (Redevelopment)	CS	Turnpike, Pa.	–
067	–			
068	–			
069	–			
070	–			
071	–			
072	Bay City - Midland - Saginaw	WR-CS-WR	East Central, Mich.	A (i); A (ii), (a)
	Sault Ste. Marie (Redevelopment)	CS	Eastern Upper Peninsula, Mich.	C (ii), (b)
	Alpena (Redevelopment)	CS	Northeast, Mich.	A (ii), (b)
	St. Ignace (Redevelopment)	PS	Eastern Upper Peninsula, Mich.	–
	Tawas - East Tawas	FCC-FCC	East Central, Mich.	B (ii)
	Newberry (Redevelopment)	PS	Eastern Upper Peninsula, Mich.	A (ii), (b); C (i), (b)
073	Traverse City (Redevelopment)	CS	Northwest, Mich.	A (i)
074	–			
075	–			
076	–			

077	–			
078	–			
079	–			
080	–			
081	–			
082	–			
083	–			
084	–			
085	Marquette - Negaunee - Ishpeming	CS-CS-CS	Central Upper Peninsula, Mich.	A (i); B (ii)
	Escanaba - Gladstone Area (Redevelopment)	CS-CS	Central Upper Peninsula, Mich.	A (ii), (b)
	Iron Mountain - Kingsford - Norway Area (Redevelopment)	CS-CS-PS	Central Upper Peninsula, Mich.	–
	Houghton (Redevelopment)	PS	Western Upper Peninsula, Mich.	–
	Iron River (Redevelopment)	PS	Western Upper Peninsula, Mich.	–
086	–			
087	Duluth	WR	Arrowhead, Minn.	A (i)
	Ironwood - Bessemer - Wakefield (Redevelopment)	WR-PS-PS	Western Upper Peninsula, Mich.	–
	Ontonagon - White Pine	FCC	Western Upper Peninsula, Mich.	A (ii), (b); B (ii); C (ii), (b)
088	–			
089	–			
090	–			
091	–			
092	–			
093	–			
094	Havre	CS	Bear Paw, Mont.	A (ii), (b); C (ii), (b)
095	Hardin	PS	Big Horn, Mont.	C (i), (a)
096	–			
097	–			
098	–			

(continued)

Table A–8. (continued)

OBE Area	Name of Center	Level in Hierarchy	EDA District	If actual growth center in the 1960s category under which EDA center is classified
099	–			
100	–			
101	–			
102	–			
103	–			
104	–			
105	–			
106	–			
107	–			
108	–			
109	–			
110	–			
111	–			
112	–			
113	–			
114	Carbondale	CS	Greater Egypt, Ill.	B (ii)
	Mount Vernon	CS	Greater Egypt, Ill.	B (ii)
115	Paducah	WR	Purchase, Ky.	A (i)
	Poplar Bluff	CS	Ozark Foothills, Mo.	–
	Sikeston	CS	Boothill, Mo.	–
	Mayfield (Redevelopment)	CS	Purchase, Mo.	–
	Dexter - Bloomfield	CS	Boothill, Mo.	–
	New Madrid (Redevelopment)	PS	Boothill, Mo.	–
116	Springfield	WR	Lakes Country, Mo.	A (i)
	Harrison	CS	Northwest, Ark.	–
	West Plains	CS	South Central Ozark, Mo.	–
	Vinita	CS	N.E.C.O., Okla.	–
	Mountain Home	FCC	Northwest, Ark.	B (ii)

117	Little Rock - North Little Rock	WR-WR	Central, Ark.	A (i)
	Pine Bluff - Sheridan	WR-FCC	Southeast, Ark.	A (i); B (i)
	Hot Springs	CS	West Central, Ark.	–
	Conway	CS	Central, Ark.	B (i)
	Russellville	CS	West Central, Ark.	A (ii), (b); B (ii)
	Searcy (Redevelopment)	CS	White River, Ark.	–
	Malvern (Redevelopment)	CS	West Central, Ark.	–
	Newport	CS	White River, Ark.	–
	Batesville (Redevelopment)	CS	White River, Ark.	–
	Brinkley (Redevelopment)	PS	Central, Ark.	–
118	Fort Smith - Van Buren	WR-CS	Western, Ark.	A (i)
	McAlester (Redevelopment)	CS	Kiamichi, Okla.	A (ii), (b); B (ii)
	Mena	PS	Western, Ark.	B (ii)
	Dardanelle	FCC	West Central, Ark.	B (ii)
119	Muskogee (Redevelopment)	WR	Eastern, Okla.	–
	Fayetteville - Springfield	CS	Northwest, Ark.	A (ii), (b)
	Stillwater	CS	Central, Okla.	B (i)
	Claremore	CS	N.E.C.O., Okla.	–
	Sapulpa - Bristow	CS-PS	Central, Okla.	–
120	Shawnee	CS	Central, Okla.	–
	Ardmore	CS	S.O.D.A., Okla.	–
	Chickasha	CS	South Central, Okla.	–
	Ada	CS	S.O.D.A., Okla.	–
121	Duncan	CS	South Central, Okla.	A (ii), (b)
122	–			
123	–			
124	–			
125	–			
126	–			
127	Durant	CS	S.O.D.A., Okla.	–
	Sulphur Springs	CS	Northeast Tex.	B (ii)
128	Waco	WR	Central, Tex.	A (i)
	Temple	WR	Central, Tex.	–
	Killeen	CS	Central, Tex.	–

(continued)

Table A–8. (continued)

OBE Area	Name of Center	Level in Hierarchy	EDA District	If actual growth center in the 1960s category under which EDA center is classified
129	Bryan - College Station	CS	Brazos Valley, Tex.	A (i)
130	Nacogdoches - Lufkin - Diboll	CS-CS-PS	Deap East, Tex.	A (ii), (b); B (ii)
	Marshall	CS	North East, Tex.	C (i), (a)
	Jefferson (Redevelopment)	PS	North East, Tex.	C (i), (b)
	Northeast Texas Municipal District (part, Upshen Co.)	–	North East, Tex.	–
131	Texarkana (part)	WR	North East, Tex.	A (i)
	Texarkana (part)	WR	South West, Ark.	A (i)
	Hope (Redevelopment)	CS	South West, Ark.	–
	Northeast Texas Municipal District (part)	–	North East, Tex.	–
132	Shreveport - Bossier	M-WR	North West, La.	A (i)
	Natchitoches (Redevelopment)	CS	North West, La.	–
133	Monroe - West Monroe	WR-CS	North Delta, La.	A (i)
	Alexandria - Pineville (Redevelopment)	WR-CS	Kisatchie - Delta, La.	A (i); A (ii), (b)
134	Greenville (Redevelopment)	WR	South Delta, Miss.	A (i)
	Cleveland (Redevelopment)	CS	South Delta, Miss.	B (i)
	El Dorado	CS	Southwest, Ark.	A (ii), (b)
	Greenwood (Redevelopment)	CS	North Central, Miss.	–
	Grenada	CS	North Central, Miss.	A (ii), (b); B (ii); C (ii), (b)
	Crossett - Hamburg	CS-PS	Southeast, Ark.	–
135	Jackson	WR	Central, Miss.	A (i)
	Vicksburg	CS	Central, Miss.	–
	Forest	PS	East Central, Miss.	–
136	Meridian	WR	East Central, Miss.	A (i)
	Hattiesburg	WR	Southern, Miss.	A (i)
137	Pascagoula	CS	Southern, Miss.	A (ii), (a); B (i)
138	Baton Rouge	WR	Capital, La.	A (i)
	Natchez	CS	Southwest, Miss.	A (ii), (b)
	McComb	CS	Southwest, Miss.	–
139	Lafayette - New Iberia	WR-CS	Evangeline, La.	A (i)
	Opelousas (Redevelopment)	CS	Evangeline, La.	–
140				

141	–			
142	Victoria	WR	Coastal Bend, Tex.	A (i); B (ii); C (ii), (b)
	Del Rio (Redevelopment)	CS	Middle Rio Grande, Tex.	B (ii); C (ii), (b)
	Uvalde (Redevelopment)	CS	Middle Rio Grande, Tex.	–
143	Corpus Christi - Aransas Pass	M-CS	Coastal Bend, Tex.	A (i); B (i); C (i), (a)
	Laredo (Redevelopment)	WR	South, Tex.	A (i)
144	Brownsville (Redevelopment)	WR	Lower Rio Grande Valley, Tex.	A (i)
	McAllen	WR	Lower Rio Grande Valley, Tex.	A (i)
	Harlingen	WR	Lower Rio Grande Valley, Tex.	A (i)
145	–			
146	Santa Fe	CS	North Central, N. Mex.	–
	Las Vegas (Redevelopment)	CS	North Central, N. Mex.	–
147	Pueblo	WR	Southern, Colo.	A (i)
	Trinidad	CS	Southern, Colo.	–
	Alamosa	CS	Southern, Colo.	A (ii), (a); B (i); C (ii), (a)
148	–			
149	Moab (Redevelopment)	PS	Southeastern, Utah	A (ii), (b)
150	–			
151	Price (Redevelopment)	CS	Southeastern, Utah	–
	Richfield (Redevelopment)	PS	Six-County, Utah	A (ii), (b)
	Delta	FCC	Six-County, Utah	–
152	–			
153	Butte - Anaconda (Redevelopment)	WR-CS	Inter County, Mont.	A (i); A (ii), (a); C (i), (a)
154	Lewiston	CS	Clearwater, Ida.	–
	Colville (Redevelopment)	PS	Trico, Wash.	–
155	–			
156	–			
157	–			
158	–			
159	–			

(continued)

Table A-8. (continued)

OBE Area	*Name of Center*	*Level in Hierarchy*	*EDA District*	*If actual growth center in the 1960s category under which EDA center is classified*
160	–			
161	–			
162	–			
163	–			
164	–			
165	–			
166	–			
167	–			
168	Grass Valley - Auburn (Redevelopment)	PS-CS	Sierra, Calif.	B (i)
	South Lake Tahoe (Redevelopment)	–	Sierra, Calif.	–
169	–			
170	–			
171	–			

B Areas of accelerated relative growth during the 1960s
(a) within the OBE center's labor market
(b) beyond that labor market

C Areas partially successful in offsetting decline in the 1960s
C (i) Population decline or emigration took place, but incomes increased and/or poverty population declined
C (ii) Simply, less rapid relative decline
(a) within the OBE center's labor market
(b) beyond that labor market

As table A–8 reveals clearly enough, EDA's record in picking out likely growth centers on the basis of their regional role and growth experience in the 1960s was mixed at best. Fifty percent of the designated economic development or redevelopment centers fall into *none* of the above categories. Less than 25 percent were centers that displayed accelerated growth in the 1960s.

APPALACHIA'S CONCENTRATED INVESTMENT CENTERS

Table A–9 shows the complete set of designated regional and primary district centers in Appalachia. Seventy-five percent of the growth area investments of the Appalachian program were concentrated in the centers identified by asterisks in this table. As we indicated in Chapter 2, some but by no means all of these centers experienced accelerated growth as a consequence of the ARC efforts. The particular combination of factors distinguishing the real growth centers from the others were: size and diversity of the labor supplies; availability of developable sites; an attractive living environment; good access, especially to a regional metropolis; and a modern and responsive local governmental structure and leadership (Fuller, 1970).

Table A–9. District Centers in Appalachia

Regional Centers	*Primary Centers*
* 1. Greater Binghamton (N.Y.) (includes Endicott, Johnson City)	1. Ithaca-Cortland (N.Y.) 2. Oneonta-Bainbridge (N.Y.) 3. Cobleskill-Schoharie (N.Y.) 4. Cooperstown (N.Y.)
* 2. Greater Elmira (N.Y. & Pa.) (includes Corning, Waverly, Athens, Sayre, and Towanda)	5. Hammondsport-Bath (N.Y.) * 6. Hornell-Alfred (N.Y.) 7. Olean-Bradford (N.Y. & Pa.) 8. Ridgeway-St. Marys (Pa.) 9. Warren-Jamestown (Pa. & N.Y.)
* 3. Greater Erie (N.Y. & Pa.)	*10. New Castle-Sharon-Mercer (Pa.) 11. Meadville (Pa.) 12. Franklin-Oil City-Titusville (Pa.)
* 4. Scranton-Wilkes Barre-Hazleton (Pa.)	13. Stroudsburg (Pa.) 14. Pottsville (Pa.)
* 5. Greater Williamsport (Pa.) (Lock Haven-Sunbury-Berwick)	

(continued)

Table A-9 (continued)

Regional Centers	*Primary Centers*
* 6. Altoona-Johnstown (Pa.)	15. Somerset (Pa.) 16. Bedford (Pa.) 17. Clearfield-Dubois (Pa.) *18. State College (Pa.)
* 7. Hagerstown-Martinsburg (Md. 7 W. Va.)	19. Hancock-Berkeley Springs (Md. & W. Va.)
* 8. Greater Cumberland (Md. & W. Va.) (includes Keyser, Frostburg, and Westernport)	20. Romney (W. Va.) 21. Oakland (Md.) 22. Elkins (W. Va.)
9. Tri-Cities (W. Va.) (Fairmont-Clarksburg-Morgantown)	23. Buckhannon (W. Va.) 24. Philippi (W. Va.)
*10. Greater Pittsburgh (Pa.) (All SMSA)	25. Indiana (Pa.) 26. Uniontown-Connellsville (Pa.)
11. Upper Ohio Valley (W. Va. & Ohio) (Wheeling-Weirton-Steubenville)	*27. New Philadelphia-Dover (Pa.) *28. Zanesville-Cambridge (Ohio)
*12. Greater Charleston (W. Va.)	*29. Coshocton (Ohio) 30. Covington-Clifton Forge-Lewisburg-White Sulphur Springs (Va. & W. Va.) 31. Bluefield-Princeton-Beckley (Va. & W. Va.) 32. Williamson-Logan (W. Va.)
*13. Mid Ohio Valley (W. Va. & Ohio) (Parkersburg-Marietta)	33. Athens-Nelsonville (Ohio) 34. Jackson-Wellston (Ohio) 35. Gallipolis-Point Pleasant (Ohio & W. Va.)
*14. Lower Ohio Valley (W. Va., Ohio, & Ky.) (Huntington-Ashland-Ironton)	36. Portsmouth-Lucasville (Ohio) 37. Chillicothe-Waverly (Ohio)
(Lexington)	*38. Paintsville-Prestonburg-Pikeville (Ky.) 39. Winchester (Ky.) 40. Morehead-Midland (Ky.) 41. Hazard-Whitesburg (Ky.) 42. Campbellsville (Ky.) 43. Somerset (Ky.) *44. London-Corbin (Ky.) *45. Middlesboro-Barbourville (Ky.)
*15. Tri-Cities (Tenn. & Va.) (Briston-Kingsport-Johnson City-Elizabethtown)	46. Norton-Wise-Appalachia (Va.) 47. Marion-Wytheville (Va.) 48. Galaz-Hillville (Va.)
(Roanoke)	49. Pulaski (Va.) 50. Greeneville (Tenn.) 51. Morristown (Tenn.)
*16. Greater Knoxville (Tenn.) (Knox, Blount, Anderson Counties)	*52. Cookeville-Crossville-Sparta (Tenn.) 53. Jellico-LaFollette
*17. Greater Chattanooga (Tenn., Ga. & Ala.) (includes Cleveland)	54. Tullahoma-Manchester-McMinnville (Tenn.) 55. Athens (Tenn.) 56. Dayton (Tenn.) 57. Dalton-Calhoun (Ga.)
*18. Greater Asheville (N.C.) (includes Canton and Waynesville)	58. Murphy-Andrews-Hayesville (N.C.) 59. Sylva-Bryson City (N.C.) 60. Hendersonville-Brevard (N.C.) 61. Rutherfordton-Spindale-Forest City (N.C.)

(continued)

Table A-9. (continued)

Regional Centers	*Primary Centers*
	62. Morganton-Lenoir (N.C.)
	63. Wilkesboro-N. Wilkesboro (N.C.)
19. Greater Winston-Salem (N.C.)	64. Mt. Airy (N.C.)
	65. Elkin-Jonesville (N.C.)
	66. Boone (N.C.)
	67. Anderson (S.C.)
*20. Greenville-Spartanburg (S.C.)	68. Gaffney (S.C.)
	69. Clemson-Seneca (S.C.)
	70. Gainesville (Ga.)
(Atlanta)	*71. Carrollton (Ga.)
	72. Rome-Cartersville (Ga.)
*21. Greater Birmingham (Ala.)	*73 Gadsden-Anniston (Ala.) (includes Talladega & Guntersville)
	*74. Tuscaloosa (Ala.)
*22. Huntsville-Florence-Decatur (Ala.)	75. Corinth (Miss.)
	*76. Pontotoc-Tupelo (Miss.)
	77. Starkville-Columbus-West Point (Miss.)
	78. Amory-Aberdeen (Miss.)

*Centers in which 75 percent of the growth area investments of the Appalachian program were concentrated.

References

Appalachian Regional Commission (1970). *The Urban-Rural Growth Strategy in Appalachia.* A Commission Staff Summary Report.

Beale, Calvin L. (1969). Statement before the Subcommittee on Urban Growth, House Committee on Banking and Currency, June 24, 1969.

—— (1971). Statement on Population and Migration Trends in Rural and Nonmetropolitan Areas, submitted to the U.S. Senate Committee on Government Operations, April 27, 1971. Economic Research Service, U.S. Department of Agriculture. Mimeographed.

Berry, Brian J.L. (1966). *Strategies, Models and Economic Theories of Development in Rural Regions.* Washington: Agriculture Economic Report No. 127.

—— (1967a). *Geography of Market Centers and Retail Distribution.* Englewood Cliffs, New Jersey: Prentice-Hall, Inc.

—— (1967b). "Spatial Organization and Levels of Welfare." Paper presented to first Economic Development Administration Research Program Conference.

—— (1968). *Metropolitan Area Definition: A Re-Evaluation of Concept and Statistical Practice.* Working Paper No. 28, U.S. Bureau of Census.

—— (1969). *Growth Centers and Their Potentials in the Upper Great Lakes Region.* Washington, D.C.: Upper Great Lakes Regional Commission.

—— (1971). "DIDO Data Analysis: GIGO or Pattern Recognition?" In H.D. McConnell and D. Yaseen, eds. *Models of Spatial Variation.* DeKalb, Illinois: Northern Illinois University Press, pp. 105–131.

—— (1972). "Latent Structure of the American Urban System, with International Comparisons". In Berry, ed. *City Classification Handbook.* New York: John Wiley and Sons, pp. 11–60.

Bird, Alan R. (1968). *Growth Areas and Development Districts of the Upper Great Lakes Economic Development Region.* Washington, D.C.: Upper Great Lakes Regional Commission. Mimeographed.

Bluestone, Herman (1970). *Focus for Urban Development Analysis: Urban Orientation of Counties.* Washington, D.C.: Economic Research Service, U.S. Department of Agriculture.

Bohm, Robert A. and David A. Patterson (1972). "Interstate Highway Location and County Population Growth." Urban Research Section, Oak Ridge National Laboratory.

Borchert, John R. (1967). "American Metropolitan Evolution." *Geographical Review,* Vol. 57, p. 324.

—— and Russell B. Adams (1963). *Trade Centers and Tributary Areas of the Upper Midwest.* Upper Midwest Economic Study Urban Report No. 3.

Borts, George H. (1967). *Patterns of Regional Economic Development in the United States, and their Relation to Rural Poverty.* Report to the National Advisory Commission on Rural Poverty, U.S. Department of Agriculture.

Cumberland, John H. (1971). *Regional Development. Experiences and Prospects in the United States of America.* The Hague: Mouton.

Duncan, Otis Dudley et al. (1965). *Metropolis and Region.* Baltimore: Johns Hopkins University Press.

Economic Development Administration (1967). *Directions of the District Program.* Office of District and Area Planning. Mimeographed.

—— (1972). *The Economic Development Administration Growth Center Strategy.* Washington, D.C.: U.S. Department of Commerce.

Friedmann, John. (1966). *Regional Development Policy.* Cambridge: The M.I.T. Press.

—— and John Miller (1965). "The Urban Field." *Journal of the American Institute of Planners,* Vol. 31, pp. 312–19.

Fuller, Stephen S. (1970). *Impact of Appalachian Regional Commission Assisted Public Investment in Selected Growth Centers.* Report to the Appalachian Regional Commission.

Gustavson, Neil C. (1973). *Recent Trends/Future Prospects. A Look at Upper Midwest Population Changes.* Minneapolis: Upper Midwest Council.

Haren, Claude (1972). "Current Spatial Organization of Industrial Productivity and Distribution Activity." Economic Research Service, U.S. Department of Agriculture.

Harris, Chauncy D. (1954). "The Market as a Factor in the Localization of Industry in the United States." *Annals of the Association of American Geographers.* Vol. 44, pp. 315–48.

Henderson, James M., and Anne O. Krueger (1965). *National Growth and Economic Change in the Upper Midwest.* Minneapolis: University of Minnesota Press.

Hodge, Gerald (1966). *The Identification of 'Growth Poles' in Eastern Ontario.* Ontario Department of Economics and Development.

McClelland, David C. (1961). *The Achieving Society.* New York: Van Nostrand

National Advisory Commission on Rural Poverty (1967). *The People Left Behind.* Washington, D.C.: U.S. Government Printing Office.

Perloff, Harvey S. et al. (1960). *Regions, Resources and Economic Growth.* Baltimore: Johns Hopkins University Press.

—— and Lowdon Wingo (1963). "Natural Resource Endowment and Regional Economic Growth." Washington, D.C.: Resources for the Future, Inc.

Perroux, Françoise (1961). "Les pôles de croissance." *L'économie du XX siècle.* Paris.

Pred, Allan (1966). *The Spatial Dynamics of U.S. Urban-Industrial Growth, 1800–1914.* Cambridge: The M.I.T. Press.

Tidemann, T. Nicolaus (1968). "The Theoretical Efficacy of 'Potential' and Transport Cost Models of Location." Center for Urban Studies, University of Chicago. Mimeographed.

Thompson, Wilbur (1968). "Internal and External Factors in the Development of Urban Economies." In Harvey S. Perloff and Lowdon Wingo, Jr., eds., *Issues in Urban Economics.* Baltimore: Johns Hopkins University Press.

Ullman, Edward L. (1954). "Amenities as a Factor in Regional Growth." *Geographical Review,* Vol. 44, pp. 119–32.

—— (1957). *American Commodity Flows.* Seattle: University of Washington Press.

Upper Great Lakes Regional Commission (1968). *Strategy for Development.* Washington, D.C.: The Commission.

U.S. Department of Agriculture. (1971a). *The Economic and Social Conditions of Rural America in the 1970's.* Economic Development Division, Economic Research Service, U.S. Department of Agriculture. Prepared for the Committee on

Government Operation, U.S. Senate, 92nd Congress, 1st Session. Washington, D.C.: Government Printing Office.

—— (1971b). Table of Nonmetro places with 1970 population between 25,000 and 50,000, intercensal growth rate of 13.3 percent or greater, and 75 miles or more from an SMSA, and Table of Nonmetro places with 1970 population between 10,000 and 24,999, intercensal growth rate of 13.3 percent or greater, and 75 miles or more from an SMSA. Population Studies Group, Human Resource Branch, Economic Development Division, U.S. Department of Agriculture. Mimeographed.

U.S. Department of Commerce (1965). *Growth Patterns in Employment by County, 1940–1950 and 1950–1960.* Office of Business Economics, U.S. Department of Commerce. Washington, D.C.: U.S. Government Printing Office.

Index

access, 45, 54; filtering, 158; in Fuller, 185; in Tidemann, 1; and tourism, 114
agglomeration, 45
agriculture, 17, 36; in Applachia, 43; and Upper Midwest, 149
Alpena, 91; growth, 114
amenity resources, 151
annexation, 171
Appalachia, 36; geographic definition, 53; strategy, 41
Appalachia Development Highways System, 41–45
Appalachia Regional Development Act, 1965, 42–44
ARC (Appalachian Regional Commission), 43; and financial support, 54; growth center definition, 48
area: defined by Berry, 52
Area and Regional Economic Development, 173
Arkansas: and filtering, 155
Ashland: growth, 114
autonomy, 7

Baltimore, 36
Bay City, 91
Beale, Calvin L., 165
Berry, B.J.L., 8, 55; area definition, 52; 1960 census data, 134; commuting areas, 45; urban hierarchy, 1, 60, 117
Bird, A., Upper Great Lakes Development District, 56–58
Bluestone, H., 122
Bohm, R., and Patterson, D., 151
Borchert, J., 4
Borchert, J. and Adams, R., 59; trade centers, 104
Borts, G., 4
Boston, 36

centers: primary and secondary defined by ARC, 51
central place theory, 15
Chicago, 36; Milwaukee complex, 114; Milwaukee, Twin Cities regions, 92
City Classification Handbook, 117
classification, by Rand McNally, 63
closure, 7; and DUS, 15
clusters, 11
colleges: and growth in Upper Midwest, 150
Commission on Crimes of Violence, 39
Commission on Population Growth and the American Future, 36
commuting: hierarchy, 122; patterns in Berry, 63; and urban growth, 149
Cumberland, 157

decentralization, 40, 59, 145; dynamics of, 41; and minorities, 155
decline, as in Lincoln Center, 140
development: definition, 56
Detroit, 36, 91; Grand Rapids complex, 114
differentiation, 40
diffusion, 145, 158; hierarchical, 75
disadvantaged, 91
dispersion, 36, 45, 134; and spread effects, 74; and Upper Midwest, 150
districts, development, 51
diversification, 5, 21; lack of in Appalachia, 43
Doxiadas, C.A., 11
DUS (Daily Urban System), 11; description, 15, 16
Duluth: as primary growth center, 108

education, 42
employment, 56
exports, 7
expressways: and access, 114

Fargo: as primary growth center, 108
filtering, 104; concept of in growth center strategy, 114; and integration, 115; mechanism, 9; and small towns, 155
Flint, 91
Florida: and retirees, 151
Fox Valley, 92
Friedmann, J., 6
Fuller, S., 53, 185

Georgia: and filtering, 155
geography: definition of Appalachia, 53
ghetto, 39

government, support of, 21
gradients: and spatial interdependencies, 122
Grand Forks: as a primary growth center, 108
Green Bay: as a region, 92
growth: and Beale, 172; centers, 140; and DUS, 17; and primary centers, 41, 108; regional history, 6; strategy in Appalachia, 43; in Thompson, 10

Harris, C., 1
heartland: in Harris, 1; as a primary growth center, 108
Henderson, J. and Krueger, A., 56
hierarchy, 8, 136; definition in Borchert and Adams, 59; and urban and growth centers, 41, 51, 114, 158
highway, improvement of, 51; and penetration, 122
hinterland, concept of, 6, 48, 55
history, economical review, 4
homogeneity, 39

immigration, 36; in Nashville, 134; of poor into core city, 151
income: low in Appalachia, 42
infrastructure, 114, 158
innovation: and spread, 8; in Thompson, 10
integration: and filtering, 115
Interstate Highway System, 158, 170
intervention, 157
investment, 108; needs, 56; private, 54

Johnson, L.B., 173

Kentucky: Cumberland River Valley, 45; east, 47

labor: market, 8
Lincoln Center: decline of, 140
Lindsberg, 140
location: and DUS, 15; and growth, 168

McClelland, David, 36
McPherson, 140
manufacture, 17; in Appalachia, 43
Marquette: growth, 114
megalopolis, 151
Memphis: OBE area, 120
methodology, 55; and gradient information, 136; and hierarchy, 117
Michigan: Dept. of Commerce, 92; Upper, 149
Midland-Bay City, 104
migration, 5, 36; and filtering, 158; patterns, 92
military bases: and growth in Upper Midwest, 150
Miller, J. and Friedmann, J., 5
mining: in Appalachia, 43
minorities: and growth, 155
Minneapolis:-St. Paul complex, 114
Minnesota, 149; and amenities, 150
Mississippi Delta, 36
mix: industrial, 168
Montana, 149; and amenities, 150

NASA, 170
National Advisory Commission on Rural Poverty, 108
North Dakota, 149

OBE: economic area boundary and geographical distinctions, 120
Office of Management and Budget, 120
Ohio: southeast, 45
outmigration, 115

penetration, 75
performance: and economic welfare, 91
Perloff, H., 6
Perloff, H. and Wingo, L., 1
Philadelphia, 36
Pittsburgh, 36
population, 36, 42
Population Commission, 167
poverty: and regional growth, 157
Pred, A., 5
productivity, 56
public facilities, 43
Public Works and Economic Development Act, 173

railroads: and access, 158; in Appalachia, 43
relocation: of soft goods manufacturing, 155
resources, 4; and DUS, 15
retail trade, 21, 151; and technology, 104
'rimland', 36
Rockies, 45

Saginaw, 91
St. Louis, 36
Salina, 140
segregation, 40
services, 6, 21; centers, 41, 58; delivery area, 48; roles, 136; sector, 44
shopping centers, 114
size: and DUS, 17
social dynamics, 40
South, the Deep, 36
South Dakota, 149
Southwest, 45
space: economy, 9
spatial organization, 55; and regional growth, 136; and retail centers, 150
spread effects, 8; and spatial organization, 134; and Upper Midwest cities, 150; and urban-rural differences, 151
specialization, 5
standard of living, 42, 51
status, 39
strategy, 1; for growth centers, 41, 52, 53; regional development, 9
suburbanization, 36

technology, 44; and market shift, 43; and retail pattern, 104
Tennessee: Cumberland River Valley, 45
Thompson, Wilbur, 9
Tidemann, T., 1
tourism, 58; and growth, 114
travel behavior, 45

UGLRC (Upper Great Lakes Regional Commission), 41, 44, 56
Ullman, E., 5
unemployment, 42
Upper Midwest Council, 149
urban region: definition, 10
urbanization, 42, 44, 122; in Borchert and Adams, 59; inducement of, 45
USDA (United States Dept. of Agriculture), 122, 165
utilization: rate and services, 55

Virginia: southwest, 45

water resource planning, 15
welfare, 91, 136
West Virginia, 45
Wichita, 140
Widner, Ralph, 41
Wisconsin, 149; amenities, 150; Upper Midwest Economic Development, 92
work, pattern of, 11

About the Author

Brian J.L. Berry is the Irving B. Haris Professor of Urban Geography at the University of Chicago. He also directs the academic programs of the university's Center for Urban Studies and is a Fellow of the Center for Policy Study. Professor Berry received a B.Sc. degree in Economics at University College, London in 1955, and M.A. and Ph.D degrees in Geography at The University of Washington in 1956 and 1958 respectively. He joined the University of Chicago faculty in 1958, and is now a naturalized U.S. citizen.

Among his publications are:

1959 *Studies of Highway Development and Geographic Change*
1961 *Central Place Studies*
1963 *Commercial Structure and Commercial Blight*
1965 *The Science of Geography*
1966 *Essays on Commodity Flows and the Spatial Structure of the Indian Economy*
1967 *Geography of Market Centers and Retail Distribution*
1967 *Goals for Urban America*
1968 *Metropolitan Area Definition*
1968 *The Impact of Urban Renewal on Small Business*
1968 *Spatial Analysis*
1969 *A Strategic Approach to Urban Research and Development*
1970 *Geographic Perspectives on Urban Systems*
1971 *Comparative Factorial Ecology*
1972 *City Classification Handbook*
1973 *The Human Consequences of Urbanization*

Professor Berry is a member of a number of professional societies, and has held offices in the Association of American Geographers and the Regional Science Association. He is a member of the editorial boards of several journals, including the *Journal of the American Institute of Planners, Journal of Regional Science, Journal of Urban Economics, Geographical Analysis, Growth and Change, Progress in Geography, Progress in the Mathematical Social Sciences, Regional Science Perspectives,* and *L'Espace Geographique.* He was given the Association of American Geographers' 1968 award for Meritorious Contributions to the Field of Geography. He is also a member of the Behavioural Sciences Assembly and the Building Research Advisory Board of the National Research Council (National Academies of Science and Engineering).

He has been and is a consultant to agencies of the U.S. Government, to State and local governments, to private businesses, and to governments overseas, on matters of urban and regional development and planning, facilities locations and program evaluation.